JACQUELINE PEPPARD'S

New Era Healthy Eating Cookbook

RECIPES WHEN YOU WANT HEALTHY
but LOVE food

Stay healthy or lose weight
without mind-numbing calculations along the way.

Gourmet, veggie-packed, low-carb and paleo-friendly
recipes designed to satisfy body and soul.

Includes an ingredients chapter
empowering you with sustainable healthy-eating
practices for yours and the planet's wellbeing.

A NEW ERA HEALTHYEATING® PUBLICATION
www.NewEraHealthyEating.com

Thank you for your interest in my book and to show my appreciation, I would like to give you the: *New Era Healthy Eating Resource Guide.*

In it, I share my go to websites, books, and product suppliers to propel you along in building a healthier you and planet.

Please visit www.NewEraHealthyEating.com
and download your **FREE** copy.

PUBLISHER'S CATALOGING-IN-PUBLICATION DATA:

Author: Jacqueline Peppard
Title: New Era Healthy Eating Cookbook
Library of Congress Control Number: 2017910249
ISBN: 978-0-9990244-0-9 (PAPERBACK)
Summary: Recipes when you want healthy but LOVE food
Includes: References and Index
Publisher: New Era Healthyeating, Auburn, CA
Subjects: Low-Carbohydrate Diet-Recipes/Cooking/Health/Weight Loss
BISAC: COOKING / HEALTH & HEALING / LOW CARBOHYDRATE

For more information about New Era Healthyeating® or Jacqueline Peppard, please visit www.NewEraHealthyEating.com

Email: postmaster@NewEraHealthyEating.com
I like hearing from you and do my best to respond as soon as possible to your email and comments on blog posts or social media.

PHOTOGRAPHY BY JACQUELINE PEPPARD

GRAPHIC DESIGN BY OLIVIA PEDERSEN
www.OliviaPedersen.com

TABLE OF
CONTENTS

Frittata Fun, page 98

Lettuce Jus, page 236
Teriyaki Shrimp, page 124

INTRODUCTION

TO EAT IS STILL SOMETHING MORE THAN TO MAINTAIN BODILY FUNCTIONS. PEOPLE MAY NOT UNDERSTAND WHAT THAT 'SOMETHING MORE' IS, BUT THEY NONETHELESS DESIRE TO CELEBRATE IT.

SCHMEMANN 1973

THE PROBLEM WITH DIETS—AND A SOLUTION.

Stressing out and adhering to a specific diet regime is exhausting! All thoughts of fun race out the window, and you can almost hear the sucking sound as they go. So how are we to navigate through the morass of healthy eating cookbooks? It's hard to know which nutritional philosophy holds the answer without worrying if we'll be duped again by yet another fad. On one hand, we're told to consume whole grains, while other persuasions insist we eliminate them and go low-carb, paleo, or gluten free. Are we relegated to coconut flour pastries for the rest of our lives, or worse yet, no sweets at all—forever? I'm the type of person who will dutifully choke down most anything if I believe it's good for me, but is that sustainable long term? Nope, doomed to failure. Does it feel good and enrich our lives? Probably not.

In a world of increasingly impersonal technology, where our work hours are spent staring at a computer or conversing with the person down the hall via text messages or email, cooking offers us a warmhearted human connection. It encompasses a myriad of life experiences and provides a place where we can delight all of our senses. Flavors, smells, colors, and textures come alive in a setting where we enjoy the pleasure of intimate conversation and touch. It is a joyous adventure, an exploratory journey, a call to action, a venue for personal expression and creativity. A place to indulge ourselves in moments of success or comfort ourselves in difficult times. Cooking serves as a key element in celebrations, feasts, and communion with family and friends. But most importantly, it is a way to share our love.

Free yourself from calorie and carb counting. Eat sensibly, but without obsessing over forbidden food. Be inspired by delicious edibles based on sound yet flexible dietary practices designed to assist you in preparing amazing cuisine. This book is not just about eating better, but also serves as a path to self-expression and entertainment. It is beyond the "food-is-fuel" concept of deprivation and rigid meal plans, with their inherently repetitive rules, condemning us to relentless boredom. The recipes here will please the palate and soul, as well as nourish and inform.

MY CULINARY JOURNEY.

While cooking intrigues my creative propensities, what keeps me engaged are the smiles my dishes bring to faces. I do not cook so much for myself as I do for other people. Nothing brings me more happiness than witnessing the joy a delicious dish elicits in others. My fascination with food and its correlating mind/body connection began at 11 years old when introduced to *Prevention* magazine by my grandmother. Cooking has been a lifelong pursuit beginning in my pre-teen years and I have been a whole-foodie ever since.

Always passionate about healthy food, its production and preparation, I watched fads come and go. I am a living laboratory and have the scars to prove it. I'm on a mission to expose the damage "science" teamed up with corporate agribusiness has inflicted upon my grandparents' generation to the millennials and show you a better way to eat. We are not science projects and we all deserve better.

Today I must be doing something right, because I do not count calories or carbs, keep a food diary, measure food, eat a low-fat diet, use small plates, weigh myself regularly, eat large quantities of protein, or take any medication. I skip meals all the time (supposedly a big no-no) and my fat and protein intake is predominately animal-sourced. And no, it is not that my genes are particularly good – adult onset diabetes, cancer, stroke, heart and thyroid disease runs in my family.

WHY THIS BOOK IS DIFFERENT

Perhaps you have hit the low-carb or paleo wall and need more ideas? Maybe you just want to eat healthier without a weight-reduction plan? Inside are seemingly indulgent options that you can enjoy guilt-free. While not espousing any one "diet," you are enticed by tasty transitions containing fiber-rich vegetables and fruits, with moderate amounts of animal-sourced proteins. Here you will find practical yet innovative dishes created with whole foods readily found in most grocery stores.

Budding cook and seasoned veteran alike will find delectable alternatives to recipes from cookbooks based on misguided USDA food guides. You will learn how to choose the best ingredients and distinguish marketing hype from reality. Confusing food labeling terms are demystified. Not only are the recipes low-carbohydrate and paleo friendly, they are suitable for those seeking to reduce sugar, grain, and nut consumption. Humanely raised, sustainable, and organically sourced ingredients are emphasized. Revealed inside is scrumptious fare distinguished by fresh color and flavor pairings that bridge the gap between epicurean and nutritious.

MY PROMISE TO YOU. This is a health-motivated cookbook, but it is not about making you "eat your veggies." It entices you in a healthier direction with a diverse array of yummy creations to satisfy cravings, and gently nudges you into sustainable eating habits. The recipes along with nutritional information, will help you revamp your food choices, lose weight, improve your health, and heal your body with little sacrifice. Offered are eating patterns to last a lifetime, that will prevent disease from beginning in the first place. It is possible to live an energized life free from disease, medication, and pain well into your nineties.

NOW IS THE TIME. Increasing numbers of people, some younger than ever before, are encountering health crises induced by environmental toxins, unhealthy fats, excessive carbohydrate and protein consumption, and genetically modified food products. Will you be one of them? Maybe you will be the person who gets away with bad eating habits for decades and then, from out of the blue, slammed with disease at age fifty? Will you take a chance with your health and that of your loved ones, or will you start now and take control of your happiness? It is never too early or late to begin.

Healthy homemade meals are the best preventive medicine. All the things you hope for, dream about, and that make you the happiest are so much easier to manifest with a sound body and mind. Your guide is complete with hints, workarounds for special dietary needs whenever possible, a how-to section, and a comprehensive ingredients chapter. Misinformation is dispelled, and you will find references to the most revolutionary minds of our time. People who have both confirmed my worst suspicions and validated my life experiences and beliefs. Feel better and have fun along the way – let's get cooking!

Winter Borchst, page 192

INGREDIENTS

FIRST WE MUST SEARCH FOR THE WIDEST VARIETY OF THE BEST GROWN FOODS WE CAN FIND, IN THEIR FRESHEST CONDITION, AND THEN LOOK FOR FOODS WITH MINIMAL BUT SAFE PROCESSING AND PRESERVATIVES AND WITHOUT SYNTHETIC ADDITIVES...IF FRESH FOODS IN GOOD CONDITION ARE AVAILABLE TO YOU, CHOOSE THEM EVERY TIME

ROMBAUER AND BECKER 1975.

LEARNING THE LANGUAGE. Ingredients, the basis of all recipes, underlie the never-ending question of what you should put in your mouth today. Food, how it's produced, what we buy, and what we cook cannot be separated. However, the food choices we make only form part of the picture and often fail to ask a darker question: How are we to make informed decisions when information is purposely omitted, obscured, or outright falsified because of lack of regulation and oversight? In conjunction with the introduction of the *Genetically Engineered Food Right to Know Act*, Dennis Kucinich, a former US Representative, perhaps sums up this dilemma best when he stated, "We're looking at a dramatic transformation in food. If we are what we eat, so we are told, then we sure better know how our food is made and what is in it, so we know what we are to become. The right to know is a fundamental" (Kucinich).

Be careful out there—it's a jungle. As crazy as it sounds, you must almost become an investigative reporter to find out exactly what is in your food. Labels contain all manner of buzzwords, which do not honestly portray the contents and are designed to prey on the concerned consumer. The biggest travesty perpetrated upon the public by the food industry has been to manipulate them into paying for expensive "healthy" food products that aren't. Government regulatory agencies like the USDA, FDA, and the EPA are not fully protecting you, and the food industry preys on the ignorant.

Here, I help you unravel the fabric of deception. This section puts you in rubber hip boots and helps you wade through the manure of labeling and health claims as you navigate your way through grocery store aisles. You will be able to make informed choices that are in your best interests, not the manufacturers'.

I cannot stress enough how important it is to read labels before you purchase. If you don't know what a listed ingredient is, buy the product at your own peril and assume the worst. However, even scrutinizing labels proves problematic. For example, take sour cream, a rather innocuous item. It's a milk product from a cow—how bad can it be? After giving its label a face lift, a large California dairy selling "All Natural" Sour Cream no longer lists its ingredients as "Cultured Grade-A Pasteurized Cream, Milk, Non-Fat Milk, Corn Starch, Guar Gum, Carrageenan, and Locust Bean Gum" and NOW lists its ingredients as "Grade A Cultured Cream, Contains Milk." Okay, they are not technically fibbing, because their product is predominately cream and milk, and the USDA allows them to label in this manner. However, you would never know from its label it also contains a laundry list of additives, nor can I find any product information on their website. So much for transparency and the right to know.

Now check out Wallaby Organic Cultured Sour Cream's ingredient list: "Organic Cultured Pasteurized Cream and Live and Active Cultures." Wallaby's website emphatically states, "We craft our organic sour cream using only two ingredients: cultures and fresh organic cream." Which one would you want to buy if you were properly informed by the label?

In a perfect world, it would be nice to be able to visit a local farm or ranch to assure yourself you are purchasing organic, humanely raised, pastured meat and vegetables grown by individuals who value sustainable stewardship of the land, but this is not always possible. In this section, you are armed with information organized by category, so you can make the healthiest choices possible—without getting ripped off. I have highlighted the most commonly encountered ingredients, providing a solid foundation for you to build upon. Don't become overwhelmed. It is like learning a new language, and wending your way through a complex food industry maze does get easier.

Finally, I leave you with this question when weighing your options: Quality raised and produced food is going to cost a bit more, but what good is cheap food if the ultimate result is poor health and a mountain of doctor's bills?

ADDITIVES

As you scrutinize the labels on bottled, wrapped, frozen, and canned products, you'll notice it's hard to find any processed food that doesn't contain at least one additive. Food manufacturers use these to make a fast buck at the expense of your health. I have yet to find a single additive that provides any health benefits whatsoever, and all seem to lead directly to health problems. Most are modern creations, ranging from artificial sweeteners to emulsifiers, thickeners, and preservatives.

Think sulfites, tricalcium phosphate, propylene glycol, dextrin, dextrose, guar gum, xanthan gum, cellulose, citric acid, azodicarbonamide, and MSG. Most are by-products (don't even want to call them food) extracted from GMO corn, grain, and soybeans by way of highly industrialized manufacturing methods. Don't be duped by industry assertions these are healthy, "natural" products. Buying organic isn't going to protect you either. Calcium sulfate, calcium chloride, glucono delta lactone (whatever that is), and cellulose are all allowed for use in producing "organic" products.

The USDA, in their infinite wisdom, has determined many additives are exempt from labeling if present in a food at insignificant levels. Additionally, in August 2016 the FDA issued a final ruling and in it stated, "Unlike food additives, GRAS [generally recognized as safe] substances are **not subject to FDA pre-market approval**" [emphasis mine]. Wow, the USDA and FDA has our backs or what. Never mind we are exposed to a myriad of toxins steadily and incrementally accumulating in our bodies that exponentially compound our risk of disease. Studies are finding these chemicals, organic or not, can alter gut bacteria and cause intestinal irritation. The chronic, low-grade inflammatory response they induce may increase the likelihood of developing irritable bowel syndrome, metabolic syndrome, ADHD, allergies, cancer, celiac disease, and weight gain. While it is beyond the scope of this book to expose each and every additive used in food products, provided here are some of the most ubiquitous ones.

BROMINES. Part of the group of elements known as halides, bromines are every bit as toxic as their siblings fluorine and chlorine. Used in everything from plastics and fire retardants to medications and food, this endocrine disruptor is hard to get away from. We ingest it via drinking water, pesticides, flour conditioners, soft drinks, and food emulsifiers. Many countries have already banned the use of bromines, but here in the US, they are still allowed in our foodstuffs, sprayed directly on crops (methyl bromide), and used for shipping and packaging purposes.

Strawberries are routinely sprayed with methyl bromide. The National Pesticide Information Center includes this statement in their 2000 technical fact sheet on methyl bromide: "Human experience and use history indicate that methyl bromide is highly toxic" (NPIC 2000). This stuff has been poisoning us since 1932, yet it still isn't outlawed even though its toxicity is common knowledge.

Bakery goods are notoriously enriched with it, and you can bet your bottom dollar the cupcake you just ate was spiked with one of these lovelies: potassium bromate, calcium bromate, or sodium bromate (a.k.a. brominated flour).

CARRAGEENAN.   One of the most insidious additives, carrageenan is found in dairy products such as cottage cheese, sour cream, ricotta cheese, yogurt, and ice cream. It is made from Irish moss, a seaweed vegetable that technically should be good for you, right? Wrong. Many plants contain poisons that are not safe to consume in any quantities, and this is one of them. It is used in place of fat to thicken, gel, and stabilize food products. This allows food companies to cut corners and still charge a premium by using less whole foods and eliminating or speeding up traditional food processing methods. It adds a seductive creaminess to the "low"- or "non"-fat dairy products, so you don't spit them out on first bite. It lurks about in low-fat deli meat and is used as an emulsifier in salad dressings, infant milk, and coconut milk to prevent them from separating. No sir, no need to worry about shaking your chocolate milk, only the colitis or colon cancer that mysteriously appears later down the road.

To begin with, this bad boy's chemical structure is unlike anything found in other seaweeds, and once it hits the stomach's acid environment, it transforms into something nasty. Dr. Joanne Tobacman published a review of carrageenan scientific literature where she concluded: "The widespread use of carrageenan in the Western diet should be reconsidered" due to evidence that "exposure to undegraded [food grade] as well as to degraded carrageenan was associated with the occurrence of intestinal ulcerations and neoplasms" (Tobacman 2001).

Perhaps, if cooked and consumed in its most natural form, uncorrupted by industrialized processing, it might be okay to eat. Maybe the researchers are missing something. I know Irish moss is a favorite among vegans and raw foodists, but, you must realize, once it is transformed into powders and flakes, you are not eating food anymore. God only knows what variety it is, what has been done to it, and whether it originated from Asia, South America, or Europe.

A report created by the Cornucopia Institute describes the negative responses carrageenan induces in our bodies: "Many individuals experiencing gastrointestinal symptoms (ranging from mild 'belly bloat,' to irritable bowel syndrome, to severe inflammatory bowel disease) have noticed that eliminating carrageenan from the diet leads to profound improvements in their gastrointestinal health." The report further identifies other reactions, such as: "...[carrageenan] triggers an immune response in the body, which is similar to the effects of pathogenic bacteria like Salmonella" and "...contact with carrageenan reduces the activity of certain beneficial enzymes in human cells" (Cornucopia 2013). A recent updated report by Cornucopia highlights new studies which support earlier findings connecting carrageenan to inflammation, cancer, and diabetes (Cornucopia 2016).

Interference with the natural enzymes present in dairy, whether it be from pasteurization or additives, is a big reason many can't digest it. It is no wonder milk products cause so much intestinal distress when you combine the triple whammies of pasteurization, homogenization, and carrageenan. The "healthy" low-fat yogurt you just ate may not have been so healthy after all.

CELLULOSE.   Cellulose, also known as microcrystalline cellulose, MCC, carboxymethyl cellulose, or cellulose gum, is another crazy, "natural" additive. The food industry tries to disguise its true origins by calling it plant sourced, and while it can be made from vegetables, don't be hoodwinked into believing it is. This stuff is extracted from wood pulp or even cotton by an industrial chemical process, added to our food, and amazingly enough, deemed safe by the FDA for human consumption. It moves in and out of our bodies undigested and rates zilch on the nutritional scale.

Despite food manufacturers' claims the use of cellulose is a healthy way to boost fiber, here is the real story: They use it because it adds cheap filler or binder to products such as cheese, meats, breads, crackers, tortillas, and the French fries at your local fast food joint. When added with water, a manufacturer can use less of the real food and substantially cut their costs. Evidence is mounting, linking cellulose to gut disease, obesity, cancer, and diabetes. In a study published by *Nature*, researchers fed common emulsifiers carboxymethyl cellulose and polysorbate-80 to mice, and "...induced low-grade inflammation and obesity/metabolic syndrome in wild-type hosts and promoted robust colitis in mice predisposed to this disorder" (Chassaing et al. 2015). While deer may do fine eating bark off a tree in the dead of winter, humans were not designed to eat sawdust, and come to think of it, I have never observed a deer eating it either.

GUMS. No, not the sugary ones you chew, but substances like xanthan, guar, and locust gum. They are used as emulsifiers and are generally viewed as innocuous; however, they are largely indigestible. The guar and locust gums derive from legume endosperm grown in tropical climates. Xanthan and gellan gum are usually products of the corn-refining process and are bacteria created from fermentation of corn sugar. Sprinkling them in and amongst other additives on a continuous basis further contributes to gastrointestinal stress in our bodies. Studies suggest guar gum and other gums can induce intestinal problems such as poor nutrient absorption, bloating, flatulence, and reduced intestinal enzyme activity. It has been long known that viscous fibers such as psyllium and guar gum interfere with fat digestion in both humans and animals (GRAS 2005). Generally, there is a lack of data supporting safe usage, even in small amounts, and the bottom line–they are not a whole food.

DAIRY PRODUCTS

Cattle domestication is at least 10,500 years old, beginning maybe as early as 12,000 years ago. You can resolve many of milk's problems by purchasing unpasteurized, organic, additive-free milk products from 100% grass-fed and pastured cows. It may be you eat less dairy, but that is a good thing. Casein sensitivity is growing, but is it any wonder when you factor in grain-fed feedlot cows, additives, pesticides, and pasteurization?

UNPASTEURIZED. Shop locally at a co-op or health food store or even the dairy itself to find unpasteurized milk, cream, and cheese. Per the Raw Milk Institute, unpasteurized raw milk contains biologically active gut-friendly bacteria, enzymes, proteins, vitamins, and other dynamic components, all so vital for digesting and metabolizing milk. In particular, the Wulzen factor (a plant steroid) protects against calcification of the joints, arthritis, hardening of the arteries, cataracts, and calcification of the pineal gland but is destroyed with temperatures over 106°F. Quality raw milk dairies will not heat their milk beyond 103°F. Fats become oxidized, enzymes and vitamins are lost, and proteins mutate with pasteurization. The resultant degraded nutritional elements no longer resemble the milk of our ancestors: "It is designed for shelf life and not gut life" (McAfee 2013).

IS UNPASTEURIZED DAIRY SAFE?

UC Davis researcher and founder of the International Milk Genomics Consortium Dr. Bruce German says this about pasteurization: "Pasteurization is an 18th century solution to an 18th century problem and we have the technology and standards to do much better" (McAffe 2013). Tuberculosis, typhoid, and diphtheria are largely diseases of filth and contaminated water supplies. Husbandry practices and standards set for the production of raw milk today are a far cry from the feedlot dairies of the late 1800s, riddled with diseased cows and unsanitary conditions. Instead of barring disreputable practices that promoted disease, pasteurization came into widespread use to meet the demand in growing urban areas and to maximize profits. Advances in technology, transportation, sanitation, and food safety hazard reduction protocols eliminate the need for pasteurization. Yet the practice persists, along with environmentally unsustainable feedlot dairies filled with cows pumped full of antibiotics and spreading antibiotic-resistant superbugs.

COOKING WITH RAW DAIRY.

Here is the dilemma if you are cooking with raw dairy: Temperatures above 106°F destroy, denature, or damage nutrients in raw milk. Pasteurization temperatures vary between 145°F for 30 minutes and 280°F for two seconds. A simmer is maintained between 175° and 195°F, which in the case of making clarified butter, would effectively pasteurize raw butter. This is why dairy should be primarily eaten in its raw, uncooked state or fermented to avoid health issues. I have come to believe, though, using unpasteurized to begin with for cooking purposes is still healthier. It is only cooked once, as opposed to twice.

GRASS FED AND PASTURED VS FEEDLOT DAIRY.

Cows' digestive systems are not designed to eat grain, and the quality of their milk and health suffers as a result of doing so. Research and locate dairies that pasture cows year-round (except in the dead of winter) in continually rotated fields or practice "mob" grazing to obtain nutrient-rich milk. Be aware most "pastured" milk-producing cows are not 100% grass fed and are given supplemental feed to increase a cow's milk yield. The larger the producer, the more they must supplement with grain. When fed exclusively on grass, the milking herd size is smaller and cows must be constantly rotated in and out of intensively managed pasture. In the winter months, they will be fed dried grass and forage. There are few 100% grass-fed dairy cow operations in the US (just so you know). Even so, cows living in pastures with room to roam and fed minimal grain supplements are still producing nutritionally superior milk. The practice is 100 times more humane than those of feedlot dairies.

One of the benefits of consuming predominately grass-fed, pastured dairy products is the fat-soluble vitamin it contains called "Activator X," originally discovered by Dr. Weston Price and which is now known as vitamin K2. Pasteurization doesn't appear to destroy the X-factor, but it totally disappears in grain-fed cows. K2 is necessary for the manufacture of vitamins A and D and assimilation of calcium (Masterjohn 2007).

100% Grass-fed milk is higher in omega-3, conjugated linoleic acid (CLA), vitamin E, selenium, and zinc. The ratio of omega-6 to omega-3 fat content ranging between 2:1 and 1:1 is far superior to the 8:1 or higher ratio in feedlot cows or those fed predominately grain. An overabundance of omega-6 relative to omega-3 interferes with our bodies' ability to metabolize omega-3. Grass-fed, pastured dairy cows also produce milk with higher levels of cholesterol-neutral stearic acid as opposed to the cholesterol-elevating palmitic acid.

LACTOSE INTOLERANCE. Many believe Asians are largely lactose intolerant, but this is grossly inaccurate. It is the Southeastern Asians and cultures in warmer, predominately tropical climates and isolated populations such as the Australian Aborigines or the Japanese who have the high rates of lactose intolerance. Where there were grasslands and conditions conducive to raising animals, humans developed genetic variants that allow adults to continue producing lactase, the enzyme needed to break down lactose. In addition to genetic adaptations, the human gut can produce beneficial bacteria that are effective at metabolizing lactose when one consumes fermented products like yogurt or sour cream containing live cultures (de Vrese et al., 2001).

Asian populations inhabiting the steppes of Russia, the Han regions of China, Tibet, Nepal, and Northern India thrive on the milk, butter, and cheese products they obtain from reindeer, yak, water buffalo, or cow. Do all these people have chronic diarrhea and stomach cramping they haven't told us about? People in Northern India have no more substantially different lactose intolerance than the Swedes (30% as opposed to 25% respectively). From the John Hopkins Center: "Testing of DNA from Neolithic individuals who lived roughly 4000 to 5000 years ago has shown a very low prevalence of the mutation. This strongly suggests that there has been strong evolutionary pressure in those with the gene surviving to reproduce at much higher rates. For example, the Neolithic DNA from Sweden showed 95% of those studied were lactose intolerant, whereas the modern Swedish population has only 25% of individuals with [lactose intolerance]... This is just one of many fascinating examples of how our bodies do interact with food and how rapid evolution can occur" (Vogelsang).

BUTTER. See under Fats: Butter, page 18.

CHEESE. Unpasteurized cheese should be eaten unheated with meats, vegetables, fruits, and jams or at temperatures below 106°F—e.g., sprinkled on top of a dish after it comes out of the oven—to realize optimum health benefits. Most nutritionists agree that naturally aged hard cheeses have virtually no lactose. The milk sugars have been consumed by the bacteria to make it a low-carbohydrate lactose free choice. So enjoy your sharp cheddar, Parmesan, and Pecorino cheese.

LOW-FAT OR SKIM MILK. Drinking fat-depleted milk is detrimental to your health. Vitamins D, A, K2, and calcium, along with other minerals in the milk, are fat soluble. If you don't have fat in the milk to metabolize these nutrients, much of them will pass out of the body unutilized and/or the body will draw the necessary nutrients from your bones. Whole milk is the healthiest choice.

SOUR CREAM. A true sour cream contains full-fat cream that has been fermented—and nothing else. It is lower in carbohydrates than a yogurt made with whole milk because it is lower in naturally occurring milk sugars. It is for this reason I choose to use sour cream over yogurt in a recipe. This is one product that is hard to purchase unpasteurized. When buying any fermented dairy product, try to find those that clearly state they contain live cultures. Many sour cream products do not have a full ingredient list and are exempt from listing them according to FDA regulations. Beware of additives.

EGGS

CHICKENS ARE NOT VEGETARIANS. Did you know chickens aren't vegetarian by nature, so they need supplemental protein in their feed? When you see the designation "Vegetarian Fed" or "All Vegetable Diet," it means no animal by-products, such as proteins and fats derived from chicken or cow, are mixed into their supplemental feed pellets. Feeding chicken by-products to chickens would be akin to what caused mad cow disease, so the FDA allows producers to incorporate bovine meat and bonemeal into non-ruminant feed. Why feed manufacturers don't incorporate insect protein instead of animal by products is beyond me. However, chickens will eat just about anything, and one time a chicken ran away with my brownie–it was hilarious! I suppose the chicken's prehistoric ancestor might have randomly stumbled upon a dead animal carcass and feasted upon it, but protein other than bugs, seeds, and legumes is not the preferred fare–that is, unless you are talking about my brownie.

PASTURE RAISED. The "Natural" egg designation means absolutely nothing. Zilch. Of course an egg is natural! It comes out of a chicken's butt, doesn't it? Besides producing the best-tasting and most nutritious egg you will ever have, pasturing chickens is the most ecologically sustainable and humane method of egg production. A certified "Pasture-Raised" label should mean each laying hen *actually* is outdoors every day, on *rotated* pasture where they can forage for insects, seeds, and fresh vegetation. However, even pasture-raised assurances can be deceptive. The devil is in the details, and "rotated" pasture is the key term here.

The only way to keep chickens on rotated pasture is to house them in mobile units. None of the pasture-raised certifications require pasture-raised chickens be housed in mobile units. Pastured operations may house their chickens in fixed barns with decidedly questionable access to rotated pasture. Rotational frequency is a big question mark as well. This is why supposedly pasture-raised chicken eggs will oftentimes taste or look no different from the eggs of free-range or uncaged hens. This fine line sometimes leaves me wondering why I am paying more for eggs from pastured hens–especially when many of the larger operations source their eggs from co-operatives, with each individual farmer using different methods to "pasture raise" on "rotated" fields. The bigger a brand name becomes, the harder it is to police their sources, and some unscrupulous companies who label their eggs as pasture raised (without certification) have bought eggs on the open market, without confirming they were truly raised under humane and pastured conditions.

FREE RANGE. Do not be fooled by "Free Range" or "Uncaged" labels–there is nothing free range about either of these. While both of these methods are more humane than eggs from factory-farmed hens relegated 24-7 to tiny cages, the hens are oftentimes debeaked or have their beaks clipped and live in buildings without ever venturing outside. The certified Free Range labels only require the hens have "outdoor access" but don't require that they are herded out of buildings every day into rotated grass pastures. In reality, chickens raised all their life in confinement will stick close to their food and water located in the warehouse, never wondering what's outside. In some instances, they might be fairly happy and healthy relative to caged hens, but they are definitely not producing nutritionally superior eggs living indoors all day. Nor is this arrangement environmentally sound; all that chicken litter and poop has to go somewhere. You will never guess where, and it ain't in the fields! Hint: Read the meat and fish section to find out.

The USDA has not defined the terms "pastured" or "free range" or "free roaming" for eggs, so buyer beware when purchasing eggs without certification labels. Basically, any egg farmer could designate their eggs as from free-range chickens. Eggs carrying the Certified Humane® in conjunction with the Pasture Raised label and when also paired with the USDA Certified Organic eliminates a lot of headaches in deciding which eggs to buy. All eggs with the Certified Humane® label AND with the Pastured Raised designation must be raised on rotated pastures with 108 square feet for each hen. Birds must be outdoors 12 months per year, every day, for a minimum of 6 hours per day (weather permitting). The Certified Humane® label doesn't permit hens, whether pasture raised or free range, be given antibiotics or feed with animal by-products of any kind. But here is the glitch: Unless the eggs are marked USDA Certified Organic or Demeter Certified Biodynamic™ in addition to any pasture raised claim, the chickens' feed, while free of other nasty stuff, could be and most likely is GMO ridden and may contain horrific chemical residues like atrazine and glyphosate.

HOW TO BUY. For true transparency, a listing of farmers who supply eggs to the various companies should be on those companies' websites. I ran across one website where they had a page for their farmers, but once I arrived it had nothing more than a search box—no listings. Once there, you must put a search term in to find them. Wow, this is a chicken-and-egg conundrum. How do I know the farm to search for if I don't know the farm I am searching for? Hmmm. . . Research the brands available in your area the best you can and don't rely upon companies to accurately represent their products. Look for egg farmers stating they use mobile housing in order to provide the hens access to rotated pasture. Shell color makes no difference when considering nutritional value. Is your head spinning yet? And you thought buying eggs would be simple.

FATS

Bear with me. This is a long section, but it is extremely important, not only in relation to your health but in creating awesome-tasting food. Fat may be more important than any other ingredient you use.

While it is good to use as little mechanically processed fat as possible and obtain the bulk of dietary fats in their naturally occurring form from food, when cooking we just gotta use extra fat—and sometimes lots of it. Let's get a grip—we are talking cooking here. This section will help you make informed choices sans fabricated hype.

Whether made in the home or factory, all fats are all technically processed. Once they are exposed to light, air, and heat, beneficial qualities are progressively lost. Even the most minimally processed animal fats and plant-based oils don't provide significant amounts of vitamins A, C, E, or D (it says so right on their labels). Hey, unless you are eating like the Inuit, that is, blubber completely uncooked, truly "raw" with skin on—you are not getting vitamins from your fats. What you are getting, though, are substances that enable vital processes throughout the body, like hormone production and assimilation of the fat-soluble vitamins.

WHAT SHOULD I LOOK FOR WHEN SHOPPING?

In both animal- and plant-sourced fats, look for organic, unpasteurized, raw, non-hydrogenated, unbleached, and non-deodorized designations. Search for plant oils displaying extra-virgin and first cold-pressed labeling, meaning it is unrefined (no *high* heat and chemicals, e.g., solvents like hexane were used). Animal fat should be from pastured, humanely raised animals for the best fatty acid profiles.

Be aware that even organic products may still undergo a process of bleaching and deodorizing to remove gums, non-fatty materials, water-soluble and acidic pigments.

Processed at Low Heat. Whether animal- or plant-based, even the most primitive, low-technology methods of extraction subject the fatty acids to varying degrees of heat. All "raw" and "cold-pressed methods" generate heat to a certain extent. Heat denatures the flavor and nutritional qualities of all animal- and plant-sourced fat.

Most reputable producers will explain their processes and the temperatures the various fats are subjected to and for how long. When you purchase extra-virgin, cold-pressed plant oils, unpasteurized dairy, and kettle-rendered animal fat like lard, the manufacturers are required to keep processing below temperatures ranging from 98°F to 118°F so the fatty acids will not substantially degrade. What is also critical is the length of time a fat is exposed to heat; the longer the time, the greater the degradation.

You may ask, "Why bother finding low-temperature processed oil if I am going to heat it anyway?" Because *you* get to control the heat, and whether you heat it at all. Low-heat methods used to express the fats from the animal- or plant-based material minimize the loss of valuable nutrients and toxic by-products formed from oxidation and protein mutations. Fats stay in a form that nurtures and nourishes the body instead of stressing it out.

Insist On Organic. There is a distressing trend in the oil and fat industry whereby manufacturers proclaim their product GMO free and then proceed to charge high prices as if it were organic. Organic is not synonymous with GMO free. A GMO-free product, while a step in the right direction, can be grown with any manner of chemical fertilizers and pesticides.

No Hydrogenated or Partially Hydrogenated Trans-fats. All hydrogenated fats (a.k a. trans-fats) were removed from the FDA Generally Recognized as Safe list (GRAS) and are scheduled to be phased out completely by 2019. In the meantime, you still must read labels to protect yourself.

HOW SHOULD I STORE THEM?

Time, air, heat, and light increase the oxidation rate of fats. Inspect expiration dates before buying, and buy in small quantities. Don't buy products exposed to light and temperature variations near windows in stores, and keep them away from light sources and heat spots in your kitchen. Keep your fats in a cool, light-protected place and not set out on the counter, even if they are in a tin or tinted bottle. Recap them ASAP after using, and while the cool-looking little spouts for pouring are handy for chefs for speed and mass production, they unnecessarily expose the oil to oxygen in home applications. Finally, a big no-no: Don't reuse oil.

WHAT FATS SHOULD I USE?

I encourage you to use in moderation the fats that suit your dietary needs and genetic makeup, are minimally processed, and best fit the recipe at hand. This will ensure you have a well-rounded diet and eliminate the confusing dietary recommendations that are all over the board and largely unsubstantiated. I say, "in moderation" because fats, while so critical to health, are nutrient-dense foods. If you are not expending huge amounts of energy in your everyday life, the extra not burned, just like too much protein or carbohydrates, will be stored as yet more fat. By "minimally processed," I am talking about oils you could make in your own kitchen if you desired, and "genetic makeup" refers to the fact that humans have mutated over thousands of years and adapted to the food in their geographic location. For example, I imagine West Africans are genetically superior converters of the carotenoids contained in palm oil, while others like Northern Europeans or Northern Asians might be less efficient. It is interesting to note that lactose intolerance is high in West Africa, where palm oil is prevalent, and in East African herders, lactose intolerance is virtually nil.

While some authorities claim that prior to the 1950s, coconut and palm oil were common in Western kitchens, I see no evidence of that in my grandmother's older American cookbooks. I suppose it depends on where in the world you are talking about. The shortening called for in my great-grandmother's ginger cake was "sausage grease" (oh my!) and some of her recipes, like her mincemeat pie, called for suet. It is hard to find dietary fault with a woman who lived to be 93, did not use medications, didn't go to the gym, wasn't overweight, and still relished her animal fat right to the end!

SATURATED FATS—THEY'RE BAAACK!

After almost 65 years of institutional demonizing, the pendulum has swung and dietary fat is now your friend again. OMG—is this crazy or what? "Science" has failed to prove that eating a low-fat diet will stem heart disease. Back on the menu are traditionally processed saturated animal and tropical fats such as lard, butter, and coconut oil. Not all saturated fat is created equal, and it appears in different forms and ratios in the various sources. We have saturated palmitic acid in palm oil, stearic acid in pastured animals, lauric acid from coconuts, and the monounsaturated fats that predominate in olive and avocado oil, with each of these having been used by ancient societies.

These fats have different fatty acid profiles from one another, and each provides varying health benefits, depending on how it is processed.

Dentist Dr. Weston Price, in his book *Nutrition and Physical Degeneration*, written in the 1930s, was perhaps one of the earliest to explore the beneficial effects of saturated fats, even in the presence of grains in the diet. Cardiologist Dr. Atkins, in his book *Diet Revolution*, and later Dr. William Davis, in his book *Wheat Belly*, reveal it is the high consumption of grains and sugar, and not fats, that have created widespread heart disease and diabetes in recent times. Dr. Atkins realized we need fat to burn fat. Loren Cordain and Nora Gedgaudas, in their books The Paleo Diet and Primal Body, Primal Mind, respectively, describe how grass-fed animal fats are critical for healthful omega-6 to omega-3 ratios and the assimilation of the fat-soluble vitamins A, D, E, and K and minerals. In *Grain Brain*, neurologist Dr. David Perlmutter extensively explores the role of fat in promoting brain health. Fat is brain and endocrine fuel, and it is vital for your body to function optimally. Prominent doctors, nutritionists, and others have collectively given us pause to rethink and return to ancestral fats.

DRAWBACKS TO PLANT-BASED OIL. Although I do use plant-based oils, for the most part they should be used sparingly. Historically, they were seasonally obtained in concert with plant fruiting cycles, in contrast to animal fat, available any time of year.

Omega-3 Fatty Acids. The omega-3 fatty acids in plant-based oils are largely unavailable to metabolize. We have been led to believe nuts, avocado, olive oil, chia seed, and flaxseed are a rich source of omega-3 fatty acids. While they may have varying amounts of omega-3 (some like coconut, hazelnut, peanut, sunflower, safflower, and almond have none at all), the type obtained from plants is in the form of alpha linolenic acid (ALA), the omega-3 precursor to or parent form of EPA and DHA.

Okay, so what does this mean? Humans are grossly inefficient at converting ALA into EPA and DHA, and many individuals have no genetic ability whatsoever to convert ALA into a usable form of omega-3. For those who can convert, research suggests less than 15% of ALA is converted to EPA and DHA. Animals like 100% grass-fed ungulates and wild-caught cold-water fish are extremely efficient at converting ALA into the metabolically available forms of EPA and DHA humans so desperately need.

Omegas in the Wrong Proportions. Additionally, many plant-based oils contain a disproportion amount of omega-6 relative to omega-3. Take grape-seed oil for example, which has close to 700 parts of omega-6 to one part omega-3. Yikes! It is generally agreed among experts that omega-6 to omega-3 ratios in our diets should not exceed a ratio of 5:1 and preferably no greater than 2:1. Excessive amounts of omega-6 metabolically inhibits the availability of omega-3. Deficiencies in omega-3 have been linked to over 300 diseases, most notably chronic inflammatory responses, depression, Alzheimer's, and heart disease.

Modern Innovations. Oils such as safflower, canola, corn, soybean, flaxseed, grape-seed, and avocado oil are modern creations for "human" consumption and weren't considered culinary staples in the past. To mass-produce, most of them require highly industrialized processes that were only available as recently as the late 1800s and early 1900s, and in the case of avocado oil, the year 2000 for first cold-pressed versions.

The refining process will partially—and in some instances, completely—denature any beneficial properties the oils might possess, but it increases their shelf life and smoke point proportionate to the amount they are processed. Many companies assert their refining techniques are "natural," however they fail to describe what exactly their "natural refining" techniques entail or the temperatures the oil is subjected to. We have discussed this "natural" designation before, and it essentially means nothing in the food industry and is used to snow job the consumer. It is reminiscent of "natural" factory-produced eggs. The FDA does not police or define the "natural" designation as it applies to food production methods.

While many manufacturers claim their product undergoes testing to verify nutrient density and fatty acid profile, to ensure their "natural" refining processes produce the highest-quality, most nutrient-packed oil possible, they neglect to post these tests on their websites or direct us to third-party testing results.

Sneaky Hormone Disruptors. Some individuals are exceedingly sensitive to the high levels of phytoestrogens in flaxseed, sunflower, safflower, soybean, cottonseed, or canola oil and must avoid them completely. These mimic, displace, or disrupt the manufacture of hormones in our bodies. When you consider all the toxic chemicals we are constantly bombarded with daily, which also induce hormone disruption, consuming oils high in phytoestrogens just might be the final trigger in short-circuiting our endocrine systems.

WHAT IS SMOKE POINT?
The smoke point is the irreversible point in time when an oil or fat has been heated until it begins to burn and emit smoke, and if left long enough, it will eventually flame. From experience, and I have been there more than once, when unrefined plant-based oil starts to heat, its color gradually changes from golden or pale green to colorless, and if left to do so continuously, it will smoke, stink up the kitchen, and burn the pan. I am sure you would never do this, but should it occur, your fat or oil is wretchedly beyond reclamation.

The more an oil or fat has been refined, the higher its smoke point will be. So, don't be fooled by certain products claiming higher smoke points than one another. The more a plant-based oil is refined, the less color it will have because the phytonutrients have been cooked and strained right out of it, and the more tasteless and nutritionally void it becomes. It's best to cook with all fats at the lowest temperatures possible, especially if you have gone to all the expense of purchasing raw and/or minimally refined fats for their health benefits.

When researching smoke points, I found they are all over the board. For example, when comparing cold-pressed olive oil in one chart to that of another chart, I ended up with smoke points between 220° and 385°F! It was like playing pin the tail on the donkey, with some analyses making no distinction for whether the oils were unrefined vs. refined or unfiltered vs. filtered. My own experience tells me butter is the least stable and tolerates medium-low to medium heat; clarified butter, olive oil, and coconut oil can tolerate medium to medium-high heat for longer; and an animal fat like lard is the most stable for occasional deep frying. When discussing the smoke point for any particular oil or fat in the following sections, I have tried to identify the unrefined smoke points, though it is a hard task at best.

WHICH FATS ARE THE HEALTHIEST?

To review: It is the type of fat, the omega-6 to omega-3 ratios it contains, how it is produced and processed, how you use it, and your individual genetic adaptation, that determines how healthy any one fat will be for you. The takeaway on this: Use centuries-old, time-tested fats that could be made in any kitchen or with primitive equipment, such as butter, ghee, leaf lard, tallow, and cold-pressed plant-based oils such as coconut and olive oil, processed at the lowest temperatures possible. Instead of trying to choose the "healthiest" one based on the latest fad or scientific claims, cook with a variety of quality-produced fats mated with the flavor profile or ethnic origin of the recipe. Below are reviewed some of the most popular and commonly used fats in today's world.

Avocado Oil. Do not be confused into thinking this oil has superior health benefits over the homely olive oil. It has essentially the same fatty acid profile as olive oil, except it is about 40% higher in polyunsaturated oil, but that is nothing to get excited over because both are low in polyunsaturates. Its oleic fatty acid (omega-9) profile is one and the same as olive oil. Its omega-3 is in the ALA form, just like olive oil.

A truly first cold-pressed extra-virgin product should have a green color to it and, contrary to manufacturer claims, will have the same smoke point as olive oil. These will not be any less distinctive in taste than first cold-pressed/extra-virgin olive oil, just different in flavor. Oils with a higher smoke point have been heated to higher temperatures and refined to remove some or all their solids and phytochemical pigments, such as chlorophyll and carotenoid. This oil simply cannot be compared to unfiltered non-deodorized olive oil, it is like comparing apples to oranges.

Unlike olive oil, avocado oil has no watchdog organizations that provide testing, set standards, define terms, and certify quality. The *proposed* standard for unrefined extra-virgin avocado oil is that it not be processed at temperatures higher than 122°F, but again, there is no watchdog overseeing compliance. Compare that to 80.6°F for first cold-press extra-virgin olive oil. Let me remind you: Avocado oil's fatty acid profile is the same as that of olive oil, a predominately oleic monounsaturated fat.

This is not an ancient dietary oil, and its historical use was limited to cosmetics. It wasn't until 2000 that New Zealand developed an extra-virgin cold-press process similar to the mechanical extraction method used for olive oil. A whole new category of culinary oil was born and heavily marketed as a "healthy" oil suitable for high heat cooking purposes.

Some manufacturers do disclose it is "lightly refined," and by this they mean their cold-pressed extra-virgin avocado oil undergoes additional processing to remove chlorophyll and sediment. This produces an oil with a milder flavor, a lighter color, a higher smoke point, and a longer shelf life. The expensive mayonnaise versions contain oil that has been heated and refined beyond what would be considered "cold-pressed extra-virgin" for other high quality oils and should be viewed in the same category as "light" olive oil.

That said, the flavor is creamy and avocado-like and works well in salad dressings or mayo. I am skeptical of health claims, and given its short track record, undefined standards, and lack of regulatory oversight for manufacturers, I prefer olive oil.

Butter. Butter has a low smoke point and burns easily, so use with medium to low cooking temperatures. If you don't need to sauté with it, add as close to the end of the cooking process as possible. While it is my main go-to, in any of my recipes you may substitute an equal amount of clarified butter, coconut oil, olive oil, lard, or tallow for butter as best suits the recipe, your constitution, and taste buds. To receive the best bang for your buck with unpasteurized butter, eat it uncooked or at its melting point (95°F).

As with all dairy products, raw, unpasteurized butter is the best choice for obtaining maximum digestibility and nutrients. Oftentimes when savoring the goodness of raw, grass-fed butter, I reminisce that this was the butter my great-grandparents consumed as children. Prior to 1900, lard and butter were the main fats used in American cooking—that is until plant-based shortening, margarine, and peanut oil hit the markets. "Between 1920 and 1960, the incidence of heart disease rose precipitously to become America's number one killer. During the same period butter consumption plummeted from eighteen pounds per person per year to four. It doesn't take a Ph.D. in statistics to conclude that butter is not a cause" (Fallon and Enig 2000).

In addition to unpasteurized, I purchase cultured butter as well. The culturing process allows live bacteria to eat up some of the hard-to-digest and allergenic milk solids before it is made into butter, plus I feel it enhances the flavor. But, here is another Catch-22 where the American consumer is usually duped yet again. A cultured butter should be left to ferment prior to churning, but this is not what manufacturers within the United States typically do. It is far faster and more profitable to churn the butter, and then add cultures and diacetyl (hazelnut compound) to recreate the same flavor as slow fermentation. Contact the producer directly to determine the culturing process they use.

Butter contains the fat-soluble vitamins A, D, E and K. It is composed of 3 to 4% preformed butyric acid, making butter a far superior source than grains or vegetables. Butyric acid reduces gut permeability, feeds the colon cells, and assists with the production of healthy gut flora. Grass-fed butter has a small but proper balance of omega-6 to omega-3 fatty acids and substantial amounts of conjugated linoleic acid (CLA). It is now well recognized how important fatty acids are to brain health, but it is now believed CLA may help with long-term weight management and may inhibit cancer formation. Heck, it can't be all bad—look at Julia Child, a famous chef, author, television personality and a devoted butter advocate who lived until two days short of 92.

Clarified butter or Indian ghee is an ancient food tied to the domestication of ungulates, and its use wasn't necessarily tied to landlocked farmers. Nomadic shepherds would have most certainly used clarification to preserve precious butterfat, particularly during the warm summer months. To this day, it remains a staple food for shepherds living on high Tibetan grasslands. Records dating back at least 5,000 years document its use for culinary, healing, and religious purposes. They both are created by simmering butter until all moisture has evaporated and the milk solids have separated from the liquid fat. The milk solids will foam, sink to the bottom, and are then strained off. This process renders it largely, but not totally, casein and lactose free. Removing milk solids and moisture creates a higher smoke point. This is useful for applications where higher heat and prolonged cooking times are necessary, such as browning or frying meats and sautéing.

Contrary to what some may believe, the milk solids are not caramelized in highly prized ghee and a nutty flavor indicates low quality. Ghee is simmered slightly longer than a European clarified butter to totally remove all moisture, giving it a longer shelf life in hot climates. The most highly prized ghee is gently simmered from cultured butter, and in some cases, it is aged as well to render it virtually casein and lactose free.

There is no getting around the heating process during clarification, and it essentially pasteurizes the butter. This destroys the enzyme lactase that digests the milk sugar lactose. The destruction of lactase is not really an issue in this instance because the lactose is strained off anyway. However, the heating process will also destroy butter's anti-stiffness properties, a.k.a. the Wulzen factor, unless temperatures are kept below 106F. If you read the Dairy section you might remember the discussion about the X-factor found in milk from pastured dairy cows that graze on fresh, not dried, grass. The good news is heating doesn't eliminate this nutrient. This leads to the question: Should I worry about finding a product that uses cultured and raw (unpasteurized) butter prior to clarification? The answer is yes, but it's hard to find. Pasteurization adds one more denaturing element to the picture—essentially, cooking the ghee twice. This is an instance where you might want to make your own to obtain a quality product.

Canola Oil. The supposed benefits of canola oil are nothing more than flimflam foisted upon unsuspecting health-conscious consumers. Rapeseed oil is a member of the mustard family and has been cultivated for about 4,000 years. Its use was limited to nonfood purposes such as cleaning and lubricating tools and in oil lamps and paint. Its high erucic acid content made it toxic and inedible for human consumption.

In the 1970s, the Canadians crossbred rapeseed varieties and developed a never-seen-before low erucic acid strain. It later became known as "canola" and hit the US markets in 1985. This new, virtually untested, oil was hyped as "heart healthy," when in reality, alternative studies suggest canola oil produces heart and liver damage in animals and humans—just great. Many doctors and nutritionists who previously recommended the oil have now reversed their positions.

While the food industry insists canola oil is not rapeseed oil, the FDA defines it as follows: "Low erucic acid rapeseed oil, also known as canola oil, is the fully refined, bleached, and deodorized edible oil obtained from certain varieties of Brassica Napus or B. Campestris of the family Cruciferae. The plant varieties are those producing oil-bearing seeds with a low erucic acid content. Chemically, low erucic acid rapeseed oil is a mixture of triglycerides, composed of both saturated and unsaturated fatty acids, with an erucic acid content of no more than 2 percent of the component fatty acids" (GRAS Sec. 184.1555 Rapeseed oil). Notice the oil is refined, bleached, and deodorized, and the code further describes this oil as "used as edible fats and oils in food." Sounds like rapeseed to me.

Unless the label specifically states it is cold pressed, refining temperatures reach 450°F or above. Okay, any oil refined at such high temperatures is going to be completely devitalized, end of story. If you insist on buying this product, look for a rich amber color, but it is kind of hard to tell when they are packed in tinted bottles. Of course, as with all the cold-pressed oil markets, the FDA doesn't regulate this designation, and they can basically claim whatever they want. There are no independent third-party organizations to oversee and set standards for the canola oil industry. Most cold-pressed manufacturers call their oil "raw" or "unrefined" but artfully don't define these terms.

North Prairie Family Farms Gold Cold-Pressed Non-GMO Canola Oil is an exception, and assures us, on their website, their oil never exceeds 122°F. They adhere to the European Cold Crush Standards. This is good, but 122°F still exceeds the 98° to 118°F temperatures generally considered as cold pressed for other oils. They do not offer an organic variation, so I must assume it contains pesticides. After the cold-pressed oil is extracted by expeller, it is then exposed to some type of filtration to make it palatable. Some producers use a steam filtration process—but wait a minute. Steam is created at 212°F, isn't it? Raw oil submitted to hot steam would be an oxymoron, right? Yes, I thought so.

GMO glyphosate-resistant canola was first introduced in 1995, long before consumers really knew what the heck glyphosate or GMO was. The Canola Council of Canada admits "about 80% of the canola grown in Canada has now been modified using biotechnology to make it tolerant to some herbicides" (Canola Council 2016). They qualify this statement with assurances that GMO canola is perfectly safe. Yeah, right.

Coconut Oil. The flavor of coconut oil is perfect for use in Asian- or Polynesian-based recipes. It's useful for cooking at a slightly higher heat like ghee, but then again, high heat should be avoided whenever possible as it will destroy the beneficial properties of the raw coconut oil you paid so much money for. The smoke point of unrefined coconut oil is 350°F, compared to olive oil's 320°F, and butter's 300°F. But there again, what is the point of going to higher temperatures if you are purchasing unrefined oil cold pressed at or below 113° to 118°F? No matter how you plan to use it, purchase the raw, first cold-pressed, unbleached, non-deodorized, organic, fair-trade products.

It is made up of 90% saturated fat and contains no omega-3 or 6 fatty acids, but not to worry. Since it contains virtually no omega-6, it will not contribute to the overload of this fatty acid so prevalent in modern diets and negatively impact omega-3 availability. When you combine coconut oil with pastured, grass-fed meat and cold, wild-caught fish, its fats are not believed to complete for omega-3 receptors and uptake. What makes this oil so beneficial is the high content of lauric acid it possesses. This type of saturated fat is believed to improve brain function and possess antimicrobial properties that protect against leaky gut and the accompanying autoimmune/ inflammatory responses associated with it.

Raw coconut oil, like raw animal butter, retains active enzymes and the structure of its fatty acids is not compromised. Raw varieties are also purported to contain higher percentages of lauric acid and medium-chain fatty acids than coconut oils treated at higher temperatures. In primitive kitchens, you can be sure as little heat as possible was used to produce oil. Fuel for fire is labor-intensive to obtain, making it a precious commodity that would have been used in an economical manner.

Upon opening, raw coconut oil will have a delicate, fresh, coconutty smell and a sweet taste. However, these properties will deteriorate within the week if left on the counter or in the cupboard. Its smell and taste definitely degrades at room temperature, no doubt about it. Unless you use it every day, I would recommend storing it in the fridge until ready to use it and putting it back in when done.

This oil is not cheap, but rightly so, as producing coconut oil by any method is labor intensive. First the coconut must be harvested from the tree, which is no small feat. The tough, fibrous casing is then removed to expose the brown shell casing. This casing must be cracked and the coconut water drained before the meat can be removed. Homemade versions are made with fresh coconut meat that is cleaned and grated while still wet and then hand kneaded and squeezed to separate the milk from the meat. The liquid is then either left overnight to separate (less oil is obtained this way) or low simmered (the oil collects at the top, and the curdled solids sink to the bottom). The clear oil is then skimmed off and strained. This is not what you are buying in the grocery store, of course.

The commercially produced "raw" coconut milk is cold expeller-pressed or centrifuged at 118F or below. No chemicals are used to facilitate the extraction process with organic cold-pressed varieties. Depending on the oil-extraction machine used, it may be left to separate several hours before the oil is skimmed off. A low temperature limits how much oil can be extracted, hence the higher price for the extra-virgin, first cold-pressed, uncooked oil. "First cold pressed" just means the coconut pulp will not be run through a machine extraction process more than once. All presses are going to generate some type of heat due to friction. If the pulp is run through multiple times to extract the maximum amount of milk, degradation of nutrients will occur with each press.

Flaxseed Oil. While ancient peoples like the Egyptians cultivated flaxseed for rope, cloth, and as feed for livestock, it is not clear to me whether it was a preferred food for human consumption. I have not found any definitive archaeological studies to support this supposition. The Greeks and Romans certainly would have preferred their olive oil. Flaxseed is one of the oils hyped as healthy—but only recently. Like soybeans, its seed contains a significant amount of phytoestrogens (mimicking the human hormone, estrogen). Whether they play a beneficial role in the body is a controversial topic, but many believe they cause imbalances in our hormonal system. They have been tied to infertility as well as breast and prostate cancer and appear to aggravate hormone-sensitive conditions like hypothyroidism. Studies suggest flaxseed alters estrogen metabolism more than soy products (ASCN 2004).

To further complicate matters, it contains a cyanide-like compound that is only neutralized by heat, it is high in polyunsaturated fats that are destabilized by heat, and its high ratio of omega-3 is in the form of ALAs (remember, those are the guys that need conversion before they are metabolically available, and few individuals can convert those). Given all the negatives stacking up against flaxseed, I am thinking it is better left to chicken feed than human feed.

Grape-seed Oil. Another so-called health food, grape-seed oil owes its popularity to marketing nonsense. Grapeseed is a by-product of the wine-making process that has been profitably repurposed for human consumption. This oil is primarily composed of heat-sensitive polyunsaturated omega-6 oil, which we receive way too much of in modern diets, and it contains essentially no omega-3. Unlike olive oil, it contains little monounsaturated fat, and there are no independent certification programs setting standards as to purity and quality. So, while you may think you are buying a first cold-pressed product, odds are you aren't.

Leaf Lard and Lard from Pork. Leaf lard is prized for baking due to its neutral flavor and the flaky, tender texture it imparts to pie dough and pastries. It is rendered strictly from the fat surrounding the pig's kidneys and is regarded as the purest form of lard. Regular lard is made from the back fat and other areas of fat from the hog and has a strong distinct flavor. Both types have high smoke points, making them great for sautéing and deep frying.

To obtain their important benefits, be sure your lard is sourced from pastured hogs for the best fatty acid profiles, is not bleached, deodorized, or hydrogenated, and has no added stabilizers. Pastured pig pork lard is about 38 to 43% saturated fat and 47 to 50% monounsaturated fat (the same fatty acid present in olive oil). It is conjectured lard's high saturated fat content stabilizes the monounsaturated and polyunsaturated fats and prevents them from oxidizing with air and heat.

Okay, all this sounds great, but it is seriously hard to find a local supplier in my area, let alone a national producer who can guarantee an organic or pesticide-free product in combination with a humanely pasture-raised (non-CAFO) animal. There are many that provide GMO-free products, but this doesn't ensure pesticide-free products. This is one product you might have to search locally for or render yourself. Don't pay more for expensive products unless the producer can assure you with third-party independent certifications or from statements made publicly on its website and packaging, their product is sourced from organic, humanely raised, pastured hogs.

Macadamia Oil. The macadamia nut is native to Australia's rainforests, but you are probably more familiar with those grown in Hawaii. As always, organic, extra-virgin, cold-pressed is the only way to go, but this is another oil that is hard to find at a reasonable price. Be careful. While many oils claim they are cold-pressed and non-GMO, relatively few brands are organic. The extra-virgin will be golden in color and not white like the more processed, ersatz "cold-pressed." I have been fooled by this once, but they won't get me again. It is really too bad, because it is such a great oil. Its rich, buttery flavor is perfect for use in salad dressings and mayo. Its omega-6 to omega-3 ratio is better than olive oil and contains up to 79% monounsaturated fat with little polyunsaturated fat. It is hard to tell what the smoke point is, because I suspect the ratings are for the more refined versions. Mostly likely it has the same smoke point as olive oil, given its high monounsaturated fat content and similar shelf life.

Olive Oil. You should know the drill by now: Purchase organic, extra-virgin, first cold-press, and preferably unfiltered. The omega-6 to omega-3 ratio is okay for a plant oil, though again, it's in an ALA form. Many paleo recipes specifically state they have substituted olive oil for coconut, but it leaves me wondering why. Uh, both are vegetable oils, global usage of both oils is the result of agriculture and innovations in transportation, and neither really is "paleo" per se. Olive oil has a smoke point of 320°F while coconut has one of 350°F, so not a huge difference there. Olive oil contains lots of monounsaturated fats, while coconut oil has few. Both are low in polyunsaturated fats although coconut's high saturated fat content makes it slightly more stable when heated. It is believed by some that olive oil should only be used unheated, because it is quickly oxidized (this is bad) during any cooking process due to its high monounsaturated fat content without an equal balance of saturated fat to stabilize it. None of the recipes in this book require olive oil to be used in extreme heat situations such as deep frying. This oil has been used for culinary purposes for 6,000 years, and I just don't worry about it. They both have beneficial properties, so unless you have a health condition that requires the saturated lauric fatty acids, pick the oil that best blends best with the flavors in the recipe at hand.

You can be sure your modern-day, first cold-press, extra-virgin olive oil is made in centrifuges, and not in traditional presses. The International Olive Oil Council regulations consider a method to be "cold extraction" if the olives are kept at a temperature at or under 80.6°F, while the California Olive Oil Council believes milling temperature should not exceed 86°F.

Fraud is rampant among olive oil producers, and there is little governmental oversight with regard to label claims. The top brands in US grocery stores and the imported brands are the worst offenders! The USDA does provide certification, but it is voluntary, not mandatory. An oil that does not pass extra-virgin testing could still be sold and labeled as extra virgin, just without the USDA certification. Let me put this a different way: If USDA testing results in a fail, sellers are not forced to re-label their products as not being extra virgin. The FDA has informed the USDA that olive oil grades are not viewed as dangerous health concerns, and they will not take action if false labeling is reported! However, a USDA certification does ensure the product has passed testing, and you can be sure of its authenticity.

You can also increase the odds of purchasing quality by choosing an oil within 15 months of the harvest date, looking for a certification seal from the North American Olive Oil Association (NAOOA), the International Olive Council (IOC), or the California Olive Oil Council (COOC), and oils that are protected from light in opaque tins or dark glass bottles. I formerly bought oil in large tins to save money, but I realize now that purchasing smaller quantities provides less opportunity for the oil to go rancid.

Palm Oil and Palm Kernel Oil. Talk about a confusing and little-understood topic. This oil has been used in the South American and West African regions for about four to five thousand years but didn't enjoy widespread use until the mid-1990s. You have to be careful when purchasing this oil, as oil is obtained from both the flesh and the kernel, and each has a different fatty acid profile. The oil from the flesh is a dark red color and semi-liquid at room temperature, while the seed oil is white and solid like vegetable shortening. In the case of modern machine extraction, both the seed and flesh may be pushed through, creating a combination of the two. Not only do the flesh and seed have different fatty acid profiles, the two varieties do too: The South American version is different from its African cousin. Now here is where the waters get murky. The hurried consumer will find it hard to distinguish from most labels exactly from what variety and from what portions of the fruit the oil originates.

The fibrous, red, fleshy portion of the fruit is predominately composed of saturated palmitic acid. Many red palm oil manufacturers advertise it as containing high amounts of monounsaturated fat to balance out the palmitic acid, but in reality, it only contains approximately 36%, as opposed to olive oil, which contains up to 83% monounsaturated and relatively little palmitic fatty acids. Alternatively, the kernel oil contains 48.2% lauric acid (the same fatty acid found in coconut oil), 8% palmitic, and about 15% monounsaturated.

Traditional versions made by hand use the wet method to extract oil from the pulp, pretty much leaving the seeds intact. The laborious process involves soaking and hand massaging the pulp and seeds, straining while pouring hot water over it, or boiling at least once. The technique somewhat resembles primitive methods for extracting coconut oil, while low-tech machine extraction processes remove oil from both pulp and seed using either the wet- or a dry-press method. Either way, the oil is extracted by heat, no getting around it. The raw, cold-pressed products are usually defined as being produced at temperatures at or below 118°F.

While at first glance, palm oil contains many nutrients such as alpha-carotene and beta-carotene, these carotenoids can't be readily utilized by all persons. They first need to be converted by the human body into vitamin A, a process that the human body is terribly inefficient at. Contrast this against the readily absorbable preformed vitamin A present in animal sources like cod liver oil, butterfat, liver, and eggs, which requires no conversion. But the most damning feature of palm oil is its omega-6 to omega-3 fatty acid ratio: off the charts at a totally unbalanced 45:1. If mixed with the omega-three fatty acids found in fish, the inordinate amounts of omega-6 will hinder the uptake of omega-three.

Like other plant-sourced oils, palm oil is a product of agriculture and was most likely used to supplement dwindling animal fat sources. It has a distinctive taste that is a defining feature in West African cuisine. When used in moderation and balanced out by quality animal-sourced fats, it probably won't adversely affect your health, given the fact West Africans have been using it for centuries.

Perhaps most disturbing attribute of all, palm oil's recent popularity has led to widespread deforestation of the tropical rainforests. Certified sustainable palm oil carrying the CSPO label by the WWF or the Round Table on Sustainable Palm Oil (RSPO) label is your assurance the oil meets sustainable standards. Be on the lookout for and avoid highly processed palm oil and its fractional derivatives. They hang out in oodles of food and other consumer products. The World Wildlife Fund has identified palm oil as appearing under these names: Vegetable Oil, Vegetable Fat, Palm Kernel, Palm Kernel Oil, Palm Fruit Oil, Palmate, Palmitate, Palmolein, Glyceryl, Stearate, Palmitic Acid, Palm Stearin, Palmitoyl Oxostearamide, Palmitoyl Tetrapeptide-3, Sodium Laureth Sulfate, Sodium Lauryl Sulfate, Sodium Kernelate, Sodium Palm Kernelate, Sodium Lauryl Lactylate/ Sulphate, Hydrated Palm Glycerides, Ethyl Palmitate, Octyl Palmitate, and Palmityl Alcohol (WWF 2017).

Sesame Oil. One of the older oils used for human consumption, sesame oil dates back about five thousand years. It is best used in conjunction with lard, olive oil, or coconut oil as a flavor enhancer, and not as the predominate fat—a little bit goes a long way. Organic roasted sesame oil is a staple in my pantry and indispensable for stir-fries or adding an Asian twist to dishes.

Suet and Tallow. With suet and tallow, we are talking beef or lamb "lard" instead of pork lard. They have a distinctly different flavor profile from that of pork lard. Suet is the kidney fat and tallow is the muscle fat from ungulates like cows or lamb that has been rendered (simmered at low temperatures to remove meat solids) to produce a purified fat for cooking. Non-rendered or raw suet is sometimes finely cut up and used in traditional mincemeat pies as well as puddings.

A quality product is non-hydrogenated, has no added stabilizers, and was produced at low temperatures. Low-heat rendering produces a milder-tasting suet and tallow with superior fatty acid profiles. Like pork lard, suet and tallow are best sourced from organic pastured animals for the healthiest ratios of saturated, monounsaturated, and omega fatty acids. Suet and tallow contain relatively low levels of polyunsaturated fat, but like pork lard, they are comprised of about 50% monounsaturated fat. In research funded by the Weston A. Price Foundation, it was found, "Grass-fed tallow had 45 percent less total PUFA, 66 percent less omega-6 linoleic acid, and four times more omega-3 alpha-linolenic acid...[and] saturated stearic acid was 36 percent higher" (Masterjohn 2013).

FISH

Little oversight is given to the seafood industry, and there is no assurance labeling is accurate. Are you getting tired of hearing this? Me too, but this is the state of our food supply. Sometimes seafood is labeled as from the US when it is really from South Asia or another region. Fish labeled "fresh" may have been thawed and frozen 2 to 3 times before it reaches you. Haddock is sold as cod, Asian catfish and tilapia as red snapper, and escolar as white tuna. Sushi venues are the worst offenders, where 74% of sampled fish were mislabeled (Oceana 2013).

The best we can do here in the USA is search for Alaskan wild-caught, and avoid farmed fish and shellfish. Buying wild-caught from the Alaskan fishery will ensure a high eco-rating, the lowest rate of labeling fraud, the highest amounts of omega-3 (DHA and EPA) and vitamin D, low mercury levels, and in the case of salmon, astaxanthin (naturally occurring carotenoid/antioxidant). Wild salmon forage crustaceans, plankton and algae, and these creatures naturally color the salmon's flesh with the red-orange color.

BEST OMEGA-3 SOURCES. The highest levels of omega-3 fatty acids are found in the oilier (fattier) fish caught in cold water, such as mackerel, herring, sardines, salmon, black cod (sable fish), bluefin tuna, and rainbow trout. Fish such as halibut, pollock, blackfin tuna, flounder, sole, and albacore tuna contain moderate amounts. Yellowfin tuna, ocean perch, and snapper contain low amounts. The omega-3 levels of any one type of fish are dependent upon their fat content, which is determined by the temperatures and/or depth of the water they inhabit.

RADIOACTIVE FISH? The Alaska Department of Environmental Conservation (DEC), in conjunction with other governmental agencies, continue to test Alaskan seafood for any potential impacts resulting from the 2011 Fukushima nuclear disaster in Japan. Testing conducted in 2016 showed no detection of Fukushima-related radioactive material in Alaskan fisheries. While scientists are still detecting trace levels of Fukushima-related radioactivity in Californian and Oregonian fisheries, the DEC said in a press release: "[These waters] do not indicate a threat to Alaska waters or the safety of consuming marine fish" (Alaska DEC 2017). I sure hope they are telling us the truth, but I worry they aren't.

CHEMICALLY TREATED. Most likely your fresh fish has been treated with chemicals or gas to preserve freshness, and you know what? There is just no way to tell with unpackaged fresh fish. These chemicals may include antimicrobials, nitrites, sulphites, sorbates, benzoates, and citric acid. Fresh fish from Asia, whether farmed or not, have been known to be treated with formalin (formaldehyde, an embalming fluid) or carbon monoxide gas, so it retains that fresh-caught look. Asia is notorious for its use of formalin, and one in four fish slips into the US containing levels far exceeding the naturally occurring trace amounts allowed (Andrews 2013). The US doesn't prohibit the use of carbon monoxide on fish to preserve them, and has approved formalin to control pests in fish farms.

To make your shopping life a bit easier, the organization Seafood Watch offers a free phone app where you can search for up-to-date seafood recommendations quickly by using the common market name.

CANNED FISH. Do you ever wonder if canned fish loses its omega-3 content and whether it's better to buy fish canned in water or oil? Should you really buy it at all?

Canning processes will degrade nutrient values to a certain degree. Processing varies from one company to the next, and the methods used ultimately determine what nutrients will remain. Most canned fish is not packaged raw. All brands freeze the fish on the fishing boats and then defrost it prior to processing. After defrosting, most of the conventional brands precook the fish by deep frying or steaming and then dry it at 110-degree temperatures. If necessary, as in the case of salmon and tuna, it is then deboned, cut into chunks, and heated for yet a third time by the canning process.

Cooking, drying, and canning exposes the fragile polyunsaturated omega-3 fats to high temperatures varying from 100° to over 200°F for long periods of time. Not only does this destroy the omega-3 content but it degrades other heat-sensitive nutrients as well. Some of the more gourmet and health-conscious brands will pack their fish raw without a cook-and-dry method, and their products most likely contain more omega-3 fatty acids and other nutrients. You can only determine how any one brand processes their fish by visiting their website and exam their FAQ section.

Some studies suggest omega-3 levels are greater in water-packed canned fish than in oil packed, and others indicate completely the opposite. While fish packed in olive oil seems like a good idea, it is not going to retain its beneficial properties either once the canning heat is done with it. The trouble with water-packed fish is there may be other liquids added along with the water. These may include vegetable broth, hydrolyzed vegetable proteins, and fillers—all made from corn and soybeans. Additionally, fish packed in water will lose many of its water-soluble vitamins, particularly the highly volatile B1 and B2.

I have found a company that packages their tuna without adding any liquids, and this would be the preferred choice whenever possible. I really am at a loss, because there is no concrete data out there suggesting whether water or oil would be a better choice. If money is an issue, it would be better spent shopping for fresh fish on sale, dividing it into portions, vacuum sealing it, and then freezing it for later.

FARMED FISH. Wild fish forage and eat other small fish, plankton, and shellfish (including shrimp, krill, and other crustaceans). In contrast, farmed fish are fed grains and legumes (most likely GMO soy and corn protein and vegetable oil), given antibiotics, and treated with pesticides to control parasites. Their feed may also contain chicken litter. Oh yeah, they are eating chicken poop, too. Just wonderful. Farmed fish are fed soy, corn, and chicken litter—things they would never, ever find in the wild. Genetic modifications are increasingly being explored as well, to make fish more adaptable to an unnatural environment and food supply.

Fish-fed grains and legumes lose the beneficial ratios of omega-3 in their fat much in the same way a cow would, and in salmon, these totals are half of those found in wild caught. Those fed meal fortified with anchovies or other small, oily fish to increase omega-3 content usually carry high levels of mercury in their flesh. Anchovy populations are declining in response to overfishing to supply fish farms. I know it's tough at times, since farmed and GMO fish are so cheap and available, but please, don't create a market for it. Watch sales to find wild-caught from sustainable fisheries instead.

A pretty reliable way to distinguish farmed salmon from wild is the preponderance of white, fatty streaks in the meat. This isn't normal for a healthy, wild-caught fish. Another (but less accurate) measure is the flesh color. Wild salmon will have a deep red-orange color to its raw meat, while farmed will have a pale or light orange color. Sometimes the flesh will have light brown or gray mottled spots scattered throughout. Sockeye salmon is always wild and cannot be farmed; however, disreputable producers have taken to coloring salmon and calling it sockeye or wild caught.

Cheap as it is, tilapia is one fish you should avoid. Since it is a warm-water-loving, non-oily freshwater fish, its meat contains relatively little omega-3 fatty acid. There is no such thing as wild-caught tilapia. While one of the oldest aquaculture fish, it is guaranteed to have all the same issues surrounding modern-day farmed fish.

SUSTAINABLE FISHERIES. Sustainable fisheries can also mean farmed fish, so be sure to look for the "Wild Caught" designation. Fish and shellfish with the certified sustainable label Marine Stewardship Council (MSC) are supposedly responsibly caught, handled with care, and can be traced back to a sustainable source. However, many feel that MSC is continually lowering the criteria, and they have been criticized for their sometimes-deceptive practices of certifying fisheries that are not sustainable at all. MSC denies these claims. After reading the pros and cons, I am thinking they are better than nothing and will slowly lead to a higher level of awareness. Perhaps with the public eye now on them, they will work harder to ensure compliance with their own standards—let's hope. Other businesses have opted instead to use the guidance provided by the Monterey Bay Aquarium Seafood Watch program. Although they offer no labeling certification and oversight, fishing and seafood related businesses can join the Seafood Watch Business Partner program and learn to become environmentally responsible.

IMPORTED ASIAN FISH. Avoid imported wild and *all* farmed species from any source originating from Asia, certified sustainable or not. Not only must fish be harvested in a sustainable manner, they must be obtained ethically. Many of the Asian boats, including New Zealand foreign charter vessels but particularly those from the Maldives, Thailand, and Cambodia, use slave labor. Horrible atrocities are perpetrated upon those workers, and it is unbelievable slavery still exists. Boycott those sources until there is a certification process in place to protect workers. I would rather not eat fish than perpetuate slavery, no matter how inconvenient it is for me to do otherwise.

COOKING. The general rule for cooking fish fillets is four minutes per inch of thickness on each side when grilling at 425°F and eight minutes per inch when oven roasting at 425°F. For example, when grilling a ½-inch-thick fillet, which is what we most often find in the grocery store, figure two minutes on each side, and then let rest covered for a few minutes before serving. It will cook further as it cools a bit, and like a steak, the juices will stay in the meat instead of running out.

Grilled Cod with Meyer Lemon Butter, page 116

FLOUR

See also under Nuts or Cassava. In this section we'll devote attention to the much-maligned wheat flour. Frankly, I usually avoid using any type of flour product, but when the occasional need arises, I prefer einkorn wheat over any flour derived from tubers, pseudo-grains, or nuts, including coconut. Unless you have celiac disease or a gluten intolerance, experiment with einkorn wheat, and you may find yourself a whole lot happier.

WHEAT FLOUR. The late 1870s revolutionized milling machines. Technology went from grinding wheat grain with primitive stone burrs and sifters to using steel rollers and new-fangled purifiers. These innovations could now mass-produce flours cheaply, increasing consumption as never seen before in human history. Fine bran and germ particles were now separated from the endosperm to create a fluffier texture and lighter color without compromising the protein strength (the elastic quality of gluten) so highly prized by bakers. It sure changed the face of pastries and accessibility, but at what peril to our health? However, the final death blow to this ancient grain was not cast until the 1950s, with the advent of the super-hybrids and GMO wheat.

WHAT TO LOOK FOR. Fortunately for us, small growers have returned to farming the original strains of einkorn, emmer, and the simpler hybrids such as Fife. Choose unbleached, non-enriched, and unbromated flours. Chlorine gas (chlorides) and bromates used as bleaching agents and dough conditioners contribute to endocrine dysfunction (see discussion under **Additives**-Bromines). Chemical additives fool the consumer and allow millers to sell inferior flour made from cheaper, undesirable wheat grades.

While some organic flours, particularly the hard red wheat varieties, claim they are non-hybrid, I wonder how this can be true. I suspect the labels mean they are not "ultra-hybrid" and are one of the heritage wheat varieties in existence prior to the 1850s. Einkorn and emmer wheat can now be found in grocery stores and should be used in every application except when making pie crust or when desiring a flaky pastry crust or a chewy brownie. In that case, choose the all-purpose heritage hard red wheat hybrids. I use Fife, an heirloom hard red wheat, for my holiday pie crust. Are these more expensive? Well, yes, but worth it in the long run. Like organic food, if demand increases, the price will eventually drop.

EINKORN WHEAT FLOUR. If you are wheat sensitive, but not yet at the extreme end of the spectrum suffering with celiac disease, you just might be able to eat wheat again by choosing einkorn. For individuals with no sensitivities, eating this wheat may very well protect you against future intestinal damage or autoimmune disease as you age. It's not for every day, of course, but it is sure great to be able to whip up a special treat on occasion. This wheat is the original non-hybrid ancestor to all hybrid, ultra-hybrid, and genetically modified versions of wheat. Its digestibility lies in its simple chromosome structure, highly soluble proteins, and the fact it contains less starches than other wheat varieties. While not gluten free, it has substantially less than conventional all-purpose flour. Plus, its gluten affects the immune system differently, insofar it doesn't seem to induce elevated antibody production like modern wheat. (Pizzuti et al. 2006)

Einkorn performs wonderfully when making anything fluffy like breads, muffins, cakes, scones, biscuits, and some types of cookies (soft, not chewy). Einkorn's proteins and starches are denser, so it behaves somewhat like a cake flour by absorbing less liquid. The dough presents as gooey and wet, but resist the temptation to add more flour to make up for it. Baked goods made with it have a characteristic golden tint due to its high lutein content.

You won't get a decent flaky pie dough or a chewy brownie out of it, because it doesn't contain enough gluten. When baking with einkorn wheat, less fat is needed than your regular recipe calls for. Fat tends to break the long strands of gluten in the dough into shorter units (this is why it's called "shortening"). Its gluten is less elastic and will break down faster, so it doesn't require kneading or the "double in volume" proofing rule like typical breads risen with dry active yeast.

For best results with cookies and biscuits, use shortening that has softened enough to work with but still has a chill to it when cutting into flour (not refrigerator hard but not room temperature either).

Orange Nut Cake, page 255

FOOD LABELS

As you may have gathered when we touched on this topic earlier, trying to decipher food labels is like wandering around lost in the wilderness without a map. Some of them like "All Natural," "Heritage," and "Free Range" can embody storytelling at its finest and mean only what any individual food producer says they mean. Take the Heritage Hybrid Tomato: It sounds heirloom, doesn't it? There may be nothing heirloom about the product, but the label is a marketing ploy designed to prey upon your natural inclination to buy a healthier product. Certified labels ensure food products are raised in compliance with a set standard, but they don't always guarantee testing or rigorous regulatory oversight. There is much ambiguity surrounding the question of what we are actually paying for, given the differing standards from one certifying body to the next.

In the following pages, I cover a few major labels commonly found in the grocery store. While many of these labels provide valuable assurances, no one program unilaterally protects or addresses the complete shopping bag of concerns. Product packaging may display up to five different labels we must interpret. On the positive side, they have raised our collective consciousness and, ideally, will increase market demand for well-regulated, sustainable, healthy, as well as ethically produced food products we can count on. I encourage you to support these labels, but at the same time become familiar with the ones available in your area. Research their websites, send them emails with questions, and give praise when due—or alternatively, encourage them to do better.

Contact the various certifying agencies and companies when you observe discrepancies between what is advertised and the product you receive. Take field trips and visit local small companies or farmers. A drive out to the country will be a pleasant and relaxing experience. Emails sent to companies usually get a response, but sometimes it is nothing more than a superficial gobbledygook regurgitation of what is on their website. Ask pointed questions: Is the supplementary feed they and their co-operatives give their animals free from pesticides as well as GMOs? Do they spray around the farm perimeters with pesticides? If they won't answer these questions in writing, you can be sure they are hiding something.

I have contacted a few companies advertising humane, sustainable practices, no pesticides, and no GMOs who have dodged these questions or dropped the email correspondence completely. Others have explained that while they don't apply pesticides, they do apply herbicides around pasture perimeters or irrigation pipes. Give me a break. Pesticides are toxic or nontoxic chemicals that kill a broad spectrum of plant "pests." These substances include herbicides, fungicides, and insecticides. A weed is a pest. What am I missing here? While you may run into brick walls at times, at least they know they are being watched—and their evasion answers your question.

AMERICAN GRASSFED. AGA's standards apply to beef, bison, goat, lamb, and sheep. Animals are fed only grass and forage from weaning until harvest, are raised on pasture without confinement to feedlots, and are never given antibiotics and growth hormones. Animals must be bred and raised in the US, and genetically engineered and/or cloned animals are prohibited. Producers are audited annually by independent third parties to ensure compliance. While this is a great program, it would be even better if organic grass and forage was required or if pesticide and synthetic fertilizer use was also prohibited. This label is only valuable in conjunction with one of the "organic" certified programs.

CERTIFIED NATURALLY GROWN. USDA Organic certification can be prohibitively expensive and the hoops difficult to jump through. This certification offers small local farmers and ranchers a low-cost alternative to the National Organic Program. Certified farmers don't use synthetic fertilizers, pesticides, or GMOs, just like certified USDA organic farmers. Inspections are peer-based, conducted immediately after acceptance into the program and annually thereafter. Like any program, it may be abused, but it offers a certain degree of transparency and feedback you don't find with the USDA program. For example, farmers are required to explain their operations clearly on their farm's public profile on the CNG website. Profiles include contact information, certification records, dated status reports, and inspections.

DEMETER ASSOCIATION INC. This organization is recent on my radar screen, but it appears to be an excellent one you may rely upon. Its principles require deep ethical and philosophical commitment from its members and promote a sustainable, holistic approach to agriculture. The products carrying this label are produced organically using environmentally sound regenerative practices, with animal welfare foremost in mind. It specifically prohibits genetically engineered organisms. Certified Demeter regulates two labeling categories: 1) "Demeter Certified Biodynamic" and 2) "Made with Demeter certified Biodynamic (ingredients)."

IRRADIATED FOODS. The FDA has approved virtually all foods for irradiation in the US: beef, poultry, pork, shellfish (oysters, clams, mussels, and scallops), crustaceans (lobster, shrimp, and crab), fresh fruits and vegetables, lettuce and spinach, seeds for sprouting (e.g. alfalfa sprouts), shell eggs, spices and seasonings, and additives, to name a few. The FDA, in all their wisdom, has assured us food treated with radiation is perfectly harmless. What a bunch of baloney. The FDA safety assurances are based upon the fact that irradiated foods have been on the market for 30 years, and we are all fine, right? Just forget about the fact cancer is skyrocketing, and science has yet to prove long-term use is safe. Never mind irradiation creates a cheap solution and covers up production, handling, storage, and shipping problems the food industry should solve.

The Department of Energy originally advocated the use of irradiated food in order to provide a market for the waste product cobalt-60. Absolutely brilliant! Let's create a toxic, dangerous power source for corporations to make money off, without taking responsibility for anything, and then make more money by selling its radioactive waste to food manufacturers. The FDA didn't stop there with gamma radiation. It approved two other radiation sources for use on food: 1) x-rays produced by reflecting electrons off heavy metals and then streamed into food and 2) electron beams (similar to x-rays) streamed from an electron accelerator into food.

Fortunately, the FDA still requires irradiated foods to bear the international Radura symbol along with the statement "treated with radiation" or "treated by irradiation" on the food label. However, the symbol depicts a plant in usually a benign green color and looks healthy. It does nothing to alert the uninformed consumer their food was treated with a potentially hazardous material. The FDA also allows the word "pasteurization" as an acceptable substitute for the word irradiation. Conduct an internet search for this symbol and familiarize yourself with it.

Bulk foods, such as nuts, grains, and produce, are required to be individually labeled or to have a label next to the sale container. But of course, there are always loopholes for the food industry jokers. The FDA does not require labeling of individual ingredients in multi-ingredient foods or by the person second in line after the initial purchase. So, processed foods like your granola bar from the health food store, or foods sold in restaurants, schools, or fast food joints won't bear consumer labels warning you. What can you do about this? Just about nothing if you eat out regularly, but you can protect yourself with home-cooked meals made with fresh, whole organic ingredients, and by packing lunches and snacks for you and your family.

FREE-RANGE OR CAGE-FREE. I have touched on these topics under individual ingredients like eggs or meat. Terms like free-range and cage-free more often than not mean thousands of chickens and pigs are confined to warehouse-style buildings. These designations provide huge loopholes to the unethical producer. The USDA only regulates chickens and turkeys carrying this label, but not the eggs from poultry or cattle and pigs. In the case of chickens, the regulations only require access to the outside with no requirement for how long they must be outside. This outdoor "access" is broadly interpreted, and some outdoor systems leave animals in overcrowded conditions with no meaningful full-body exposure to sunlight, fresh air, or grass.

I plain don't recommend this label, certified humane and organic or not. If you are left with no alternative but to buy free-range or cage-free, look for a brand with both the "Humane" and "Organic" certified labels on the packaging.

HUMANE. These labels provide varying degrees of assurance an animal has not been mistreated or abused during breeding, life, transport, and slaughter. The USDA provides no standards or regulation for the "humanely raised" label, and basically anyone can use this label without any oversight. Certified labeling doesn't always mean the animals spend most of their days in idyllic pastures or aren't subjected to procedures, such as disbudding horns, branding, or castration. Pain relief is not always provided. Nor do these labels mean the animal has been raised on organic feed or ban the use of genetically modified and/or cloned animals and their offspring. Dairy cows oftentimes will have their calves separated from them within 24 hours of giving birth. Standards also vary widely regarding the treatment of breeding animals, animals during transport, and animals at slaughter.

Animal Welfare Approved, Certified Humane, American Humane Certified, Demeter, and the Global Animal Partnership are some of the labels you will find. These organizations update their standards annually, and I recommend personal investigation for those concerned. The USDA provides no standards for them to follow and merely verifies each certifying body is complying with its own labeling standards.

On the upside, the practices of debeaking (severe beak trimming), ear splitting and notching, tail docking, and nose rings are largely discouraged, and in some cases, prohibited. Ranchers and farmers are required to take other measures such as environmental enrichment and reducing stock densities to eliminate factors necessitating physical alterations. There are requirements surrounding the reasons for and the actual procedures themselves when physical alterations are permitted. Oddly enough, the various organizations differ in their definitions of "humane." For example, Animal Welfare Approved allows castration and ear-notching without pain relief, and American Humane Certified permits debeaking. While these two improve their standards yearly, I find American Humane Certified one of the least reliable in interpreting humane animal handling.

Certified Humane has some of the better standards by limiting or prohibiting debeaking, ear splitting and notching, tail docking, and nose rings. Dairy calves must not be weaned from their mothers before five weeks of age. They still allow beak clipping under their free-range/cage-free standards for birds ten days or younger. The Demeter certification is the only one I have found that provides extremely high humane standards with a holistic approach, where all farm or ranch animals must be organically fed and pasture raised.

The Global Animal Partnership's 5-Step Animal Welfare with its number and color coding is perhaps the easiest system to remember, once you are familiar with it. Look for a class 5 or 5+ and a green label, and you are good to go. On the downside, they provide no standards regarding treatment during breeding or slaughter or any assurance the animal was raised organically without pesticides or chemical fertilizers.

NATURAL. The term "natural" is not regulated by the FDA. In a nutshell, the FDA has NOT formally defined the "natural" designation on food products as of this writing. The FDA in a Federal Register Notice requesting comment states this:

"Although the FDA has not engaged in rulemaking to establish a formal definition for the term 'natural,' we do have a longstanding policy concerning the use of 'natural' in human food labeling. The FDA has considered the term 'natural' to mean that nothing artificial or synthetic (including all color additives regardless of source) has been included in, or has been added to, a food that would not normally be expected to be in that food. However, this policy was not intended to address food production methods, such as the use of pesticides, nor did it explicitly address food processing or manufacturing methods, such as thermal technologies, pasteurization, or irradiation. The FDA also did not consider whether the term 'natural' should describe any nutritional or other health benefit." (FDA 2015)

Artificial and synthetic? Well what does that exactly mean? Well, we would have to look those definitions up in the FDA manual for their interpretations and what exceptions to the rule they allow. For example, cellulose is considered a "natural" ingredient, but do we want to eat that? Not really. To add insult to injury, the Grocery Manufacturers Association has filed comments with the FDA requesting the label "Natural" to include foods that are genetically engineered or contain foods derived from genetic engineering (GMA 2016). In contrast, the Consumers Union (CU) comments filed with the FDA suggest: "consumers are currently misled by the 'natural' label on food and nearly 90 percent expect it to mean much more than it does." They believe the term should be banned altogether, because it is false and misleading under the Federal Food, Drug, and Cosmetic Act (CU 2016). The fun never ends, and it will be interesting to see what the FDA does with this.

NON-GMO. Genetically modified organism (GMO) free is NOT the same as pesticide free. While non-GMO verified food is a step in the right direction, it is not enough. A non-GMO food can be as riddled with pesticides as a GMO product. Non-GMO Project Verified means there is less than .09% GMO contamination, but it doesn't mean there are no pesticides like atrazine, chlorpyrifos, or glyphosate on it or in it. Look for a Certified Organic label in addition to Non-

GMO certifications. Many people confront me with the argument that all our food is essentially genetically modified via hybrids for thousands of years, so what am I so whipped up about? What they maybe missed or fail to understand is the profound difference between GMO and super-hybrids vs. simple hybrid seeds. Let's take a look at each one individually in relation to the plant world.

Hybrids. In the case of plant seeds, hybrids are the result of cross-pollinating two similar but unique plant varieties to create a new one. This process does occur within nature without human intervention, or can be nudged along by humans employing low-technology methods in the field. Take, for example, the evolution of wheat: It occurred gradually over thousands of years. The original wild einkorn wheat pollen mingled with goat grass pollen to produce emmer or faro wheat, and from there, emmer cross-pollinated with *Triticum* grass to become the wheat that was pretty much the standard for centuries until the late nineteenth century. The length of time it took primitive wheat, over countless generations, to adapt and evolve into unique new varieties, and the ability of each subsequent hybrid to reproduce exact copies of themselves, represent two critical distinguishing traits separating the hybrid from the super-hybrid.

Super-Hybrids. The techniques used to create super-hybrids, in contrast to traditional hybrids, were not discovered until the late 1800s and didn't become refined until the 1950s. To create today's super-hybrid requires high-tech gene restructuring within a laboratory environment. They are the first offspring after crossing two parent lines, or what is called an F1 hybrid (first generation). But before the parents of the F1 are mated, each of the two lines of breeding stock are inbred over multiple generations until two separate strains with desirable characteristics are consistently duplicated. Then, and only then, are they mated to produce the F1 hybrid. The offspring seeds are genetically unstable, and they are unable to reproduce a vital, consistent subsequent generation. Seed saving becomes impractical for farmers, because the super-hybrid's offspring often devolve and may not retain the beneficial attributes of their parent, such as resistance to insects or dry conditions. The F1 hybrids are not tested or evaluated by the USDA or FDA for food safety risks, and potential negative health and biodiversity impacts have not been explored.

Genetically Engineered Organisms. There is so much confusion over what exactly defines a genetically engineered organism because not even scientists themselves can agree. When you combine that with corporate profit interests, it's no wonder there is such controversy. GMO plants are different from simple hybrids, in that their genetic manipulation requires radical and highly complex technology. In simplistic terms, it is gene splicing, where desirable genes from one species are artificially extracted, duplicated or cloned (they may or may not be altered at this point), and then placed by unnatural means into another species.

Engineering genes is so much more than carefully manipulating a sexual reproduction process like cross-pollination, and the genes could come from something totally unrelated. For example, genes extracted from bacteria are inserted into food crops to make them pest resistant. Take glyphosate-tolerant plants, engineered by introducing genes isolated from a soil bacterium. Something like this would never occur in nature. Plants are not going to cross-pollinate with bacteria but with another similar plant that has become more resistant by producing a unique enzyme or protein within itself to thwart a threat. Additionally, while DNA transfer can occur naturally in organisms, this exchange has progressed slowly along the evolutionary timeline. It is a fine line, but one that has been crossed, and the long-term consequences are unknown.

Where the scientists get the gene from and what they do to with the gene during the cloning process distinguishes the bright line in separating out a modified organism from a clone or super-hybrid. This distinction is superfluous. A gene artificially taken out in a high-tech lab environment, manipulated or not, and placed in another organism, whether of the same family or not, and destined for the food supply may set off unintended consequences. Both GMO and super-hybrids require highly sophisticated gene manipulation, the benefits of which are either unstudied or remain unproven. Both could profoundly—and in some cases, irrevocably—impact the entire world's economic, animal, and environmental health for the worse.

Unlike super-hybrids, their offspring can and do go on to reproduce. This is the scariest aspect about them, and already there is growing concern GMO salmon farm escapees will unleash havoc among wild salmon populations. The reality is we just don't know. Neither the USDA nor the FDA conduct independent GMO research—instead, they rely solely upon manufacturers to provide evidence as to the safety and efficacy of their products. An extremely limited subset of the population—scientists, corporations, and politicians—are risking the entire world's food supply. It is an unacceptable risk, and one the consumer should have a choice in. Throughout history, horrific atrocities have been committed in the name of science, only later to be debunked. Seed supply and animal breeding should be taken out of the labs and put back into the fields. There, selective evolutionary pressure can be applied by forces far more intelligent than humans.

ORGANIC CERTIFIED. The organic label conjures visions of happy animals lounging in verdant fields where farmers employ holistic, regenerative agriculture practices. Unfortunately, this is more of a fairy tale than not. On a national level, the USDA Organic Certified designation gives you peace of mind that you are buying the most antibiotic-, pesticide-, synthetic fertilizer-, and GMO-free product commercially available, short of growing it yourself or knowing your local farmer.

Although organic produce has substantially less pesticides than conventional, the USDA Organic Act approves the use of various non-synthetic and synthetic pesticides on crops and permits the residues of these in products designated organic. Yikes! Some states and organic certification agencies have tighter rules, but the consumer is given no guarantee they are purchasing completely pesticide-free food. Take rotenone for example. Formerly touted as a "safe" and natural insecticide compatible with organic gardening, studies have now proved it causes neurodegenerative diseases like Parkinson's. I remember first reading about rotenone in a 1978 *Organic Gardening* magazine and then liberally dousing my broccoli with it to control cabbage worms. It was eventually banned in 2005, then reapproved for limited use in 2010, and not completely phased out until January 1, 2016. For years and years, consumers unwittingly consumed a dangerous yet "organic" neurotoxin.

Most drugs, including antibiotics and growth hormones are prohibited under the National Organic Program. However, regulations don't preclude administering antibiotics and other medications to sick animals when it is medically necessary. You can be sure some farmers broadly interpret this rule.

The USDA allows a 5% concentration of the gnarly prohibited substances (this includes GMO and glyphosate) in organic foodstuffs. This means organic produce could possibly contain more than one prohibited substance, as long as each one is present in a 5% concentration or less. Think about that: When multiple prohibited nasties are combined, that's quite a bit of poison.

Organic doesn't always mean testing has been done for GMO contamination. Only a Non-GMO Project Verified label, in addition to the USDA Organic label, offers peace of mind. Dwarf super-hybrid grains are totally unregulated, and organic offers zero protection against that issue. Not all organic farmers practice what would be considered sustainable holistic agriculture. Large factory farms, organic or not, use feedlots for meat and dairy animals, and pastures may be little more than large, fenced dirt lots. Crop rotation is loosely interpreted for vegetable production and trucking in compost to enrich depleted soil is a common practice.

Are We Getting Ripped Off? Well, a little bit, yes, but there are compelling reasons to buy organic despite the drawbacks. The bad boys like antibiotics, hormones, GMOs, glyphosate, chlorpyrifos, neonicotinoids, and atrazine are limited to a 5% concentration, while conventional farm products usually contain much higher levels. One of the most worrisome concerns with purchasing conventional produce is the use of systemic pesticides like glyphosate. They aren't *on* your food; they are *in* it and cannot be washed away. Antibiotics are routinely used in conventional food animals, not only to prevent, control, and treat disease but to accelerate growth rate, even though it has been shown antibiotics are not necessary or effective (CDC 2013). Organic certification ensures animals will be fed organically grown feed made with no added animal by-products and raised without the use of hormones or antibiotics (the USDA already bans use of added growth hormones in conventionally raised hogs and poultry, but they can still use these in conventional beef and dairy cattle).

The reality is many people cannot find and/or afford it, but I will tell you, it is considerably cheaper and more available than it was in the 1980s. What to do, especially if you can't grow your own or have close access to small organic farms? The next best thing is to shop for crops requiring the least amount of pesticides to grow, and buy the rest organic. The EWG's shopping guides identify conventionally grown fruits and vegetables, which test the lowest and highest levels of pesticide residues. Their studies are conducted by washing and peeling produce (when applicable; e.g., a banana) prior to testing. Their reports change yearly, and these can be found on their website.

Consumer Reports also offers a comprehensive list of the good, bad, and ugly on their website. In their "Risk Guide," the conventional vegetables and fruits listed in the low- or very low-risk categories are "essentially equivalent to organic."

SMARTFOOD. This minor brand reminds me of the "Natural" label, and I include it to illustrate how labels oftentimes are simply marketing techniques used to manipulate you into buying a product. They make you "think" you are getting more than you are. As you may well know, Smartfood® is a popcorn line. This label completely fooled my daughter and almost got me too. She brought home a bag of this stuff, and we both mindlessly munched away. The front of the bag assures us it contains no artificial flavors or preservatives, is 100% whole grain, and is gluten free. Okay, so far so good. Following my own advice (albeit a bit late), I turned the bag to the backside and read the ingredients list, which displays quite prominently, "partially produced with Genetic Engineering." I pointed out this warning and alerted my daughter to the fact that nowhere on the packaging did it say or certify its ingredients were organic or free of chemical fertilizers or pesticides. My daughter disgustedly threw the not-so-smart popcorn into the garbage.

SUSTAINABLE. The word implies attention to issues concerning human and animal health, socioeconomic impacts, and the environment (air, soil, and water health). Do the various sustainable certifications broadly address all these issues in relation to the products we purchase? No. For example, Rainforest Alliance Certified will not mean an item is organic, and the Marine Stewardship Council does not guarantee international safe and fair working environments. Unfortunately, the US has no sustainable food policy and no governmental agencies who establish standards, provide certification, and educate consumers. Some of the more common private organizations you might have encountered include: Fairtrade Certified, Rainforest Alliance Certified, Food Alliance, Demeter Certified Biodynamic, Protected Harvest, and the Marine Stewardship Council. All these different labels mean different things and are updated annually, and no one label ensures a completely sustainable product, but when combined with organic and humane labels, sustainable labels bring you one step closer to the desired end.

FRUITS

The naturally occurring sugars in fruit are a wonderful replacement for refined sugars or heavily concentrated natural ones, such as honey or maple syrup. That said, be aware they are quite high in carbohydrates and the sugar fructose. For example, take an apple. One apple contains 25 grams of carbohydrate, 4.4 grams of fiber, and 19 grams of sugar. Or how about a banana, clocking in at 27 grams of carbohydrate, only 3.1 grams of fiber, and 14 grams of sugar. Snacking on broccoli, celery sticks, carrots, or an avocado (technically a fruit) would be a far better choice on a daily basis than an apple a day.

FRUCTOSE. Even from natural sources, this substance when used in excess has negative effects on the body. For example, and per Nora Gedgaudas, "Fructose, the simple sugar in fruit, may not impact insulin much (except when it's in high fructose corn syrup), but it is extremely glycating and damaging.... In this context, the carbohydrates we are talking about here don't include fibrous vegetables and greens, which are very beneficial and have negligible sugar or starch content" (Gedgaudas 2011). Dr. William Davis also agrees fruits and vegetables shouldn't necessarily be considered in the same breath: "Eat some fruit. Notice that I did not say 'Eat fruits and vegetables.' That's because the two don't belong together...fruit should be consumed in limited quantities" (Davis 2011).

HERE'S ANOTHER DILEMMA. Three generations ago, fruits were a limited part of our diets and were only available seasonally. Late spring frosts or particularly dry weather can cause flowering buds to drop. Some trees, like the persimmon, may only bear biannually, meaning one year there is a bumper crop, but zilch the following year. Particularly in colder climates, fruits were a luxury, showing up as dried or canned, and reserved for the holidays. A fresh pineapple in the 1850s was a luxury at Christmas. Our bodies aren't designed to tolerate a constant supply of fruit.

Many of you who live in or on the edges of forests know you have to beat the animals to the punch when fruit and nuts are involved. Me? I get out and pick wild blackberries and figs before the bears find them and pray I don't turn into the main course served with fruit sauce! My experiences with foraging wild fruit and harvesting fruit from old heirloom trees assures me the perfect, polished, oversized fruit you buy in the grocery is nothing like what was eaten by Paleolithic man—or people even as recently as 100 years ago.

With modern means of transportation, fruit is never out of season. Blueberries out of season in North America? No problem. They are in season in Chile or Peru. Don't get me wrong; I am not hating on fresh fruit. I chow down on my regional favorites when in season, and going without would make life oh so boring. Fresh fruit or juice is essential for creating many of my recipes, and who could do without homemade jam? Moderation is the key: Eat them in small amounts, occasionally, and as a special treats, and not as a major component of your diet.

GRAINS

I don't think people are allergy and gluten intolerant so much as they are toxic chemical, pesticide, super-hybrid, and GMO intolerant. Our organs can only tolerate so much. Some folks tolerate these toxins better than others, and particularly as people age, their systems become less resilient to constant bombardment. This section is long, like the Fats section, but it is extremely important you understand why you can't continue with grain as a predominate nutritional element in your diet.

WHAT? GRAINS AND LEGUMES ARE PALEO. When you investigate the facts, legumes and grains are truly Paleolithic. There is evidence wild strains such as einkorn wheat were first gathered along waterways as early as 75,000 years ago–leaving plenty of time for digestive and genetic adaptations to occur. Depending on whose study you read, recent scientific research has so far dated agriculture back anywhere between 10,000 and 15,000 years ago. It is interesting to note the last Ice Age (of the Pleistocene Epoch) ended just about that time as the planet started to warm and man had spread out across all the continents. In northern climates, tropical and semitropical nuts like almonds, typically thought of as paleo, would have been nonexistent. Grains from grasses like wheat, barley, rye, and millet were and would have been the supplemental hunter-gatherer food in colder climates.

SO WHAT'S THE PROBLEM? Okay, we know grains, like legumes and nuts, have been a *minor* seasonally obtained portion of our diet for thousands and thousands of years. Trouble is, everyone today has been confused into thinking grains and legumes, thanks to corporate and governmental propaganda, should constitute a *major* source of nutrition. Grains were usually served in concert with meat. A diet heavily slanted toward grains can seriously impact our health in a number of ways. While gluten might first to spring to mind, there are so many other problematic issues.

In a relatively short span of time, less than 100 years, the grain landscape has been dramatically altered for the worse. First with the advent of chemical fertilizers and pesticides, brought to us by WWI and WWII, and then in the 1950s, when grains and legumes began their radical transformations into super-hybrids, and finally in the 1990s, when GMOs first reared their ugly heads. The environmental and health implications have not been fully studied, and massive data is accumulating, raising serious concerns about the combined negative impacts of these technologies.

Buying organic may protect you in large part from petroleum-based fertilizers, chemicals, and GMOs, but it doesn't protect you from the unfolding threats found in super-hybrid grains, affecting not only wheat but corn, millet, and rice as well. Rice, typically thought of as the "safe" non-gluten grain, is far from it. Just as was accomplished with wheat, Chinese researchers changed the basic composition of traditional tall-growing rice around 1955. They created high-yield dwarf varieties whose seed heads won't topple when nitrogen fertilizers are applied. Mind you, these seeds are created in high-tech labs that radically restructure them within a relatively short time span.

They cannot reproduce (cross-pollinate) if left to go wild, and they need human intervention to breed. And it hasn't stopped with wheat and rice; virtually all modern grains, including corn, have been genetically engineered into dwarf or semi-dwarf varieties to increase yield.

Celiac and gluten intolerance, practically nonexistent in 1900, have been on the rise since the 1950s. Advances in screening technology do not adequately explain its exponential rise. Many experts in the field conclude something else is happening. Mounting evidence is pointing directly to super-hybrids and GMO grain as major contributors to the incident rise of celiac disease. Dr. Alessio Fasano, director of the Center for Celiac Research at Mass General Hospital for Children in Boston had this to say about celiac disease in a Reuter's interview: "If you lead the lifestyle of three or four generations ago, you don't see this epidemic. I do believe what we're witnessing with celiac disease is that we're changing the environment way too fast for our body to adapt to it" (Seaman 2013).

Not only do GMO and super-hybrids raise health concerns, but biodiversity and sustainability issues are at stake. Farmers can no longer save their seed and those in undeveloped countries cannot afford to annually buy seed, chemical fertilizers, and pesticides necessary to grow these high-yield crops. Wild strains may be lost forever, and the lack of genetic diversity can and has led to massive crop failures.

SUPER-HIGH IN CARBOHYDRATES, LOW IN FIBER.

Next to super-hybrids and GMOs, this nutritional profile is perhaps the most troubling aspect of high grain consumption, and this includes *all* grains and pseudo-grains, not just wheat. Carbohydrates command the largest ratio in any individual grain's compositional profile, and you will receive more fiber gram for gram from vegetables than grain, including whole grain. Grains can cause tremendous blood sugar swings, sometimes even more so than sugar.

MAGNESIUM LOSS.

Any insulin surge in the body created in response to a blood sugar rise, triggers certain metabolic processes resulting in magnesium loss. Constant repetition of this cycle leads to an overall depletion of magnesium in the body. It's mind boggling how many bodily systems and functions require this vital nutrient. In her book *The Magnesium Miracle*, Dr. Carolyn Dean identifies fifty-six conditions a deficiency induces (Dean 2014). Magnesium impacts the circulatory and nervous systems, bone, muscles, reproductive organs, enzyme production, and the ability to utilize calcium. Before you start poo-pooing this information because your blood serum tests come back fine, know these tests do not accurately reflect the magnesium present in your body cells. "Serum levels usually do not become low (below about 2.0 mg/dl), however, until intracellular levels have been largely depleted" (Gedgaudas 2011). By the time you reach low serum levels, you may already have cellular damage, and who wants to risk that?

GLUTEN-FREE AND PSEUDO-GRAINS MAY ALSO MEAN TROUBLE.

In addition to carrying all the problematic factors attributed to grains in general, the proteins contained in gluten-free and pseudo-grains *may* cause in certain individuals what is known as a "cross-reactive" immune response. Their protein structures are so similar to gluten, a compromised immune system could erroneously identify them as dangerous. People are often surprised to find oats, barley, rye, millet, corn, teff, hemp, the pseudo-grains (quinoa, amaranth, chia, buckwheat), sorghum, and even rice sometimes provoke the same backlash as gluten in people with celiac disease, wheat allergies, and gluten intolerance.

Even given the possibility there is no cross-reactive process going on, plant proteins, particularly in grain, seeds, and legumes, are harder to digest than animal protein. When you combine this factor with the mutated proteins present in dwarf hybrids and GMOs, this could also conceivably explain the digestive havoc that ensues with gluten-free substitutes.

Others speculate the gas, cramping, bloating, and diarrhea suffered by sensitives and induced by gluten-free grains may be related to the high ratios of the fermentable carbohydrates (here we go again with those pesky carbs). Diets like FODMAP often recommend their reduction or elimination to control gastrointestinal issues.

DIGESTIVE PH IMBALANCES. Grains are believed to produce a more acidic *blood* profile and a more alkaline *stomach* environment. Do not confuse the pH balance of your blood with that of your stomach. Your stomach is supposed to be highly acidic to function properly. The high-carbohydrate, low-fat content of grains stimulates less hydrochloric acid production than would normally be produced when digesting animal protein and fat. We are designed with a little trap door at the bottom of the stomach specifically calibrated to open when a perfect acid state has been reached. Only then will the trap door open and release the stomach contents to continue their journey. When this valve fails to open in a timely fashion due to low production of hydrochloric acid, the contents are forced up, instead of down. Lack of hydrochloric acid results in inefficient processing of vitamins and minerals, gas, indigestion, acid reflux, and ultimately the destruction of the esophagus.

ANTINUTRIENTS. Many plants contain multiple internal mechanisms for self-protection and nourishing their offspring to reproductive maturity. A biggie is phytic acid. This binds to minerals such as calcium, zinc, magnesium, iron, and copper, which are present within grains, legumes, and seeds, and limits their bioavailability. So while grains might contain healthy doses of magnesium, manganese, and selenium, the amount we can actually absorb is reduced by high concentrations of phytic acid bound directly to these elements in the grain.

Some grains, especially millet, contain goitrogenic chemicals. Given the right circumstances, for example, low iodine in the diet, goitrogens interfere with thyroid function by inhibiting enzyme activity, hormone production, and iodine uptake and may lead to or aggravate thyroid disease. While to a certain degree much of the antinutrients can be mitigated by heat, consuming quality animal fats, and using ancestral food preparation techniques such as sprouting, soaking, and fermenting, these still do not negate the deleterious effects of the carbohydrate load, particularly for the relatively sedentary lifestyles we live.

INFERIOR NUTRIENT SOURCES. In the 1970s, macrobiotic and vegetarian ideologies led me to believe legumes and whole grains, in particular rice, were concentrated sources of B vitamins. One macrobiotic book specifically advised rice for brain health. NOT! How did they come up with this nonsense? Grains provide absolutely no B12, and what small amounts of B6, biotin, thiamine (B1), and niacin (B3) they do contain can be inhibited by certain factors like antinutrients and inherited genetic disorders. Again, many minerals and trace minerals like calcium and magnesium present in the grain are bound by phytic acid and limits our ability to absorb them.

HERBS AND SPICES

I am all about using fresh herbs, and they magically transform a mundane dish into gourmet. Try picking up at least one fresh herb to compliment your weekly meal plan, and prepare to be amazed. Whatever you don't use, cut up and throw in your salad for lunch or dinner the next day.

Few realize herbs freeze well and are fabulous in soups, sauces, and stews. This is particularly handy for hard-to-find exotics like kaffir lime leaves, Thai ginger galangal, or lemon grass. Dried lemon grass and cilantro are tasteless but retain their flavor when frozen. Fresh basil is another good one to freeze and can be crumbled directly into the pot while still frozen.

One of my favorite dried spices for meat or fish is powdered smoked paprika. Keep some on hand to sprinkle on top or mix with other spices to create a rub. Dried thyme, rosemary, tarragon, marjoram, and oregano retain their aromatic essential oils better than most other herbs. Buy these in small quantities, as they should be stored no longer than a year.

Tip: Keep all your old bottles, and wash and refill them from the organic bulk spice jars at the local health food store.

LEGUMES

Wild legume consumption dates back to the Paleolithic era, but like grains, they comprised a minor portion of that diet and were combined with meat. Unlike grains, legumes are high in fiber, but they share many of the same problematic issues as grains (see discussions under Grains). Soybeans have been bred into semi-dwarfs for maximum production and profit and present the same dangers as super-hybrid grains. Incredibly high in carbohydrates, soybeans cause blood sugar spikes that deplete magnesium levels in the body. Improper pH balances in the stomach are induced by heavy legume-based diets and may cause digestive dysfunction.

INFERIOR NUTRIENT SOURCES. They are profoundly inferior nutrient sources for obtaining B vitamins, protein, and fats. Antinutrients, such as phytic acid block nutrient uptake, and estrogen-like substances disrupt hormone production and function. Lima beans contain high levels of cyanide compounds and must be properly prepared to eliminate the toxin. Compounds in the fava bean can stimulate an anemic condition in genetically susceptible people and in its severest form can even cause death.

COOKING LEGUMES. If you would like to incorporate legumes into your diet, I encourage you to learn ancestral preparation methods. At the very least, soak your legumes. Large dried beans should soak for twenty-four hours before consumption. After rinsing, cover with four parts water to one part beans, bring to a simmer uncovered, and immediately remove from heat. Soak for twenty-four hours. Drain and rinse several times before cooking. For smaller legumes like lentils, follow the same procedure, but you'll need only an eight- to ten-hour soak time. Overnight or while you are at work should do the trick. Always cook lima beans uncovered to allow cyanide compounds to escape into the air.

It's important to buy fresh beans, so check the expiration date. The older they are, the less nutrients they contain and the greater the cook time. Never boil your beans for long periods of time; a slow simmer between 195F and 200F after soaking is preferred to prevent them from becoming tough. Macrobiotic cookbooks recommended cooking beans with seaweed. I am guessing it fortifies legumes with elements like magnesium and iodine to mitigate inherent phytic acid and goitrogens.

MAYONNAISE

This is the mother base to many sauces and salad dressings. Traditionally made cold-pressed extra-virgin (first-press) olive oil was the main ingredient used in the eighteenth century by the Spanish and French, the original creators of mayonnaise. Older recipes combine olive oil with vinegar, and aspic (jellied meat broth) was used as the emulsifier. Later, in the early nineteenth century, raw egg appeared as the emulsifier and lemon was added to the mix along with vinegar. The mayonnaise was "put to ice" or chilled before using.

QUALITY OIL IS IMPORTANT. What I pay attention to in the ingredient list of commercially sold products is the quality of oil used, because that is really all mayo is comprised of, along with a few eggs and lemon juice or vinegar.

Don't you believe it when others say it is okay or even healthy to use the cheaper virgin varieties of olive oil in your mayo recipe! All olive oils not labeled "extra-virgin, cold-pressed" are extracted using high temperatures, which degrades the nutritional qualities of the oil. Olive oils labeled as light, pure, or simply olive oil may also be made by using the chemical solvent hexane in conjunction with heat to remove the oil from the olive. There is nothing "paleo" about it, and no thank you, not in my food.

Soybean and cottonseed oils are also products of the toxic hexane extraction process, and unless labeled organic, are GMO and laden with pesticide. I am skeptical of the canola and avocado oils used in commercial mayonnaise, and their supposed benefits as well, for reasons discussed under Avocado Oil and Canola Oil in this section. If the manufacturer is truly using cold-pressed, extra-virgin, non-deodorized oil, the mayo will have a darker color and a distinct heavy flavor, not the light color and taste you are accustomed to.

WHY YOU SHOULD MAKE YOUR OWN.

If you read the labels on mayonnaise, you will soon realize they are predominately soybean, cottonseed, and/or canola or combinations thereof. At the time of writing this, it is impossible to find a commercial mayonnaise made solely with extra-virgin, cold-pressed olive oil. However, even if they existed, there is no real oversight limiting unscrupulous manufacturers from labeling virgin oil as extra-virgin and cold-pressed. Mayonnaises listing olive oil on their label contain relatively little olive oil.

Sometimes, I get a little lazy or jammed for time and am tempted to buy it while grocery shopping. Upon reading the label though, I always end up putting the jar back on the shelf. Remember: Mayonnaise is pretty darn high in the omega-6 fatty acids we get far too much of in modern diets, so daily consumption is probably not a great idea. As far as sandwiches go and if out of mayo, I will use unpasteurized butter on toasted bread. Try it–you just might like it.

Mayonnaise, page 242

MEATS

The human body finds the nutrients protein and fat in their most dense and usable forms in animal products. The focus is not really lean meats but meats containing high-quality proteins and fats produced in the animal's body by eating what they were designed to eat in the pasture. This is humanely raised meat, where they have access to sun and fresh air daily and fields where they can move freely. Humanely raised meat is good for the soil, air, and water, even in drought conditions when sustainable grazing methods are employed.

NATURAL MEAT. As I've discussed elsewhere in this book, "Natural" means nothing substantial or concrete. The USDA loosely interprets it with regard to meat and poultry as meaning nothing artificial or synthetic like color additives have been added. Of course, all sorts of additives are treated as exceptions to the rule of what would be considered artificial or synthetic. For a more comprehensive description, see the term under *Food Labels*-Natural.

PASTURED MEAT. While feedlots began appearing in the late 1800s, their use did not immediately become a widespread practice. Generally, all meats were pasture raised and finished until the 1950s, when a major shift occurred and concentrated animal feeding operations (CAFO) for raising animals to maturity became the standard. This arose in concert with the emergence of a megalithic grain industry that needed something to do with all their taxpayer-subsidized grain and soybeans.

The "Pasture Raised" and "Grass Fed" labeling has opened up a whole new Pandora's box of food fraud. These designations are not regulated by the USDA. Their exact definitions are nebulous and largely open to interpretation. Manufacturers display green idyllic pastoral settings on their packaging, when it couldn't be further from the truth. For the unscrupulous, "Pasture" could very well mean an overgrazed field or an outdoor dirt pen with nary a blade of green grass to be found.

On January 12, 2016, the USDA dropped the ball again and withdrew their Grass (Forage) Fed Standard for Ruminant Livestock and the Meat Products Derived from Such Livestock, and they will no longer verify applicants' programs to the Standard. Just great: No more "USDA Process Verified."

Pasture-raised, pastured, or grass-fed doesn't mean organic or free from GMOs, just like GMO-free doesn't mean free from pesticides. Lastly, this is an area where it is particularly important to understand that you as a consumer have the power to make compassionate choices and only purchase humanely raised meat bearing "Certified" humane labels or other assurances the animals were raised with their welfare in mind. Organic certifications alone do not assure this.

PH BALANCE AND MEAT. Déjà vu, and here we go again. Reminiscent of the 1970's macrobiotic diet and later, the various paleo/primal diets, these philosophies espouse controlling the body's pH balance with predominately alkaline and fewer acid-producing foods. Both diets insist vegetables alkalize the body, while meat and particularly dairy products increase the net acid load in our bodies. The Paleo Diet™ goes a step further in stressing it is only the non-starchy fruits and vegetables that increase alkalinity, which somewhat contradicts the macrobiotic diet's fondness for fermented soybeans, starchy tubers, and whole grains as alkalizing foods.

Discussions skip around from blood pH to urine pH to stomach pH, and determining what exactly we should be watching and trying to balance gets confusing quickly. Whether the blood pH changes in response to what we eat and thereby negatively impacts our health is a controversial topic. I am perplexed by how fluctuations to the left or right within acceptable urine pH ranges can adequately describe general health when viewed outside the body's complex macrocosm of checks and balances, individual environmental factors, and genetic heritage. One is left wondering why the ancient meat-eating Inuit didn't keel over dead in their igloos with overly acidic blood, eating virtually nothing but fat and animal protein during their long, frozen winters.

The primal, paleo, and ketogenic diets agree that protein, and particularly the fat in the meat, works in concert with bone-building nutrients and activates hormone production to stimulate bone, muscle, and connective tissue growth. My recipes focus on a nutrient-dense, low-carb approach incorporating abundant amounts of vegetables, and, to a lesser degree, fruits. I don't really worry about the acid/alkaline balancing act or precisely how many carbohydrates are in any particular vegetable. When I design meals, I emphasize (when practical) dishes with at least a 1:1 ratio—and preferably a 3:1 ratio—of vegetables to meat. I guess what I am trying to convey is this: My recipes get you to the same destination, without mind-numbing calculations along the way.

RUMINANTS. For meat purchases, such as beef, buffalo, elk, and lamb, look for products marked as exclusively 100% grass-fed and *finished*. If it doesn't say it on the label, it just ain't so. Ruminants with their multiple stomach chambers were designed to eat a 100% grass-based diet, not grains, so are healthiest when they do. Totally grass-fed cows sport fatty acid profiles almost identical to those found in wild ruminants. They possess notably higher levels of conjugated linoleic acid (CLA) and the cholesterol neutral stearic acid and superior ratios of omega-6 to omega-3 (more like 2:1) over their grain-fed counterparts. Eating 100% grass-fed meat means you never have to worry about consuming too much of the wrong types of fat in unhealthy proportions. 100% grass-fed pastured animals take longer to reach full maturity, and since they aren't fattened up on corn and soybeans, they won't have the rich marbling we associate with "quality" beef. The cuts tend to be smaller and sometimes tougher too, but this is the compromise you make to eat healthier meat.

Deceptive Labeling Practices. Pasture-raised or grass-fed labeling is deceptive, though. Here's the thing: Most beef and lamb is pasture raised, until they sell and ship them off to feedlots to be fattened the last few months or more of their lives (called "finishing"). Since the USDA has terminated the Grass Fed Marketing Claim Standard, companies are now free to include GMO cereal grains, grain by-products (starch and protein sources), cottonseed and cottonseed meal, soybean and soybean meal, almond hulls, and animal by-products as food for supposedly "grass-fed" ruminants. Unless it's designated 100% grass fed by a reputable company, it's finished on grain and animal products in feedlots or CAFOs.

However, 100% grass fed doesn't mean animals will be pasture raised to maturity. Reputable operations will admit they may send their animals to finishing yards to be fed dried grass for the last 30 to 90 days of their lives. The Certified Humane® standards manual allows pastured cattle and bison to be sent to feedlots for as long as 90 days for finishing. I am not saying this is right or wrong, and maybe this practice is the only practical course of action given the rising demand for pasture-raised beef. Most lamb is now feedlot finished too. Humane certification in relation to pasture requirements generally only require goats and sheep have 365-day access to pasture or an outside exercise area. The terms "pasture" or "outside exercise area" are not strictly defined and could be construed as large, fenced dirt pens situated outside and attached to an indoor facility–with not a blade of grass in sight.

Feeding Practices. Unless organic, ruminants may be fed substances to stimulate growth like ractopamine (big in the pork industry), Zilmax, steroid drugs, antibiotics, and natural and synthetic hormones. Conventionally raised ruminants are often fed composted poultry litter. That's right; this is not a typo but insanity run amok. Poultry litter is a combination of sawdust, straw, feathers, feces, rodent debris, and uneaten chicken feed that is composted and then fed to animals. Remember when I told you chicken feed could be made with bovine by-products? Well, the FDA says it's okay for ruminants to eat chicken feed containing bovine by-products if it doesn't contain any of the prohibited ones that would lead to mad cow disease. Now how in the world will the FDA enforce this if feces and feed are already in the litter, shipped from God knows where, destined for parts unknown? They can't and don't test every single batch of it, and they don't test every slaughtered animal for mad cow disease. If this isn't enough to gross you out, I don't know what is.

Many of you are probably thinking, "How do I afford 100% grass-fed, especially for a family?" One alternative is to buy in bulk. Ordering a whole, half, quarter, eighth, or a sixteenth side of beef from a local supplier allows you eat high-quality meat on a budget. Oftentimes you can customize cuts, plus it is a real time-saver. Instead of shopping weekly and trying to time sales, you simply reach in the freezer. A small, energy-efficient, free-standing freezer chest (opens at top) is inexpensive and a great choice for those with limited space. Five cubic feet is more than enough for an eighth beef side with room to spare or will fit a quarter portion with not much room for anything else. A seven-cubic-foot space will fit a quarter side of beef with more than enough room to spare for other freezer items. The bigger in size you go, the cheaper the meat becomes. You might consider sharing the purchase with friends and dividing the cuts among you. Look for farmers who price the meat at packaged weight (what you actually put in the freezer) rather than hanging weight. Expect a 35% pound loss from hanging weight pricing to actual package weight.

Fun factoid:

Did you know three types of bison once existed all over the continent of Europe? I bet you thought they were native only to the USA. Wild cattle were abundant too and finally tamed. Apparently, the European bison weren't well suited to domestication like cattle and were hunted into extinction. By the way, the original wild cattle have been hunted and bred into extinction as well.

SWINE AND POULTRY. Hormone and Antibiotic Free? Federal regulations prohibit the use of hormones in ALL poultry and pigs so don't pay more for products labeled as hormone free – they ALL are growth hormone free. But you aren't safe on the antibiotic front, even if you happen upon the label "No Antibiotics Ever" on the package. Animal health products not classified as antibiotics (such as drugs that control protozoal parasites) may and will be used if the animal doesn't live predominately outside in rotated, density-controlled pastures where the animal will naturally maintain good health. Poultry consumers in particular have grown accustomed to gigantic-sized portions bearing little resemblance to the scrawny chickens sold around 1900—or even in the 1960s. It is true, no pork or poultry may be fed hormones, but this doesn't exclude the use of antibiotics or other growth promoters like Zilmax or ractopamine, both banned in most countries around the world, including Europe, China, and Russia. Here it is perfectly legal. Unless you buy USDA Organic, you are most likely ingesting meat containing high concentrations of drug residues, even if the label states otherwise.

Free-Range or Free-Roaming Pigs? USDA hasn't defined this term for pigs, only for poultry. Any pig farmer could label their product in this manner. For non-ruminants, the American Grassfed Association recommends grass as a part of their diets. In the case of pigs and poultry, look for pasture raised certifications where the animals not only have access to forage but actually get to go outside into grass pasture. Unlike ruminants, they are omnivores and in the wild eat mostly a diet of grass and leaves but also need roots, acorns and fallen fruits, worms, insects, insect larvae, small mammals and their newborns, and the eggs and young of ground-nesting birds and reptiles (okay, maybe gross for some, but that is the reality). Organic pasture-raised poultry and pigs (this is not the same as organic free-range) are allowed plenty of foraging space where they can find the tasty tidbits they enjoy.

Farmers who don't have access to adequate year-round forest and forage areas must supplement diets with feed containing grain and legumes. This is only natural, and the pigs and chickens are designed with stomachs to handle food other than what is found in the pasture. Hunters know wild pig is often too lean to produce bacon, unless it has had access to plenty of acorns and starchy roots. Because these animals are given supplementary feed, their meat doesn't carry the same ratio of omega-3 fats as grass-fed ruminants.

Pastured, humanely raised organic poultry and particularly pork are extremely hard products to find. You must do your homework and research your supplier if you don't want to be ripped off. Truly pastured meats are as expensive as beef, if not more so. With bacon, I look for uncured to save on cost. It has half the sodium content of cured, and the taste is still amazing. I wait for sale prices on chickens and throw them in the freezer. Pork you can also purchase in quantity, just like a side of beef.

Inhumane Practices. Their ability to survive on alternate food sources has created cruel industry practices, widely considered acceptable, with little regard to the health and happiness of the animal. Chickens are debeaked and raised indoors in small cages that barely allow movement. Pigs are also raised in cages with too little room to move around in, and out of stress and frustration, end up biting or eating their cell mates' parts.

ORGAN MEATS. My mother would often share the heart and liver obtained from poultry or rabbit. My grandmother's stuffing and soups contained organ meat, including gizzards, but now it is rarely included in the package with fresh poultry. Heart, liver, and tongue were important components of the American diet as recently as the 1960s—that is to say, it was common for people to eat them, and it was easy to find at the grocery store. Take liverwurst, when was the last time you were offered it or included it in a sandwich?

Here is the thing with organ meats: They were never meant to be eaten in large quantities. You cannot feed a tribe, let alone a family, with one animal's liver, heart, brain, pancreas, kidneys, or adrenal glands. You have to realize one animal only supplies so much organ meat relative to the rest of the animal. Liver, especially from ungulates or codfish, is a dense, nutrient-rich source of vitamin A, and in large quantities it is toxic. This is because excess quantities are stored in the body rather than flushed out like vitamin C or B1. I have firsthand experience of eating beef liver or cod-liver oil and subsequently freaking out with a racing heart and shortness of breath. Apparently, I don't suffer from any vitamin A deficiencies and obtain all the vitamin A necessary from grass-fed meat, butter, and eggs. Taking cod-liver oil once a day, combined with once-a-week beef liver, almost sent me over the edge.

If beef liver is too strong for you, like it is for me, try chicken liver with its lower concentration of vitamin A. Organ meat is best used once in a while in combination with fat and other meats, such as in pâtés and in the soup pot. For example, pâté is a mix of fat and other meats combined with liver. I include plenty of celery, onion, and herbs in mine.

NUTS

Most culinary nuts like almonds, pecans, pistachios, walnuts, and Brazil nuts are not botanically classified as nuts but are known as drupes, and they are all semitropical or tropical in origin. True nuts such as hazelnuts, chestnuts, and acorns are hardy and are found in colder climates. Nope, pine nuts are seeds.

While I don't eliminate nuts out of my diet or recipes, I eat organic nuts as they were meant to be eaten: occasionally and as a special treat, not daily or even weekly. Here I dispel some common misconceptions surrounding two of the trendiest paleo nuts: almonds and coconuts. Also featured is one of my personal favorites, the macadamia. I don't really advocate one nut over another; the intention is to elevate the awareness that they are not all they are cracked up to be.

Many are promoted as rich in essential omega-3 fatty acid, vitamin E, protein, and antioxidants, but the fact of the matter is, both nuts and seeds contain unhealthy omega-6 to omega-3 ratios. Excessive omega-6 consumption has been associated with inflammation and all manner of modern illnesses. And the omega-3 is only available in its alpha linoleic acid form, which means we have to convert it before our bodies can use it, and not everyone's body is efficient at doing so. That's why it is usually healthier to receive the bulk of our omegas from cold-water fish and grass-fed, pastured animal sources–they have already done the conversion process for us.

Like grains and legumes, nuts and seeds are extremely high in mineral-binding antinutrients, such as goitrogens and phytic acid. Their protein content is hard to digest, all have substantial sugar content per ounce, and their oils are volatile (meaning they go rancid fast). They are available only seasonally, so historically, they comprised a limited portion of the diet. Early humans must have been frustrated many a time competing with animals to secure their share. I currently have almond and pecan trees in my yard, and the squirrels leave me hardly a one. Seriously, I would have to shoot all the squirrels to get a decent nut crop.

ALMONDS. Almond trees are one of the oldest domesticated trees, next to coconut trees, and are believed to have originated in the Middle East. Bitter wild almonds are deadly poisonous because of their high cyanide content, and certain preparation methods are needed to remove the toxin before consuming. They were eventually domesticated and bred into the sweet almond we all know and eat today. So really, they aren't truly "paleo," but a product of agriculture.

Do you know that all almonds are pasteurized whether marked raw or not? I thought when I bought raw nuts, they were uncooked. Wrong! California, where all the almonds are grown in the USA, requires them to be pasteurized. Other nuts, such as Brazil nuts, cashews, macadamias, pecans, pistachios, and walnuts, marked raw, most likely have been pasteurized as well, but it's hard to know for sure.

Just as in dairy products, pasteurization means the molecular composition of the oils and proteins has been changed and the enzymes denatured. There are two schools of thought regarding their enzyme content and whether they should be heat treated. Some argue once the enzymes have been destroyed, our ability to digest them has also been compromised. Contrary thought suggests the enzymes present in nuts are for sprouting the seed and are not compatible with our digestive systems. Frankly, I get a headache just thinking about this.

Organic almonds are steam pasteurized at high temperatures reaching 160F and then dried out with yet more heat. Nonorganic nuts are either sprayed with a chemical or pasteurized by a combination of hot-air roasting and infrared heat. To preserve their volatile oils, nonorganic almonds have also been treated with BHT or ethylene oxide. Unpasteurized organic sweet almonds are generally imported, and who knows what yeast, aflatoxin-producing molds, insect larvae, and deadly bacteria lurk on their surfaces. Imported sweet varieties have also been known to be contaminated with bitter almonds. As recently as 2014, Whole Foods recalled almonds imported from Spain due to high cyanide levels. Apparently, nuts need to be soaked, roasted, or otherwise processed before consuming for more reasons than eliminating phytic acid.

COCONUTS. At the time of this writing, coconut is one of the bigger trending fads in the health industry. Like almonds and walnuts, they are not botanical nuts but tropical drupes. Their meat is not really fruit but a construction of its gigantic seed. It is believed all modern coconut palms are hybrids of two original species and trace their genetic ancestry to palms off the coasts of India and Southeast Asia in the Pacific Ocean. The various varieties of coconuts found around the world are not indigenous and were dispersed mainly by human migration and trade. Today's coconuts are domesticated products of agriculture, and no more paleo than the ancient grains and seeds obtained from grasses, bushes, or other trees.

Unless you hail genetically from a region where coconut was a major part of the diet, many people just don't have the gut flora to digest it all that well. While I do okay with organic coconut milk made without additives, coconut flour is especially troublesome. Ancient peoples ate their coconut meat fresh or in stews combined with meat, and coconut flour was not really on the menu. I have endured extreme intestinal discomfort, rashes, and headaches after consuming organic coconut flour.

While slightly lower in total carbohydrates than wheat flour, coconut flour is high in fructose content. For example, every tablespoon of coconut flour contains 1.5 grams of sugar, while wheat flour contains none. Too much concentrated coconut sugar may stress the gut flora balance, but on the upside, coconut flour is much higher in fiber than either whole wheat or almond flour.

While not as common as tree nut allergies, coconut allergies are real. There is evidence coconuts may contain cross-reactive substances and the immune system identifies them as one and the same as those contained in other allergens. For example, a person with a walnut or banana allergy may have problems with coconuts. Is there something about consuming coconut I'm missing? I am certainly not advocating one do without coconut products, and I incorporate them into recipes, but don't assume it is the cure-all grain and dairy-free substitution to eat daily.

MACADAMIAS. This is another tropical nut, hailing from Australia's rainforests, and like the almond, undomesticated versions are loaded with highly poisonous cyanide compounds. The species cultivated for consumption do not contain these cyanogenic compounds and may be a great choice for you when opting for nuts. They contain a better omega-6 to omega-3 ratio of about 6:1 (ALA form) and are high in monounsaturated fat and low in polyunsaturated fats when contrasted against other nuts. They are low in carbohydrates and purportedly low in antinutrients like lectins and phytic acid. One ounce of macadamias has a net carb load of 1.52 (4 grams carbs minus 2.4 grams fiber). Compare the macadamia's stellar stats to an ounce of almonds. Almonds carry a net carb content of 2.7, contain extremely high amounts of omega-6, have no omega-3 fats, and are extremely high in phytic acid. Almonds don't look so hot now do they?

SALT

Most of my recipes require little salt, if any, and I achieve flavor with the use of herbs. Slowly decrease your salt intake, and your palate will soon become accustomed to using less. Salt is obtained by evaporating sea water, mining deposits from dried-up lakes or seas buried deep in the earth, surface-mined deposits pushed up to the surface from underground or from salt flats. The composition of salt will vary according to its source, and variations in minerals and trace elements impact flavor and color. Other factors affecting taste include mining or harvesting techniques, bleaching, additives, and the process used to remove impurities.

The anticaking agents added to keep it free flowing are particularly nasty and include silicates, ferrocyanides, and aluminum-based chemicals. Dextrose and other sugars are then added to cut the bitterness of the anticaking agents. Other additives such as coloring may be used to imitate sea salt or Himalayan salt, and this is perfectly legal as long as it is on the FDA's approved additive list. Many argue these are in such small amounts it is nothing to worry about. I take issue with that stance.

Take iodine, for example: The amount needed to maintain health is minuscule but when taken daily in excessive quantities becomes toxic. I don't care if the FDA has declared these amounts safe; pouring dextrose and aluminum on your food every day is going to add up to a negative. Instead, handle salt's natural tendency to clump by adding a few grains of uncooked rice added to the shaker and big chunks can be broken up in a food processor or blender. Many brands display the Non-GMO label but I don't know how this would be relevant if you purchase additive free salt. It is just plain silly.

IS ONE SALT HEALTHIER THAN ANOTHER? As with any food product, the less heat, chemicals, and adulteration it is exposed to, the better it is for our bodies. Soil and water are rapidly becoming degraded, and the produce arising from them contains less beneficial minerals than ever before. It only makes sense to obtain salt in its most pure form to compensate for nutrient loss in other areas of our diet, rather than exacerbate the situation by ingesting yet another denatured substance. I find merit in paying more for a low-technology-sourced, minimally processed salt, with trace minerals intact and with no chemical additives. Besides, it makes food taste better, and that's what it's all about, right?

COMMON TABLE SALT. Run-of-the-mill table salt is mined and after refining is virtually 100% sodium chloride with all trace minerals stripped. It is subjected to harsh extraction processes and treated with chemicals and extreme heat to remove impurities. The problem is, the refining process, including the addition of additives along with bleaching, completely ruins any desirable nutrient or aesthetic qualities it may have had. Gourmet, minimally processed varieties are superior to standard table salt for this reason, and to me, worth the extra money for culinary purposes. Once you stop using cheap salt, you will notice the difference after a while.

HIMALAYAN PINK CRYSTAL SALT. This is a premium gourmet salt that I find the least caustic on the tongue compared to other types of salt. It is available in coarse, fine, and extra-fine grain sizes. In contrast to refined table salt, pink crystal salt may contain up to 84 mineral and trace elements to smooth out the harshness of pure sodium chloride.

Before you get too excited about its benefits, realize pink crystal salts originate in the Himalayas from underground mines in Pakistan. Typically these salts are mined as they have been for centuries, by hand and without explosives. The work must be backbreaking! To date, I have not found any products certified as "Fair Trade" or with any other type of certification that requires companies provide safe environments, fair pay, and do not use child labor. The mines are run by the Pakistan Mineral Development Corporation, a semiautonomous corporation operating under the administrative control of the Pakistan government. Government control and oversight supposedly helps support fair employment and sustainable manufacturing practices, though this is a dubious premise. That said, I love this salt but really wish I could feel comfortable using it.

As with sea salt, there is no FDA definition for this product, and basically anyone could dye a coarse table salt, slap a bogus label on it, and call it Himalayan Pink Salt. Before you shell out good money, I would visit a brand's website, find out where and how they source their salt and the breakdown of the mineral content, and read the ingredient label to find out what else was added.

KOSHER. Certified kosher salt simply means it is pure sodium and minerals and contains no additives. It could originate from any source, whether mined or surface evaporated. The texture is larger and more granular than a regular table salt, which is a necessary element when koshering meat in the Jewish tradition. According to kosher law, blood is not allowed to be eaten, so the meat is coated with salt shortly after slaughter to absorb and assist with removal of any remaining blood. Its coarseness and the fact it contains no adulterations make it the preferred choice of many cooks.

SEA SALT. This is harvested from coastal sites along the Pacific and Atlantic Oceans, the Mediterranean Sea, the North Sea, and most famously from the Dead and Celtic Seas. Unique to its place of origin, sea salt will have different combinations of elements and color, ranging from shades of white, pink, or gray. Quality products are sun dried, hand harvested from their drying beds, and minimally refined. It is available in coarse, fine, and extra-fine grain sizes. True, minimally refined sea salt, unlike table salt, has a high mineral content and a taste preferred by discriminating palates.

Modern ocean water contains environmental pollutants like mercury, lead, petroleum, and chemicals, and this worries me about sea salt. While all types of salt must meet certain standards to be called food grade, logic would dictate the Himalayan products would contain less industrial toxins by virtue of the fact they have been buried under the ground for millions of years.

Some of the cheaper brands offer inferior sea salt from desalinated seawater, the by-product from processes used to produce drinking water. To eliminate any potential contaminates, the salt is further refined, rendering a composition and value little different from that of ordinary table salt. Canadian law requires any salt labeled as "sea salt" be from an existing sea. Salt from a mine cannot be labeled as sea salt, but US law makes no such distinction. One could mine it, refine it, dye it, slap on a label, and call it Dead Sea or Hawaiian sea salt, as long as it meets the standards of FDA Food Grade salt. Seriously, the FDA has said this is okay.

SEEDS

Seeds are fun to use in recipes and enhance the creative process by adding textural variety and interesting flavors along with nutritional benefits. While they contain no gluten, they carry with them many of the same issues as grains, legumes, and nuts. Like the foregoing, traditional preparation methods like soaking and/or roasting should be employed prior to consuming to reduce the effect of antinutrients. Their oils are highly volatile and prone to rancidity, so it is a good practice to buy them whole, keep them refrigerated, and crush them in a food processor or coffee grinder as needed.

Sesame, pumpkin, and sunflower are the most frequently used culinary favorites, with flaxseed and now chia being the two latest health-craze seeds. I have highlighted the two newest kids on the block, and when examined closely, they are really not all that special.

FLAX SEEDS. Special attention is devoted to this one, because I feel it is one of the most dangerous seeds promoted as a "health food," without providing advisories for proper preparation methods prior to ingesting. This is important because it contains cyanide, and cyanide transforms into thiocyanate inside the body, which in sensitive individuals may lead to thyroid disease. Research does not really confirm one way or another if flax was originally cultivated for human consumption; rather, historical records indicate it was used primarily for other purposes such as in animal feed, to produce cloth, rope, paper, and linseed oil for lights, for lubricating tools, and to protect wood.

That flax was not historically an important crop for human food appears to make sense, because flax cultivation dwindled to almost nothing in the twentieth century as petroleum-based products began replacing its fiber and oil used in miscellaneous products, and corn and soybean became the predominate feed for animals. If you are looking to obtain more fiber in the diet, eat more vegetables and not this seed. As far as consuming its oil and all the reasons why you shouldn't, you will find these topics covered under the Fats portion of this section.

CHIA SEEDS.   This seed boasts a low-carbohydrate profile, is high in fiber, and has no sugar content. On the upside, they fill you up with lots of fiber, but on the downside, it is at the expense of other nutrient-dense foods. For example, it is high in B3 or niacin content, and at first glance this seems great, but let's take a closer look. A 4-ounce serving of chia seeds gives you approximately 59% of your daily value (DV) requirement, yet the same amount of chicken contains 97% DV and tuna a whopping 156% DV. It is a pretty decent source of thiamine (B1), though eating a pork chop, sunflower seeds, or asparagus is going to provide substantially more, ounce per ounce. While relatively high in protein compared to other plant sources, chia still doesn't compare to animal sources, plus plant-sourced protein is harder to digest. Its high potassium and calcium content at first appears attractive, but the seed is high in phytic acid, so much of the minerals are bound and passed out of the body. The omega-3 content is in ALA form, so largely unavailable, because it has to be converted into EPA and DHA before your body can use it.

They don't have much of a taste on their own, and once you start doctoring up chia puddings and smoothies with coconut milk, high-fructose honey, or fruit, their low-carbohydrate and sugar content doesn't end up meaning much. If added to meat dishes, I guess chia adds fiber, but unlike vegetables, it won't add any flavor. For me, and others, they act like legumes and create intestinal distress—I won't go into details. Others experience allergenic responses such as hives, breathing difficulties, dizziness, and trouble swallowing. If you are eating chia seeds for therapeutic reasons, purported health benefits have not been substantiated by medical research, and frankly, there isn't much research out there to find.

They comprised a minor portion of the Aztec diet; however, they didn't dish them up with oatmeal from Europe, cold country berries, honey, and coconut milk. Seed preparation prior to consuming was more involved than whizzing them up in a smoothie or sprinkling over a salad. Most likely, it was added and soured in a maize gruel that included insects or meat to complete the nutritional profile. I am not trying to say chia is bad to eat, but if it comprises a major portion of a meal, make sure you combine it with nutrient-dense proteins, instead of high-carbohydrate complements. Oh, and make sure you get plenty of water with it. This seed will swell and absorb up to seven to twelve times its weight!

Chicken with Leek-Mushroom Sauce, page 134

TAMARI, SOY SAUCE, AND AMINOS

These sauces are simply a must for use with Asian dishes, and with all the alternatives available, one might wonder which is the healthiest option. My preferred choice in any recipe calling for soy sauce is traditionally brewed tamari or shoyu. They represent the seasoning in its most ancient form; however, I realize this might not be the best match for those with soy allergies. The next-best option is coconut aminos, assuming you don't have Candida overgrowth or another yeast-intolerant condition.

TAMARI. This is the original "soy sauce," and when made in a traditional manner, it is totally gluten free and retains its antioxidants and amino acids. If brewed and aged properly, most if not all antinutrients and phytoestrogens are eliminated. Ancient tamari was originally a by-product derived from miso (a soybean paste) production; however, the total liquid captured was minimal. Over the centuries, a brewing technique was eventually developed to create greater quantities of this prized condiment.

The brewing process I am about to describe is presented in a highly-simplified form. Soybeans are soaked, cooked, cultured with the same fungus (aspergillus oryzae) used for miso, molded for two to three days, and fermented in a brine for two to four years before they are pressed to extract the liquid and bottled. Culturing produces enzymes that break down the soy fat, starches, and proteins into simpler forms. These substances in turn provide nutrition for bacteria and yeasts during the subsequent aging process. A long aging process produces a smooth, full-bodied taste, distinguishing it from cheaper brands that age their product anywhere from three to six months.

The big brands usually pasteurize at 185°F (85°C) for three minutes before they bottle. There are a few obscure brands that don't, but they are harder to find. You will not find them at the grocery or a natural foods store. Pasteurizing will destroy many of the beneficial enzymes and probiotic bacteria and alter proteins, much like it does in dairy products, and this is a major drawback to using tamari. All the brands I have found in the US have been aged for a year or less, and this short time span doesn't allow the fermentation process to run its full course. To create a stable product that doesn't continue to age in the bottle, they must pasteurize.

TAMARI-SHOYU. If counting in centuries, this is a new kid on the block. Japanese shoyu first appeared somewhere between 1400 and 1700 and was initially referred to as tamari-shoyu. Its origins, like those of mayonnaise, are controversial, and while some believe it is a uniquely Japanese product, others believe its roots trace back to China. It is brewed with about 80 to 90% soybeans and 10 to 20% wheat or barley and fermented in the same manner as tamari. The Ohsawa brand makes an unpasteurized, organic shoyu in the traditional proportions and ages it for two years. Since it is unpasteurized, it is my pick. I always keep pure tamari on hand for gluten-intolerant folks, although I wonder if any gluten protein is left after a two-year molding and fermentation process.

SHOYU OR SOY SAUCE. Somewhere around the late 1700s, shoyu began its transformation into half soybeans and half wheat, and this ratio is what you mostly find in modern versions. Not only was the grain ratio increased, but the grain was cracked and roasted prior to fermenting. This new innovation imparted a unique flavor previously unknown in soy sauce gastronomy.

NON-BREWED SOY SAUCE. The chemical version of soy sauce we know today was first concocted around 1920 and became popular during the US occupation of Japan after WWII. Soybeans and wheat are still combined together in equal parts but are heated and mixed with a hydrochloric acid solution for a couple hours instead of undergoing a fermentation process. The liquid is drained off and the acid neutralized with sodium hydroxide. It is doctored up with corn syrup, caramel coloring, salt, and preservatives, and then this dreadful mess is pasteurized. Since there is no fermentation process, the soybean's negative attributes are not neutralized, and your body is further burdened with nasty additives and chemicals to process, in addition to dealing with soy's inherent antinutrients.

COCONUT AMINOS. This faux soy sauce is created from coconut blossom sap or nectar. The nectar is traditionally used as a sweetener or to create alcoholic beverages and has only recently been produced as a soy sauce replacement. The sap when first extracted is a milky white color and must be cooked at temperatures between 105° to 250°F until it condenses or evaporates into a caramelized liquid syrup. It is then aged anywhere from three months up to a year, and the final product is pasteurized to stop the fermentation process. Salt is added to mimic the soy sauce flavor. Coconut aminos are fairly high in carbohydrates, containing 20 grams sugar per 100-gram (about ½ cup or 3.5 ounces) serving. Or think of it this way: One tablespoon of this stuff contains 1.25 teaspoons of sugar. I cannot find data describing any antinutrient properties it might possess. Individuals with Candida issues will have the same problems with this product as with fermented soy sauce. Unless you have a soy allergy, there is no reason to replace gluten-free tamari with this product.

LIQUID AMINOS. This is another mock soy sauce made no differently from other chemically produced impostors, except they use soy protein instead of soybeans and wheat. One popular company proudly proclaims their product contains no preservatives, but at the same time shies away from proclaiming "no additives." This makes me suspicious, because the FDA doesn't require listing certain additives on the label if they are at "insignificant levels" or "incidental amounts." Why doesn't the label just say it has no additives? It would make our lives so much simpler. While they are non-GMO verified, they are not organic. The most revealing information about the product comes from the company itself: "has a shelf life of 3 years; although due to its nature, [this product] can be safely used for many years after expiration." Uhh, it contains no preservatives, yet never goes bad? Wow, not even bacteria, yeast, or fungus want to eat it. Sounds like a chemical soup to me.

SWEETENERS

For the most part, I avoid all sugar, even the "natural sweeteners," but sometimes a recipe needs a little sweetness. In many instances, you can eliminate sugar altogether, like in homemade jam or sweet berry pies. Like salt, our tongues become trained to sugar, and when we eliminate it from our diets, our palates adapt. Soon the desserts you thought were so good will gag you with sweetness.

Please do not delude yourself into thinking honey or maple syrup offers a nutritional edge over a minimally processed organic cane sugar. Claims that one natural sweetener is healthier for you because it is lower on the glycemic index are just ridiculous. C'mon, a highly-processed table sugar has a glycemic index (GI) of 65, evaporated cane juice a GI of 43, honey a GI of 50, and maple syrup a GI of 54. The differences between them are negligible and definitively not valuable for rating one as superior to the other. Sugar is sugar, and it is not a health food—it is a treat to be used judiciously.

Experts are increasingly discarding the GI as an accurate measure in evaluating the impact any one sugar will have on the body. Many factors can affect how the body metabolically reacts to sugars, and more emphasis is now put on glycemic load. Interestingly, fructose has a low GI of 25 but has a far worse impact on the body than sucrose: "[it] is an extremely glycating—or, more properly in this instance, "fructosilating"—substance that can do immeasurable damage to your arteries and tissues. In fact, fructose is 20 to 30 times more glycating (i.e., damaging) than is glucose" (Gedgaudas 2011).

Natural unrefined or minimally processed sweeteners don't offer much in the way of minerals, enzymes, vitamins, and antioxidants (I don't care what claims they make), but buying organic will eliminate toxic chemicals. At least while you are enjoying your occasional treat, your body doesn't have to process petroleum fertilizers, pesticides, antibiotics, and all manner of refining chemicals such as phosphoric acid, formic acid, sulfur dioxide, preservatives, flocculants, surfactants, synthetic defoamers, bleaching agents, and viscosity modifiers. Your endocrine and digestive system can now settle down to the serious business of synthesizing insane amounts of carbohydrate without further distraction.

ARTIFICIAL SWEETENERS. All artificial sweeteners cause a broad range of side effects from neurological damage to weight gain. Our bodies react to a sweet taste in the same way as if we were having regular sugar; the pancreas secretes insulin as soon as a sugary taste hits the tongue. This includes stevia, which some studies suggest may stimulate genetic mutations. Despite the fact many health practitioners are advocating its use, I remain suspicious of anything as highly processed as stevia. Both Splenda® and stevia have induced vertigo and stomach upset in me. No thanks! Serve me up crack in the most ancient and natural forms possible: cane sugar, molasses, honey, and maple syrup.

CANE SUGAR. I keep three variations of organic cane sugar on hand: an unrefined and unbleached whole cane sugar for use in place of brown sugar (sometimes called rapadura); an evaporated blond crystal cane juice sugar (still has a faint bit of molasses in it) as a white sugar substitute in cookies, cakes, and pies; and an organic, super-fine powdered sugar (still has a hint of molasses in it) for the rare frosting or glaze. Look for brands produced using the traditional methods of pressing and drying at low heat—no boiling—with minimal or no separation of the sugar from the molasses, and no bleaching. With cane sugar, it is particularly important to buy organic brands to ensure ecofriendly agriculture, in addition to finding ones dedicated to fair trade practices.

HONEY. You would think that honey straight from the bees would be the most natural product we could possibly use. Well, maybe and maybe not. The golden honey in the cute little bear bottles most likely has been imported from Asia and subjected to high temperatures, ultra-filtration methods, and pasteurization before packaging. Extreme processing methods eliminate the pollen content and other beneficial attributes usually present in honey. Most of this stuff enters the US uninspected, and once in, its origin becomes virtually untraceable. Imported honey may be adulterated with cane or corn sugars, illegal antibiotics, and heavy metals. The FDA is authorized to test and enforce honey labeling claims; however, they are limited in their ability to do so. To help ensure you avoid adulterated or contaminated products from abroad, try to buy as locally as possible from small companies.

Raw and Unfiltered. Sounds good, but what do these terms really mean? The FDA has no official definition of "raw" honey, but the National Honey Board defines it as "honey as it exists in the beehive or as obtained by extraction, settling, or straining without adding heat" (NHB 2003). This definition is a little deceptive. What they really mean is it will not be heated beyond temperatures the bees themselves keep in the hive.

All raw honey will be heated between 91° and 97°F to extract it from the comb and put through a strainer to remove things like bee parts, beeswax, or other particles that might have drifted into the honey during harvesting. Straining though should not be confused with high-technology filtration systems. Raw honey produced without high-heat processing still retains its pollen and phytonutrients such as propolis, enzymes, and the friendly bacteria lactobacilli and bifidobacteria. All pure honey, processed or not, will eventually start to solidify at room temperature, so this is not an accurate measure of whether it is raw. However, unfiltered versions will crystallize faster, while adulterated ones will only partially crystallize.

Organic? In the case of honey, it really is a figment of the imagination. Beekeepers might abstain from using any synthetic substances to control pests afflicting colonies, but they cannot restrict the bees' flight patterns. These industrious little guys travel incredible distances to gather nectar. In all probability, they will forage in fields sprayed with agrochemicals and drag home contaminated pollen and nectar. But that isn't the end of the story. The wax sold and used as starter comb has been found to contain inordinate amounts of pesticides.

Cooking With. If you would like to explore substituting honey for granulated sugar, there are quite a few points to consider. Honey will retain the distinct flavors from the flowers of origin. You might have noticed clover honey is more delicate than alfalfa, and wildflower is totally unpredictable in taste. Honey is best used in baking recipes where dense, moist, or fluffy textures are desired as in cakes, cookies, and quick breads. It adds and retains moisture, so you will need to subtract 1 ¼ cup liquid from the recipe for every cup honey used. In baked goods, reduce the oven temperature by 25°F to prevent overbrowning, and add an additional ½ teaspoon of baking powder or soda to help it rise. While many don't, I recommend using ¼ cup less honey than the amount of granulated sugar called for, because I find honey is more concentrated in its sweetness.

MAPLE SYRUP. There is a distinct difference between buying organic versus nonorganic maple syrup. Not only must organic maple syrup producers comply with the usual laundry list of prohibited agrochemicals and contaminants, but there are added restrictions unique to maple syrup production. Buying organic delivers you from lead or aluminum residues from processing equipment; nasty chemical defoamers, filtering agents, and disinfectants; and cross-contamination from bordering nonorganic farm land and tree lots. Buying organic also means you are supporting sustainable and responsible forest management. Organic practices prevent erosion, maintain biodiversity of tree species, and encourage healthy wildlife and insect habitats.

Defoaming Agents. Most of the large commercial operations use vegetable oil as a defoaming agent, but they also buy from smaller producers, so there is always the possibility butter or animal fat may have been used. Individuals with dairy allergies can protect themselves by purchasing brands displaying a "vegan" label, but it is a tough call for those with peanut and soybean allergies, although safflower or canola are the preferred oils. Unless you buy organic, these defoamers could also be GMO and hydrogenated.

Nutritious? Fresh, raw sap typically runs about 2 to 3% sugar, and it is boiled for about 2 hours, or until the finished syrup is evaporated to 66.5% sugar. Get this: It takes 40 gallons of sap to produce 1 gallon of condensed syrup. The boiling process leaves me questioning how many antioxidants or other nutrients are really retained when all is said and done. Frankly, B2 or riboflavin is the only vitamin present in any substantial amount, and this can better be obtained by eating nutrient-dense goat cheese, beet greens, sea vegetables, or mushrooms. Syrups packaged in clear bottles will retain less nutrients than those packed in tinted or opaque packaging. Riboflavin is particularly volatile when exposed to light. Glass packaging is best. Try to avoid plastic bottles and metal tins, because they are not inert and will leach toxins into the syrup.

Grades and Labeling Claims. The USDA changed its standards of identity in 2015 for maple syrup. Grade A is reserved for retail sale to individuals and is now divided into the Golden, Amber, Dark, and Very Dark categories. The different levels of Grade A are now associated with color and taste, whereas previously, grades were only based on color. The various tastes are categorized as delicate, rich, robust, and strong. Maple syrup's color and taste are determined by the time of season when it was harvested. Early season syrup is lighter in color and milder in taste, and it progressively becomes darker and richer as the season progresses. Grade B has been eliminated and replaced by "Processing Grade," meaning any maple syrup that does not meet Grade A requirements but meets the requirements for use in the manufacturing of other products. Processing Grade cannot be packaged in consumer-size containers for retail sale (containers of less than 5 gallons), so you don't need to be worried about avoiding it.

Many companies disingenuously state on their label "no formaldehyde" has been used in the manufacture of their product, but this substance has been banned for use in maple syrup since the 1990s. It's the pesticides, chemical fertilizers, toxic metals, production chemicals, and environmentally unsound practices you should be worried about when you don't buy organic.

Storage. Maple syrup will not keep indefinitely like honey, and once opened, it should be used within a year. Open containers should be kept in the refrigerator, and bulk quantities should be broken down into smaller units and frozen. This stuff is like liquid gold, so I usually reserve it for drizzling over a finished dish or adding a caramel flavor to puddings.

THICKENERS

Starches and gums are used for jelling or adding body to pan sauces, gravies, puddings, aspics, jams, and pie fillings. They originate from grains (wheat flour, cornstarch), roots (potato, kuzu, cassava/tapioca, and arrowroot), fruit (pectin), seeds (guar and locust bean gum), red algae (agar), fermented bacteria (xanthan gum), or animal (gelatin). Organic kuzu, arrowroot, einkorn wheat flour, and gelatin for the rare aspic or fruit gelatin dessert are common ones used in my kitchen. I steer clear of all the rest, and particularly cassava or tapioca because of their cyanide content.

Each one has its own individual characteristics and performs in different manners. Starch thickeners are somewhat temperamental. Some hold up better than others under heat, and care must be used to avoid overheating. They must be cooked long enough to eliminate their chalkiness, but if overcooked, they lose their ability to thicken. Corn and root starches impart a glistening, transparent sheen, while wheat flour is opaque. In general, thickeners don't hold up well when frozen. You may want to divide up a large batch of prepared food, freeze, and add the thickener later.

For puddings, I tend to use eggs to thicken rather than one of the grain or root starches. Lemon is useful for thickening in the case of cream- or egg-based sauces. It will instantly thicken cream, and don't worry: lemon when added to fresh cream does not curdle it.

AVOIDING LUMPS. Lumps are one of the most dreaded sins when it comes to creating smooth, silky textures. To avert disaster, mix equal amounts of starch with cold water until you have a medium-to-thin paste. Drizzle slowly into the liquid you wish to thicken, while whisking briskly to combine. I find it better to dissolve the starch slurry into the liquid while it's still on the cool side, rather than into a simmering one. Bring the mixture up to a simmer and continue to stir until thickened, then cook one minute longer; remove from heat immediately. If you still mess up, you can sometimes rescue your sauce by whizzing in a blender or food processor until it's smooth.

ARROWROOT AND KUZU ROOT. These two are included together because they are so similar. However, kuzu root starch is the superior choice in my mind. It has better jelling strength and doesn't break or separate once cooled, like arrowroot or cornstarch. In fact, it has become my number one go-to. Both kuzu and arrowroot are easily digested and allergy-free substitutes for wheat flour and cornstarch. They have no flavor of their own, so can be used to thicken any sauce, soup, stew, or pudding. Both hold up well in acidic environments. They impart a glossier finish, tolerate prolonged cooking periods, and freeze better than cornstarch or wheat flour. For sauces or gravies, use as a 1:1 substitute for cornstarch, and reduce by one-half when replacing wheat flour. For gelling or puddings, use 2 tablespoons per cup of liquid.

I have also used arrowroot starch instead of wheat flour to dredge foods in before frying them to create a crisp coating for those who need gluten free.

CORNSTARCH. This is one of the last starchy thickeners I reach for, and I have pretty much phased it out of my kitchen. On the upside, it is one of the cheaper varieties if you can tolerate corn products, but it has many drawbacks. Cornstarch loses its ability to thicken when mixed with acids and breaks (becomes watery) in a sauce after it chills. Not only is it a major allergen, it is a tad cloudier than kuzu or arrowroot, will not hold up under prolonged cooking periods, and doesn't freeze well.

WHEAT FLOUR. Wheat flour is the classic ingredient for meat gravies and stews and lends a full-bodied, velvety texture unmatched by most other thickeners. If you choose wheat flour, I definitely recommend using a non-hybrid (einkorn) or a pre-dwarf variety (Fife). It is best added after first being made into a roux, by stirring together equal parts of flour and fat. Flour is added into clarified melted butter for a few minutes to cook off the floury taste. If desired, the roux may be further cooked to develop a deeper color and a nuttier flavor; however, the darker you go, the more flour loses its thickening muscle. Once thick, the roux should then be tempered by whisking a portion of the hot liquid into the roux prior to pouring into the main pot. Incorporating the entire roux mixture directly into a large quantity of hot liquid without the final tempering step will encourage clumping. Wheat flour-based sauces or gravies are particularly prone to thinning or breaking when frozen.

VEGETABLES

These are the all-stars of the plant world. Cup per cup, vegetables have at least the same amount of fiber as whole grains, and usually more. For example, 1 cup of avocado has approximately 10 grams of fiber where a cup of cooked oatmeal has about 4 grams and brown rice 3.5 grams. A cup of cooked beets has 5.4 grams of fiber, cooked carrots 4.6, and broccoli 5.2 grams. A slice of whole-wheat bread offers little improvement over its refined counterpart, with a mere 1.9 grams of naturally occurring fiber vs. white bread at .08 grams.

Hopefully, you have read the Fruit section and the quotes from Nora Gedgaudas and William Davis's books where they discuss the virtues of vegetables over fruit. Traditional nutritionists and doctors have erroneously lumped fruits and vegetables together as being equally beneficial. "Relatively speaking, vegetables have considerably more antioxidant value per carbohydrate gram than fruits and thus represent a much more valuable dietary choice" (Atkins 2002). I never ate so many vegetables until I switched to an Atkins diet, and I was vegetarian at the time! It is amazing how many vegetarians eat so little vegetables relative to dairy, grains, legumes, and fruit. I am not dissing on you guys; just saying.

The most important factors to consider when eating vegetables or fruits are choosing those indigenous and in season specific to your geographic location. Climatic conditions induce different adaptive responses in the body, which then require certain nutritional elements to cope. Seasonal food is so much more inexpensive, and produce bought regionally has superior nutrient density over that traveling thousands of miles in cargo holds.

FAT SOLUBLE VITAMINS. Finally, it is important to remember many of the vitamins (A, D, E, K) and other nutrients in veggies are fat-soluble. Your body will not be able to synthesize these unless adequate amounts of fat are consumed along with them. This fat could be from meat, eggs, butter, olive or coconut oil, or a fat-rich avocado eaten in your salad.

CAROTENOIDS. You may be surprised to find vegetables are not good sources of vitamin A. Not everyone is a good converter of the phytochemicals beta-carotene, alpha-carotene, and beta-cryptoxanthin, the precursor forms of vitamin A. Children, the elderly, and those with gut, liver, and thyroid conditions are particularly poor at this conversion. Additionally, if you aren't eating these with enough fat, your body is further hampered in its efforts to convert carotenoids. But keep eating all the orange vegetables because they supply many other vital elements, like fiber, minerals, and antioxidants.

GREENS. Broccoli, asparagus, and spinach first spring to mind when considering greens, but there are so many more. The large leaves of the fully developed greens such as chard, kale, beet, mustard, and collard are often ignored in the store aisle. Many are left wondering what to do with them. Few realize how useful they are in stir-fries, stews, soups, or casseroles. Reserve their tender, bite-sized versions for use in salads, sautéing up as a delicate side, or as a stuffing for meats, omelets, or crêpes.

Get yourself out of the spinach rut and experiment with dandelion, arugula, or some baby greens in its place. For sauté purposes, do not confuse baby lettuces with the tender, small leaves of arugula, kale, mustard, beet, etc. (sometimes known as "super" greens). For example, immature romaine, oak leaf, red leaf, butter, and mache lettuce do not hold up well under heat and become unappetizing, soggy versions of themselves. To avoid disappointment, read the label to ensure lettuces are not a part of the baby green mix before dashing off with a box. Dandelions sauté up exceptionally nice with scallions, butter, and maybe a dash of tamari sauce.

In hot summer months, I naturally lose interest in greens and focus more on the plentiful cooling vegetables, such as cucumber, summer squash, tomato, and the slow-maturing carrots, beets, broccoli, and cabbage. Kale has become exceptionally popular recently, but you will find the mature plants particularly tough for salad use, although they are a natural for soups and stews dishes.

Tip: If you do decide to use the tougher mature greens in a salad, slice them into ¼ inch ribbons and then wilt them either by sautéing or blanching, and easier yet (and way more fun), by massaging them prior to using. Massage them for 2 minutes in a mixture of oil, lemon or vinegar, crushed garlic, a tad of salt, and your seasonings of choice; let them marinate 5 to 10 minutes prior to mixing with other vegetables.

NIGHTSHADE DILEMMA. Potatoes, bell pepper, and the luscious summer tomatoes: do you need to avoid these tropical vegetables? Most probably do not. I suspect pathological conditions supposedly induced by nightshade ingestion may be more related to other factors, such as the high sugar/carb content found in starchy tubers. Hypersensitivity may also be an allergenic response to the natural pesticides solanine and tomatine present in nightshades. There is the possibility certain individuals might already be compromised for other reasons: e.g., a preexistent pathology like leaky gut that inhibits the body's ability to neutralize the anti-nutrients found in nightshades.

The dubious correlation between nightshades and joint calcification started in the 1940s, when a vet noticed cows grazing on nightshade plants were troubled by arthritis. When he removed the suspected culprit from their diets, the cows' arthritic conditions improved. Mind you, we are talking cows here, not people, bovines who were eating leaves and not tubers. Apparently, nightshade leaves contain high levels of preformed vitamin D3, a substance toxic to cows, but not humans; however, I am not recommending you eat nightshade leaves.

There is no concrete evidence conclusively proving that eliminating nightshades from the diet alleviates nerve, joint, or stomach diseases. There is no reliable lab test to uncover susceptibility to their antinutrients. For every individual who finds relief by abstaining from them, another will not. Most of their antinutrients are concentrated in the leaves and skin, and if properly prepared, shouldn't really affect healthy individuals any more than eating any other vegetable. Since these are heat-loving vegetables, the best course of action probably lies in avoiding them out of season, eat in moderation, and purchase organic to reduce exposure to other toxins.

STARCHY VEGETABLES. All potatoes, sweet and otherwise, are high in carbohydrates and sugars. High consumption of these might be fine for athletes and physically demanding jobs, but for most of us, they are a food to consume with prudence. Their fiber content doesn't substantially negate the impact of their starchy sugars once they hit your bloodstream. Those with impaired blood sugar regulation and digestive conditions should go easy with these or consider eliminating them altogether if your body doesn't respond well to them.

Lifestyle is another big determinate. I know from experience, a sedentary, desk-bound individual who moves from their climate-controlled house, to car, to office is not able to eat a daily ration of starchy sweet potatoes without suffering negative repercussions—whereas a construction worker lifting and moving about all day might be fine with a higher carbohydrate load.

For all you paleophiles, I want to draw your attention to *The Paleo Diet*, the original paleo book where Loren Cordain specifically lists all starchy vegetables as "Foods You Should Avoid" (Cordain 2011). Sweet potatoes, yams, cassava root, and potatoes are on the list. I don't go as far as eliminating them completely but encourage you to use them with judiciousness, and you should be able to enjoy them throughout your lifetime.

Find substitutes for starchy vegetables whenever possible, so when the occasion arises and no other ingredient will do, you will happily enjoy your potato salad guilt-free. Celery root—also known as celeriac—peeled and cubed provides a fabulous substitute for white potato in salads, stews, and soups. Carrots and beets have a lower carbohydrate level than any potato, and your gut will love their fiber. The firm-fleshed flying-saucer squash makes awesome home-fried potatoes, and butternut squash or cauliflower are perfect for mashes. Shredded zucchini is a natural for fritters.

Cassava. Its flour and chips are the latest rage in gluten-free products, and I really wanted to believe it was a miracle grain alternative. I have devoted special attention here to cassava's problematic issues you may not be aware of. Its dangers are potentially troubling for everyone, but even more so for small children and individuals already struggling with compromised health conditions.

You don't really get bang for your buck when you consider its carbohydrate load is greater than wheat flour, and its nutrient density is virtually nil. But what concerns me the most is its goitrogenic properties and extremely high levels of cyanogenic compounds. These antinutrients aren't necessarily removed entirely by traditional or modern processing methods. Levels vary according to the processing method employed, and some are more effective than others for detoxification purposes. Dry or drought conditions stimulate higher concentrations of cyanogens in the root and these are higher in the bitter variety used for flour. Sustainability issues are also a concern, because large-scale, industrialized production releases large amounts of cyanide into the environment.

Confusion reigns within the food industry as to how best to efficiently and safely mass-produce a cyanide-free product. There is no consensus among world regulatory agencies as to what precisely constitutes safe levels of exposure. The international industry standard is a 0.10 ppm (parts per milligram) residue, but regulatory limits defining the maximum amount allowable in food products vary according to the country. But who can trust governmental agencies anyway, since many are swayed by industry interests and scientific research that oftentimes is suppressed or determined erroneous later down the road?

Chronic low-grade toxicity can develop in the body when cassava is used as a dietary staple, and in turn, can cause widespread health problems in the general population. Some of the most troubling disorders associated with cassava's toxins are goiter, hyperthyroidism, dwarfism, neuropathy, pancreatic lesions, and an irreversible paralytic disorder. These pathologies are prevalent in countries like Africa, where it is consumed as a major part of the diet.

Unless organic, it is grown with pesticides and later treated with preservatives and fungicides to prevent loss during storage. Herbicides may actually increase toxicity levels in the plant tissue. To date, I haven't found one cassava flour or ready-to-eat cassava chip manufacturer who displays website data regarding the cyanogen levels present in their product, and few are organic.

Given its low nutritional and high carbohydrate factors, the multitude of endocrine disruptors we are already bombarded with, and the lack of scientific data, caution is advised with cassava products, particularly for those with metabolic disorders and those with existing or family propensities to thyroid or nervous system disorders. That said, organic, sustainable products may offer you a welcome alternative to wheat flour when used on a limited basis within a balanced diet. Just make sure you obtain information from the food producers as to their processing methods and residual cyanide levels.

Sweet Potato vs White Potato. Sweet potatoes are all the thing lately and popularized as a healthier alternative to the vilified white potato. In reality, there is little difference between these two tubers. Their carbohydrate and fiber content, and corresponding glycemic load, is virtually identical when prepared in the same manner. Many sweet potatoes carry a rich carotenoid content, and this factor seemingly gives them a leg up on the white potato. However, their vitamin A is metabolically unavailable for most individuals. For both white and sweet potatoes alike, their glycemic load and carotene levels are dependent upon which variety you are talking about. This factor renders most nutritional data comparisons pretty useless and most likely accounts for the confusion between the two.

Yams and sweet potatoes are really one and the same in the United States, just different varieties, and the terms are used interchangeably, albeit incorrectly. Their skins and meat come in all shapes and sizes ranging in color from white and yellow to purple and orange. Some sweet potatoes look just as white inside as a white potato. True yams originate from Africa—and, odds are, you have never encountered one.

Sweet potatoes are tropical in origin and belong to the morning glory family (Convolvulaceae), a sub-branch of the nightshade family. White potatoes belong to a different subcategory of the nightshade family (Solanaceae) and contain the antinutrient solanine. This distinction perhaps makes the sweet potato a better choice for those with autoimmune issues. Although, the sweet potato's high sugar content may no more be a better choice for those suffering from gastrointestinal distress than a white potato.

VINEGAR

ACID CONTENT. It's all about the acidity when picking the appropriate vinegar, whether it be for reductions, marinades, sauces, salad dressings, or pickling. Quality vinegar is made by slow fermentation methods lasting as little as two months or up to a couple of years. The traditional two-stage brewing process converts sugars into alcohol, and from there, the alcohols are converted by oxidation into acetic acid. The amount of acetic acid in the vinegar will determine its acidity: for example, a robust balsamic will have a 6% ratio, a zesty apple cider 5%, and a mild rice vinegar 4%. Vinegars can be made from any fermentable carbohydrate but are most commonly derived from fruit, rice, or wine.

FERMENTING AND AGING. When purchasing vinegars, search for the naturally fermented raw, unfiltered versions and receive live, beneficial bacteria and other bioactive compounds. A bit of sediment and the "mother" bacteria will remain at the bottom. Skip using the white distilled for any cooking purpose, unless you are pickling. Break out of the apple cider rut, and have fun experimenting with various artisan fruit vinegars such as blueberry, plum, cherry, raspberry, or peach. Unlike apple cider, these fruit vinegars maintain a bit of their original character and dress up the humblest of recipes.

BALSAMIC. Most of us can't afford the traditional balsamic made with 100% reduced grape must from Modena or Reggio Emilia, Italy, which has been aged for at least 12 years. It will be labeled as "Aceto Balsamico Tradizionale" and what is important to note is the word "Tradizionale" and many cheaper varieties will fool you with various and confusing terms. You won't find these bottles in your local grocery store and it will cost at least $100, if not more—and you certainly don't want to cook with it.

There are two grades suitable for cooking purposes. The most affordable is the commercial grade labeled "Aceto Balsamico Di Modena" made by combining wine vinegar and concentrated grape must. If it carries this label and a certifying stamp it will have been aged a minimum of 2 months. Even better yet, if you can find it, is the condiment grade made in the traditional way but aged less than 12 years.

There are no official standards or labeling systems designating the condiment vinegars, and it is sometimes hard to determine quality from the label. The best way to purchase condiment grade is to taste first or buy in small quantities. Look out for products containing additives such as artificial coloring and thickeners used to simulate the taste and texture of the traditional product. Inferior vinegars can be reduced to a syrupy consistency to mock the texture and taste of the traditionally made and aged product.

WATER

TAP WATER.   If you knew what was in your tap water, you would probably never get it anywhere near your food. Tap water contains heavy metals, fluoride, pesticides, plastics, chlorine, bacteria, and pharmaceuticals. According to Environmental Working Group, they have identified 316 chemicals in U.S. tap water and more than half of them aren't regulated by the EPA. Take Vanadium and Atrazine, one of the many unregulated substances found in my tap water. Vanadium is a neurotoxin known to affect the brain, nervous system, and cause behavioral disturbances. Atrazine is an endocrine-disrupting herbicide and it adversely affects the reproductive and immune systems. These two bad boys can be present in anyone's drinking water in any amount. Scary, isn't it?

What about the fluoride added to many municipal drinking water supplies without our permission? CDC data suggests almost 50% of children ages 12 to 15 have some form of dental fluorosis. It is widely known to adversely affect the thyroid and other endocrine glands. My parents, bless their hearts, diligently provided fluoridated bottled water for their children, because dentists told them it was good for us. It blows my mind they paid hard-earned money to have a water company poison us.

While most of us don't drink tap water, how many of you cook or wash your food with it? For years, I purified my drinking water via standalone counter units, so my kids grew up in the know. One day my daughter was helping me prep dinner and commented, "So we wash vegetables in polluted tap water to remove the chemicals on the vegetables?" Wow. I had never thought of it that way, but yes, that is what we were doing.

Filtered water makes food taste so much better, and it is better for you. Not everyone can afford a whole-house water purification system, but counter units or in-line filtration systems for the kitchen faucet and the refrigerator will at least keep your food and drinking water clean. ProPur and Berkey sell excellent products and offer filters that remove virtually all contaminants. For those on the go, they also have various stainless steel counter units to suit every need, whether you are a college student, single, or have a family.

BOTTLED WATER.   There are many reasons to avoid bottled water, and chief among them is the plastic used to make the bottles. Every year it requires millions of barrels of crude oil to fuel the bottled water habit, and while recycling efforts are improving, a staggering amount of them end up in our oceans and waterways. Plastic is loaded with the endocrine disrupting xenoestrogen (estrogen mimicking) BPA. Buying BPA free will not protect you. Water packaged in PET plastic, is identified by its #1 recycling code. While this may be BPA free, there are dozens of contaminants like formaldehyde, acetaldehyde and antimony that still migrate into the water. Many of the top brands have been shown to be no freer from toxic substances than the tap water you may be trying to avoid.

At one time, I thought stainless steel re-usable bottles were non-toxic containers, but no, I have been poisoning myself with those too. Even the highest grade of 18/8 food-grade steel leaches iron, chromium and nickel into the water. While still valuable for short term storage and cooking purposes, leaving the same liquid in stainless-steel containers for periods longer than 24 hours is most likely not a good idea.

Do yourself a favor, and invest in a quality water purifier and non-toxic glass re-fillable bottles.

Hashed Browned Flying Saucer Squash, page 205

How To

Baked Winter Squash

This recipe works for any winter squash (including pumpkin), and my favorite is the sweet, meaty butternut squash. Cooked squash keeps in the refrigerator up to a week and freezes perfectly. Baking is far superior to other cooking methods as it concentrates the sugars and flavor in the pulp. You can't beat the ease of preparation, and this method provides a good base for other recipes such as soups, pies, sauces, or purees.

ESSENTIAL TOOLS:

Cookie sheet with sides or shallow baking pan

12- to 14-inch chef knife

DIRECTIONS

Wash squash. Cut in half and place on cookie sheet or baking pan. To cut a butternut, start at the round part first, where the seed cavity is. This is the thinnest area and the easiest place to insert the knife. Work around the cavity before starting on the thick neck. Once opened, do not remove seeds.

Bake between 375° and 400°F until juices have stopped running, turned a dark brown, and a wonderful aroma fills the kitchen. Don't worry about preheating the oven; just throw it in and go do something else about the house for 1 hour or so. For a large squash, it will be about 2 hours, and for smaller varieties, anywhere from 1 hour to 1 ½ hours.

You won't be able to tell if it is done from length of time cooked, since all squash are different weights and shapes. You must watch the juices and what they are doing. Cooking is completed when the juices have stopped running and turned a caramelized brown, as in the photo. Fully cooked squash will be meaty and dry, not watery.

See—the meat is not burned but soft and sweet.

After squash has cooled, remove seeds from cavity. The squash may be scooped out and mashed with butter, saved for later, or frozen.

Butterflied Chicken

Serves 4

OMG!!! Not that much effort for a moist and juicy chicken that presents beautifully on the plate! Simply scrumptious. Family and friends will think you're absolutely brilliant, and you will ask yourself why you haven't done this before. Throw on some veggies coated with olive oil on the grill or roast alongside the chicken for a one-pan dish.

A whole chicken is the most cost-effective way to buy organic, pastured chicken, or any chicken for that matter. This technique may seem a little daunting to some (maybe your butcher will cut out the spine and breastbone for you), but honestly, it's so easy.

Investing in a good pair of kitchen shears will make your life much easier and safer too, not only for this project, but for a multitude of others as well.

INGREDIENTS:

1 chicken (4- to 5-lb)

Olive oil

Dried whole-leaf thyme or marjoram

Dried rosemary or sage

Garlic powder

Salt and pepper

ESSENTIAL TOOLS:

Kitchen shears or sharp 8-inch chef knife

Paring knife

Shallow roasting pan or broiler pan (if not grilling)

DIRECTIONS

To Remove Backbone:

If Cutting with Shears: Begin by placing chicken on its breast with backbone facing you. Start by holding tail and cut up the side of backbone (not through center but to side of backbone) working your way up to the neck. Stay as close to the backbone as you can, and exert enough pressure to cut through the rib bones. Repeat on other side and lift out backbone; open up chicken to lay flat, cavity side up.

If Cutting with a Knife: Begin by sitting the chicken on its butt, backbone facing you. Starting with neck, cut down the side of backbone and work down to tail. Stay as close to backbone as you can, and exert enough pressure to cut through the rib bones. Repeat on other side and lift out backbone; open up chicken to lay flat, cavity side up.

To Remove Breast Bone:

Removing breast bone will help chicken cook faster and more evenly. At top of rib cage, at bottom of where neck would attach, is a roundish white spot composed of cartilage. With a paring knife, slice through the whitish mass down about ¼ inch to breast bone underneath; using both hands on either side of breast bone, splay the two sides of the breast back and twist to expose top of breast bone. Now run your finger down the left and right sides of breast bone to release it from flesh, and at very end of bone, use one finger to get under and pop tip away. Breast bone should now lift out easily in a single piece. If it not, use a paring knife to slice away stubborn meat clinging to it.

Cook Methods:

Generously coat all surfaces of chicken with olive oil. Don't be stingy here; generously rub both sides with dried thyme, marjoram, and rosemary or sage leaves (optional), garlic powder, salt, and pepper. Reapply if necessary to thoroughly cover with herbs. Rotate legs inward for a knock-kneed look. Tuck chicken wing tips behind back against sides of breast. Regardless of cook method, cover and let rest 20 minutes before carving.

To Grill: Preheat grill to medium high (400° to 425°F). On heated grill, place chicken cavity or bone side down. Immediately turn down flame to medium low (350°F). Close lid and cook 20 to 30 minutes (depends upon weight). Flip chicken over and cook another 20 to 30 minutes. Periodically check, and cool down grill if necessary. Better to err on the side of less cooking than more, as chicken will continue to cook as it cools.

To Roast: Preheat oven to 450°F. In a shallow roasting pan or on a broiler pan, place chicken inside with cavity down, skin up, and roast for 20 minutes; reduce heat to 375°F. Roast an additional 40 minutes for 3 to 4 pounds, and up to 45 or 50 minutes more for 5 pounds.

Caramelized Onions

Serves 4

These onions make a perfect topping or bedding for any meat. Caramelizing is a patient process that requires a medium-low-to-medium flame–and time. Resist the temptation to hurry it along by turning up the heat. If you can't tolerate any sort of butter, whether it be clarified or not, you may substitute olive oil.

INGREDIENTS:

2 large onions

4 TBS butter or ghee

⅛ cup liquid
(*water, balsamic vinegar, beef or chicken broth, wine, or beer*), plus 1 to 2 TBS water if needed

ESSENTIAL TOOLS:

12-inch skillet or sauté pan.

DIRECTIONS

Slice onions ¼ - to ⅜-inch-thick so they don't burn before they have a chance to start caramelizing.

In pan, over medium heat, melt butter.

Add onions, and toss with butter. Reduce flame to medium low, and toss periodically until onions are lightly browned and soft (about 30 minutes).

While onions are still in pan over medium-low heat, deglaze pan with your choice of liquid. Add additional water if necessary to fully dissolve any remaining browned bits on pan bottom. Cook until onions have fully absorbed all liquid.

Remove from heat and serve.

CHEF'S NOTES

You need a shallow-sided pan with a wide bottom. Much like browning mushrooms, the onions need room to breathe and release their moisture.

VARIATIONS

Substitute a large sliced bell pepper for 1 onion.

Add ½ to 1 TBS partially crushed green peppercorn during deglazing process.

Fish Skin Crackles

For years, I threw away salmon skin after grilling or broiling the flesh. Wow, was I missing out—both on a taste treat and nutrition. While you can peel and eat directly off the fish, it is more texturally appetizing to munch crispy. This is easy to prepare and takes no time at all.

INGREDIENTS:

Cooked fish fillet

Olive oil

Salt and pepper

Dried dill or
other herb of choice

Sour cream, pesto, or
guacamole

DIRECTIONS

After cooking fillet, place in a baking dish covered, skin side up. Let rest for about 3 minutes, or until cool enough to handle.

Carefully peel skin off in one piece and place on a cookie sheet.

Lightly brush both sides of skin with olive oil. Sprinkle with dill, salt, and pepper.

Place skin back on grill or under broiler, and cook at 375°F (or high broil) about 1 minute per side or until slightly brown, bubbly, and becoming crispy. It will crisp up more as it cools, so don't overdo.

Sprinkle with additional dried dill weed or other herb of choice.

Let cool, drain on paper towel-lined plate, and break into chips.

Serve with a dollop of sour cream, pesto, or guacamole.

VARIATIONS

If frying your fish, peel the skin off and lightly fry on each side with olive oil over medium-high heat until brown and crispy.

Poached Eggs

Poach eggs like a chef without a special pan. Don't fret if they don't look perfect. Before serving, you can trim them up or flip them over to the prettier side. Eggs should be fresh, the fresher the better, and the better they retain their shape when poaching. With older eggs, bits of white will collect on top of the cooking water. Just skim off and discard.

INGREDIENTS:

1 TSP distilled vinegar

½ TSP salt

Fresh eggs

ESSENTIAL TOOLS:

Large shallow saucepan, a deep skillet, or a sauté pan

Small cup or bowl

Slotted spoon

DIRECTIONS

To Poach:

In pan, add water to a depth of 2 to 3 inches; add vinegar and salt; bring to a low simmer (barely bubbling) over medium heat. Crack each egg into a small cup or bowl before gently sliding into a non-bubbling area of water. Adjust flame to maintain a low simmer.

With a spoon or heat-proof spatula, fold whites back over top of yolk until the whites start to firm up. Poach eggs for 4 to 6 minutes. When done, white will be firm and yolk soft to touch. Remove eggs with a slotted spoon and drain on a paper towel-lined plate.

If making large batches or the night before, cook eggs to slightly under done. With a slotted spoon, remove eggs from simmering water and place directly in a bowl of ice water to stop cooking action. Leave them in cold water until ready to serve; refrigerate overnight if so desired.

To Reheat:

In same pan used to poach eggs, bring fresh water to a low simmer (barely bubbling). Add eggs and heat 1 to 2 minutes. With slotted spoon, remove egg and touch yolk to test if warm. Tap gently on a paper or cotton towel to remove excess water before plating.

De-seeding Pomegranates

Yeah, yeah–I have tried every method available from spanking to drowning pomegranate seeds. No, it will not happen in one minute. It is a messy process and takes time. I don't care what the Internet gurus tell you. Presented here is the best method I have found. The older the pomegranate is, the tougher the seeds. They are best when just ripe and before they start drying out. Skin should be red, shiny, and hydrated looking.

INGREDIENTS:

Fresh, ripe pomegranate

ESSENTIAL TOOLS:

Sharp 4-inch paring knife

DIRECTIONS

Cut off the crown and bottom.

Gently score the outer pomegranate skin into equal quarters.

Gently insert your thumbs into the top part where the crown was removed and pry apart into sections.

Submerge quarters in large bowl of water and soak for a few minutes.

While underwater, gently push out the seeds to separate from white membrane and allow seeds to fall to bottom of bowl (this keeps the mess underwater and from spraying about).

Discard inner rind as you go.

Strain in a colander to remove water and pick out any remaining debris.

Place seeds on paper towels and blot gently with more paper towels. Periodically rotate them and blot them again. Let them air dry for up to an hour before using or refrigerating.

They freeze nicely.

Melting Chocolate for Dipping

If you are a chocophile, this basic skill is well worth mastering for drizzling over or dipping fruit and baked goods. Once you become familiar with the process, you will wonder what all the fuss is about.

The key to creating perfect dipping chocolate is to slowly heat at low temperature. This prevents drying out the chocolate by overheating, or worse yet, burning, from which there is no redemption.

Chocolate products vastly differ in content use of sugar, fat, and emulsifying additives, moisture content, and the temperatures they are processed at. While cocoa butter naturally occurs in chocolate, some will have added cocoa butter, some use soy lecithin to emulsify, and others may have a combination of both. Some bittersweets have sugar listed as the number one ingredient when it should be second in line to the chocolate liquor (equal amounts of chocolate solids and cocoa butter). All these factors combine to make chocolate variable in its texture, consistency, and melting point.

Some chocolate chip brands never completely liquefy to the consistency necessary for dipping. If your chocolate doesn't drizzle freely from a spoon, then you have either overheated it or have poor quality chocolate.

Microwaving is my preferred method – it is superfast and easy, but the double boiler method is also explained.

Okay, so you maybe blow it, then what?

Whatever you do, don't keep heating it – you will only make it worse. However, you can most times save thick or overheated chocolate by whisking in 1 TSP to 1 TBS hot water at a time (depending on amount of chocolate) until you reclaim the silky consistency. Hot tap water generally isn't hot enough for this purpose, so use boiled water.

Almost Healthy:
Chocolate-Dipped Strawberries, page 264

Almost Healthy: Shortbread Cookies, page 268

INGREDIENTS:

Bittersweet chocolate chips
or bars

Cream (*optional*)

ESSENTIAL TOOLS:

Microwave-proof glass bowl
or stove-top double boiler

Heatproof spatula or spoon

Wax or parchment paper

Cookie or baking sheet

CHEF'S NOTES

Choose a deep glass bowl with a bottom smaller than the top and just big enough to contain the total chocolate amount needed.

The point here is to make dipping easy by concentrating the chocolate in a deep, small area rather than having it spread out over a shallow, wide bowl. If using a double boiler, you may want to have a small bowl ready to transfer chocolate to for dipping.

All equipment should be perfectly dry to prevent moisture drops from seizing up the chocolate.

VARIATIONS

Milk Chocolate: Bittersweet chocolate, with its low sugar content, is the best choice to contrast against already-sweet fruit or pastries. However, you may prefer milk chocolate. However, you may prefer milk chocolate. In that case, add 2 TBS cream to every 3 oz of chocolate to create a creamier, lighter, milk chocolate appearance and taste without the extra sugar milk chocolate usually contains.

DIRECTIONS

To Microwave:

If using cream, warm in a small bowl for 15 to 30 seconds in the microwave; set aside.

Place chips or chocolate cut into ½-inch chunks in a glass bowl. Begin by microwaving chocolate in 30-second increments. Complete first 30 seconds, and stir non-melted chocolate into melted.

Heat for another 30 seconds, then stir and mix chunks of non-melted chocolate into melted once again.

Continue heating then stirring in 30-second increments, and stop when most of the chocolate has melted, but not all. This step is where most people fail, and overheating can occur. A small, 12-oz package of chips seems to melt faster, and they may be done in less than 1 minute. Chunks will most likely need to heat 30 seconds longer than chips.

Add optional warmed cream.

Gently stir chocolate until silky, glistening, and completely melted. Chocolate should drizzle freely from spoon. Be cautious with last increment. Too much heat will ruin the chocolate and its velvety texture.

While all microwaves and chocolate vary in nature, you really can't go wrong using the 30-second increment rule. When in doubt, go for less time and stir to finish the melting process. You can always heat it a bit more if needed in 10-second intervals.

As an example: For 9 oz of chocolate chunks, my microwave process usually takes three 30-second intervals, for about 90 seconds total. But you may need an additional 10 to 20 seconds, depending on your microwave and chocolate.

Using a Double Boiler:

Fill bottom portion of double boiler with a couple inches of water, bring to a boil over high heat, and then turn down to medium-low heat for a gentle simmer. Water should not be at a rolling boil when placing upper pan above it. Place upper pan containing chocolate bits (and optional cream) over lower pan containing water. Water in lower pan should be hot and barely simmering. Stir until smooth and glossy. Again, chocolate should drizzle freely from spoon. This will take at least 10 minutes of patient nursing.

You could also improvise by filling a small saucepan with a couple inches of water and bringing to a boil. Remove saucepan from heat, place your chocolate-filled glass bowl over it, and stir until chocolate melts. Reheat water if necessary.

Relishes, Sauces, and Jams: Making and Canning

This method is only useful for acidic based fruits. Fill jars with your choice of any acidic based relish, sauce or jam. Meats and vegetables need a water-bath or pressure cooking method, not covered here. If you choose to sterilize jars in boiling water, you will need to purchase a jar lifter in advance. A canning funnel is a handy inexpensive item, for a no-fuss-no-muss way to put jam or sauce into jars.

DIRECTIONS

Thickening:

There are two ways to thicken relishes, sauces, and jams. Use additives like cornstarch or pectin, or use the technique of reduction. A wide, shallow saucepan will allow quicker evaporation. Adding lemon juice and shredded Granny Smith apple, both high in pectin content, are invaluable for hastening along the thickening process and eliminates the need for powdered pectin in jams.

Evaporation is your friend when making relishes, sauces, and jams. Think shallow pan with lots of surface area in relation to contents. Unless you have large, shallow saucepans, it's faster to make two smaller batches than to double up on a recipe. The more fruit you use in one pot, the greater the cooking time to evaporate the water in the juices. The longer the cooking time, the more flavor is lost, and the natural fruit pectin is destroyed. High heat also destroys pectin, so keep the cooking temperature at a gentle simmer (one or two bubbles a few seconds apart) and do not boil until thickened.

You know it is done when it clings to the spoon, and the liquid resembles a thick syrup. Another test is to place a spoonful on a dish and cool in the freezer a few minutes. If the syrup thickens as it cools, you know it is done.

Sterilizing Jars:

Brand name canning jars saved from store-purchased pasta sauces, are not recommended. They are single-purpose jars (isn't that ridiculous) not designed for canning or freezing purposes.

I find it easier to wash and sterilize the lids and jars in the dishwasher, but you may also sterilize jars in boiling water. Do not boil your lids; the manufacturers no longer recommend this. Sterilize your jars by placing them in boiling water (above 185F) for 10 minutes. Leave your jars in the warm dishwasher or hot water until you are ready to fill them so they remain sterile and warm. Always use jar lifters to remove them from hot water.

If not using a dishwasher or sterilizing with boiling water, wash the jars, lids, lid bands, and tools in hot, soapy water. Let air dry on a clean towel or drainer.

Filling and Sealing Jars:

Using a canning funnel, ladle hot filling into jar, leaving ½-inch head space at top.

With a clean butter knife, gently stir sauce in jar to release air bubbles.

Remove any dripped sauce from rim and wipe clean with a clean, damp paper towel.

Place lids on jars and screw on until you feel resistance–fingertip tight.

Let filled jars cool and rest undisturbed 4 to 6 hours. Lids will invert and seal as they cool. I usually hear the pop sound after about 2 hours: Success! They have sealed. A proper vacuum seal has also been made when pressing in the middle of the lid without the top springing back. Don't fuss with pushing down on them early–until they completely cool, you may interrupt the process, and they will never seal. I hate when that happens!

Check seals on lids to make sure they have inverted (described above), and store in a dark, cool place for up to six months. If you don't have a cool area for storage, keep in a refrigerator.

Roast and Peel Peppers

When you see deals on bell peppers or chilies, stock up and buy 12 to 24 of them. This is an easy, economical way to add gourmet flair to your recipes. They keep well when packed in vinegar and olive oil or frozen.

Go ahead and burn them! Here is an instance where you want to burn them; char until blistered blackish-brown to black. I know, this just seems wrong, but unless properly blackened, the skin will not remove easily.

Can I char them too much? Well, yes you can. Stop when most of the pepper's surface is blistered and charred with only bits of color showing through. The front-middle pepper in the photo is a perfect example.

INGREDIENTS:

Any type of bell or chili pepper

ESSENTIAL TOOLS:

Shallow, rimmed baking or broiler pan *(if broiling)*

Tongs

Large baking dish or bowl

Plastic wrap, a lid, or a dish to cover baking dish or bowl

DIRECTIONS

Roasting:

Broiler: Preheat broiler to high. Line pan with foil for easy cleanup, and place whole bell peppers on pan. Position under broiler about 5 inches from heat or in upper third of oven. Some like to quarter, seed, and stem before broiling, and while perhaps easier to handle this way, I feel flavor is lost in the process. Cook 20 to 25 minutes.

Grill: The grill is my favorite way and seems to produce the best flavor. Preheat grill to 400°F. Place whole bell peppers directly on grill top and roast with cover closed. Keep grill between 375° and 425°F. Cook about 15 to 20 minutes.

Gas Stove Top: Using tongs, hold pepper directly over open gas burner and turn. Pepper should be above flame, but not in flame. This method is best used when needing only 1 bell pepper and not recommended when processing large quantities. Cook each pepper about 15 minutes.

Regardless of roasting method, check the peppers after about 3 to 5 minutes. Rotate peppers as needed until skin has blistered and charred on all sides.

Transfer peppers to baking dish or large bowl, bottoms down.

Seal tightly with plastic wrap, a lid, or a dish to prevent moisture from escaping.

Peeling:

Let roasted peppers rest, covered, for 15 to 20 minutes or until cool enough to handle. This process releases skin from pepper meat as it cools. Don't let them cool too long or skins will reattach to flesh.

Peel peppers by gently massaging with your fingers. Skin should slide off easily, and don't worry if tiny bits of char or skin remain. Open up pepper, and remove seeds and stems.

Storage:

If not using immediately, in a large bowl, toss and coat generously with two parts olive oil to one part vinegar. Pack into clean glass canning jars, and cover with additional vinaigrette mixture. These will keep up to a couple months in the refrigerator. Bring to room temperature before use.

Stuffed Burgers

Serves 4

Hamburgers take on a whole new dimension when stuffed. They become gourmet delights that are easy to make and fun to eat. Step outside the box and try using cheeses other than the standard cheddar, swiss, or mozzarella, such as brie, gruyère, gorgonzola, or blue cheese. These burgers are a bit heftier than your usual quarter pounder and require more meat per patty to keep the stuffing from oozing out.

INGREDIENTS:

1 ½ lbs ground beef, chicken, or turkey

4 oz your choice of cheese

NOTES:

DIRECTIONS

Divide ground beef into four equal portions and form into patties. Create a shallow well in middle of each patty. Leave at least ⅓ inch of meat at bottom of well.

Remove any rind from cheese and cut into equal-sized portions.

Place anywhere from ¾ to 1 oz cheese in each well center (about 2 TBS crumbled cheese, like feta). Go less on cheese if adding additional filling; don't overfill.

Bring up sides of patty to enclose cheese completely with at least ⅓ inch of meat.

Don't forget to indent patty slightly on top so your burger cooks up fairly flat.

Grill at 425° to 450°F with lid closed for 4 minutes on first side; flip, and cook an additional 4 minutes for medium.

Let rest 3 minutes before serving to allow cheese cool and set up.

CHEF'S NOTES

Add one of these items in combination with the cheese: sliced green chilies or jalapeños, avocado, roasted red pepper, fresh basil leaves, olives, or bacon pieces.

See, I told you these were fun!

For a killer topping, whip up some sautéed mushrooms or caramelized onions and pile those on. Serve on a bed of shredded lettuce, fresh baby greens, or arugula.

Washing Produce

All conventionally grown produce, including organic contain varying amounts of pesticides, wax, bacteria, and viruses. Washing with running water and/or with a vinegar rinse will substantially reduce much of it.

Bacteria, Viruses, and Molds:

A study published in the Journal of Food Protection found gentle agitation under 71-degree water for two minutes removed anywhere from 41 to 79% of pathogens from strawberries. The study also found that vinegar was the most effective substance to remove bacteria and viruses, over all the commercial washes or plain water (Lukasik et al. 2003).

Pesticides:

While vinegar is useful in removing waxy or oily residue and pathogens, commercial or vinegar washes are no more superior in removing pesticides than rinsing your produce under water. A summary of studies published by the Department of Analytical Chemistry at the Connecticut Agricultural Experiment Station (CAES) found rinsing with tap water "significantly reduced residues of nine of the twelve pesticides." The commercial wash products, such as FIT®, Organiclean, and Vegi-Clean, were not found better at removing pesticide residues than plain tap water. The study stressed it was not so much that pesticide residues were water soluble but that it was the rubbing and rinsing action under streaming water that actually removed them (Connecticut 2000).

Caution:

Many pesticides are systemic chemicals, they aren't on your food, they are in it and impossible to wash or soak away. One of the many reasons to buy organic food.

DIRECTIONS

Water Washing:

Rinse all smooth-skinned fresh produce under running water for at least 30 seconds and preferably 1 minute. Use a produce scrub brush in conjunction with running water.

Place greens and textured items such as broccoli in a large, clean bowl with water and agitate for 1 minute. Drain in a colander, and repeat the process one more time. Give a final rinse under running water. Pat dry with a clean towel or spin in a salad spinner and let air dry for at least 5 minutes before using or storing.

Vinegar Washing:

Given the high incidence of E. coli outbreaks in both conventional and organic produce, you may feel safer using a vinegar and water mixture as a preliminary wash for fruits and vegetables, especially those like apples or cherries that seem to have been coated in a waxy residue.

If you would like to use vinegar, the University of Maine, Extension Office, Bulletin #4336 advises mixing ½ cup vinegar with 2 cups water and soaking for 5 minutes (Bolton et al. 2013). You could also place the solution in a spray bottle to have handy. Spray and leave the solution on for 5 minutes, as you would with a commercial wash, and then rinse thoroughly. Here is where you can purchase in bulk the inexpensive stuff, the white distilled vinegar in the gallon bottles.

A vinegar soak is preferred over the spray for textural items like leafy greens, broccoli, or asparagus and for smaller items such as cherries, berries, or cherry tomatoes. I have used the vinegar spray wash and soak extensively and have not experienced any negative effects such as discoloration or aftertaste when rinsed adequately, even with berries.

Beyond Eggs

Asparagus Quiche

Serves 6

This quiche without the crust is a delicious brunch dish or make-ahead on-the-go breakfast that is fabulous hot or cold. Smoked salmon or leftover chicken are delicious alternatives to the usual breakfast meat of bacon or sausage. Conventional asparagus is rated as one of the "clean" veggies (extremely low pesticide residue) and is on par with its pricier organic counterpart. Pair with a fruit or leafy green salad.

INGREDIENTS:

½ to ⅔ cup cooked or smoked meat of your choice

4 large eggs

1 cups heavy cream

¼ TSP salt (omit if using salty bacon, sausage, or smoked salmon)

¼ TSP pepper

2 TBS butter, plus more for greasing

½ cup grated gruyère or jack cheese

8 stalks asparagus, ¼-inch slices cut on the diagonal

ESSENTIAL TOOLS:

12-inch skillet

9-inch glass pie dish or fluted tart pan

DIRECTIONS

Preheat oven to 400°F.

Cut, flake, or shred cooked or smoked meat into bite-sized pieces. Cook sausage or bacon (if using bacon, cut into 1-inch slices before cooking), brown lightly, and drain.

In a bowl, whisk together the eggs, heavy cream, salt, and pepper. Pour ⅓ of the egg mixture into a greased 9-inch pie pan. Bake until filling begins to set—about 10 minutes.

While egg mixture is baking, in a 12-inch skillet over medium heat, melt butter. Add asparagus and cook until just tender and it turns bright green, about 4 to 6 minutes, or microwave uncovered for 90 seconds.

Sprinkle cheese, asparagus, and meat evenly over partially cooked egg and cream base. Gently pour remaining egg mixture in a circular fashion over the cheese, asparagus, and meat.

Bake for about 35 to 40 minutes, until puffed and golden brown. Cool 20 minutes on a wire rack before slicing.

NOTES:

Chicken Breast Florentine

Serves 4

Need a break from eggs? Here a classic is reinterpreted for brunch. Get all your protein and veggies yet still feel like you are eating breakfast. Pound your chicken breast out and make the hollandaise the night before, and save yourself time the next morning.

INGREDIENTS:

4 slices smoked ham
or 8 slices bacon

1 recipe Sautéed Greens (pg. 215)

Seasoning for Chicken:

    1 TSP garlic powder

    1 TSP dried marjoram

    1 TSP dried thyme

    ½ TSP onion powder

    ½ TSP coarse ground pepper

    ½ TSP salt

Chicken Breast and Sauce:

    4 boneless chicken breasts, tenders removed

    Reserved ham or bacon grease, to fry breast

    1 TBS butter and 1 TBS olive oil, to fry breast

    1 cup Hollandaise Sauce (pg. 234)

ESSENTIAL TOOLS:

Large skillet

Plastic wrap

Rolling pin, meat mallet, or rubber mallet

DIRECTIONS

In a large skillet over medium heat, lightly brown ham or bacon; keep in warming oven, and reserve grease to fry chicken.

Prep all ingredients needed for sautéed greens and set aside.

Seasoning for Chicken:

In a small bowl, combine all seasoning ingredients together and mix thoroughly.

Chicken Breast and Sauce:

Place each chicken breast between two sheets of plastic wrap on a cutting board. Using short, even strokes, begin pounding breast starting at center and working your way outward to the edge. Repeat until they are ¼ inch thick. Make them thin, because they will become thicker as they cook. Generously rub seasoning into both sides of breast.

In skillet used for ham or bacon, heat butter and olive oil over medium heat. Add chicken breasts and cook for 2 minutes on each side, until browned and cooked through. Transfer to paper towel-lined plate to drain. Set aside in oven warmer until ready for assembly.

Prepare Hollandaise Sauce and cover to keep warm.

Prepare Sautéed Greens and cover to keep warm.

To Serve:

Place one chicken breast on each plate. Top each breast with ham or bacon and two heaping spoonfuls of greens, drizzle with hollandaise, and serve immediately.

Creamy Scrambled Eggs with Guacamole

Serves 2

INGREDIENTS:

Guacamole:

   1 ripe avocado

   1 TBS fresh lemon juice

   Garlic powder (optional)

   ⅛ TSP salt

Eggs:

   4 eggs

   4 scallions, sliced

   2 TBS olive oil or butter

   Salt and coarse ground
   pepper, to taste

   Salsa picante (optional)

ESSENTIAL TOOLS:

Large sauté pan or skillet

DIRECTIONS

Guacamole:

Slice avocado in half and scoop into a bowl. Add lemon juice, then lightly sprinkle garlic powder and salt. Mash together until creamy; set aside.

Eggs:

In a large bowl, whisk together eggs and pepper. In sauté or skillet pan, heat the olive oil or butter. Sauté scallions until aromatic and brightly colored.

Add eggs and cook over medium-low heat, lightly folding them over until all egg mixture is almost cooked but not quite—don't overdo or they'll become tough. Remove from heat and pan immediately to prevent eggs from browning.

Sprinkle with salsa picante to taste, and spoon guacamole over top. Serve hot.

NOTES:

Frittata Fun

Serves 6 as an entrée or 8 as a side

Breakfast, lunch, or dinner anyone? This all-in-one, no-brainer, no-fuss stove-top frittata adapts to whatever you have in the fridge. No need to oven bake, so it works summer or winter. And don't worry, you are not going to blow this recipe if you use too much of any ingredient. The only thing to remember is not to overcook it or the eggs become tough—but even so, no one will likely notice, it's that good.

Smoked or grilled salmon or cooked bacon, sausage, ham, chicken, or thin-sliced steak are different meat ideas, and experiment with a variety of cheeses matched to the meat and vegetables you have on hand, such as:

- Goat cheese, pancetta, mushrooms, sundried tomato, basil for Italian flavor.

- Mexican queso fresco, chorizo, Anaheim chilies, cherry tomatoes, cilantro.

- Gruyère, sausage, leeks, and tarragon for a French twist.

- Monterey jack, ham or bacon, onions, and bell pepper for American style.

- Sour cream with salmon, baby kale, and scallions for a Nordic version.

INGREDIENTS:

1 TBS butter

2 TBS olive oil, divided

2 garlic cloves, minced

1 medium onion, sliced

2 to 3 cups chopped vegetables of your choice

1 TBS fresh herbs

1 cup sliced, diced, or shredded cooked meat

8 eggs, beaten

1 cup grated cheese, or 6 to 8 TBS sour cream, or 4 oz cream cheese, softened (optional)

ESSENTIAL TOOLS:

Large skillet or sauté pan

Lid or aluminum foil

DIRECTIONS

Precooked meat should be room temperature.

In a skillet over medium heat, heat 1 TBS each of butter and olive oil. Sauté onions, bell pepper (if using), and garlic until onions are translucent and bell pepper is tender (2 to 3 minutes). Add other vegetables, such as mushrooms or broccoli, and sauté for a few minutes more. Lastly, add any greens and herbs and sauté until just wilted and reduced in size.

Add precooked meat; mix into vegetables and heat for 1 minute until warm.

Reduce flame to medium low. Drizzle the remaining tablespoon of olive oil evenly over the sautéed vegetables. Lightly toss vegetable and meat mixture to ensure oil and mixture is equally distributed around pan.

Drizzle in beaten eggs in a slow, circular fashion, starting with skillet's outer edges and working inward to center.

Cover and let steam for about 10 minutes; it should be starting to set up. Use aluminum foil to cover if you have no lid.

Distribute optional cheese equally around pan. If using sour cream or cream cheese, drop tablespoon dollops around pan. Let steam covered an additional 5 to 10 minutes. The egg will look puffy and set up and cheese will be mostly melted.

Remove from heat and uncover. The cheese will melt further as it cools.

Let rest for 5 minutes before slicing into wedges and serving.

VARIATIONS

Try vegetables like arugula, fennel, and asparagus.

Replacing butter with all olive oil or ghee and omitting cheese still produces a tasty dish.

Ricotta Crêpes with Berry Sauce

Serves 6 (2 crêpes each)

While not everyday fare, they are particularly fun for a special Sunday brunch. A hit with adults and children alike. These beauties can be prepared ahead of time, refrigerated or frozen, then baked or microwaved when you need them. Any fresh or frozen cherries or berries will work perfectly. Use no sugar or adjust to taste. For an easier throw-together, skip making the sauce and serve with fresh berries, your homemade jam, or chunky applesauce.

INGREDIENTS:

Crêpe Batter:

- 4 large eggs
- ½ cup water
- ½ cup cream
- ¼ TSP vanilla
- 2 TBS melted butter, for batter
- 1 cup einkorn flour
- 2 TBS melted butter, for pan

Lemon Ricotta Filling:

- 1½ cups whole milk ricotta
- 4 oz cream cheese, softened
- 1 TBS fresh lemon juice
- Zest of 1 lemon
- 1 TSP vanilla extract
- Pinch of salt
- 1 to 2 TBS powdered sugar, to taste (optional)

Sauce:

- 1 lb fresh berries or cherries, stemmed and pitted
- 3 TBS fresh lemon juice
- 1 to 2 TBS cane sugar, to taste (optional)

ESSENTIAL TOOLS:

6- to 8-inch skillet or crêpe pan

Wax paper

Saucepan

Baking sheet

CHEF'S NOTES

When cooking crêpe batter, keep your pan hot, and brush pan lightly with melted butter each time before pouring in batter for the next one.

This dish pairs nicely with sausage, bacon, or smoked salmon.

VARIATIONS

Substitute thoroughly drained and mashed whole milk cottage cheese for ricotta.

DIRECTIONS

Crêpe Batter:

In a bowl, whisk together eggs, water, cream, and melted butter; add flour and combine until batter is smooth. Cover and refrigerate for 30 minutes to 1 hour. Can be made night before.

Heat a 6- to 8-inch skillet or crêpe pan over medium-high heat. Once pan is hot, brush lightly with a portion of the remaining butter. Pour ¼ cup of batter into the skillet. Tilt pan to evenly coat pan bottom. Cook until crêpe bottom is light golden brown and the top is set—about 1 minute. Using spatula, flip crêpe and cook about 30 seconds more. Do not cook until crispy; you want the crêpe to remain pliable. Transfer to a plate and cover with wax paper. Repeat with remaining batter, and separate and cover each crêpe with wax paper. If making the night before, store finished crêpes in an airtight container and refrigerate until needed.

Filling:

In a food processor or bowl of standing mixer (or use hand mixer); cream the ricotta, cream cheese, lemon juice and zest, vanilla, and salt until well combined. Sweeten with sugar or honey, if desired. Set aside and refrigerate, or make the night before.

Sauce:

In a saucepan, combine cherries/berries and lemon juice. Cover and bring to a gentle simmer over medium heat until soupy, stirring occasionally (about 5 minutes). Once simmering, remove cover, add sugar to taste, if desired, and cook about 20 to 25 minutes more over medium-low heat, until juice has reduced and thickened, stirring occasionally. When using frozen cherries, thaw first and bring to simmer with lemon juice uncovered. Once simmering, add sugar if desired. Sugar is not needed to create a thick syrup. This is achieved by reducing the liquid and the action of the lemon and naturally occurring pectin in the fruit.

Assembly:

Preheat oven to 400°F.

Spread 3 TBS filling down the center, roll up like a burrito, and place seam side down on a large greased or parchment-lined baking sheet. Repeat with remaining crêpes. Bake 15 minutes, until filling is warmed through and melted. Place on individual serving plates, top with sauce, and serve.

Salmon-Poached Eggs with Greens

Serves 2

Don't despair if you lack a specially designed egg poacher, see the "How To" section under "Poached Eggs" (page 78) to make without. Directions are provided there for improvising with a large shallow saucepan, a deep skillet, or a sauté pan.

INGREDIENTS:

4 eggs

4 slices cold smoked salmon

2 TBS butter or ghee, plus more to grease egg cups

4 scallions, sliced

4 cups coarsely chopped baby greens

Coarse ground pepper

ESSENTIAL TOOLS:

Poaching pan for eggs

Large sauté pan or skillet for spinach

DIRECTIONS

To prepare poaching pan, remove the top portion of the pan that houses the egg cups or if you have individual cups that are removable, take those out. Generously grease egg cups and add 1 egg to each; set aside outside of pan.

Fill pan with water to a depth of 1 to 2 inches (or to fill line indicated on pan) and bring to simmer over medium heat; once simmering, turn off flame until ready to cook eggs.

Place 2 salmon slices side by side on each plate.

In a skillet over medium-high heat, heat the butter or ghee. Sauté scallions lightly until fragrant and bright green; add greens. Turn heat down to medium, and sauté greens until lightly wilted. Remove from heat and set aside in pan to keep warm.

Poach your eggs how you like them (4 to 6 minutes).

Place cooked greens on top of salmon, and add a poached egg. Sprinkle with coarse pepper and serve.

VARIATIONS

Substitute a thinly sliced stalk of fennel with greens for scallions.

Substitute asparagus for baby greens.

Olive oil may substitute butter.

Smoked Salmon and Baby Kale Omelet

Serves 1 to 2

The omelet shell here is made more like a giant crêpe, rather than by the traditional method of folding the eggs over upon themselves. This method is far easier for the home cook to master. Prep all ingredients before you start and set aside. The process moves quickly once you start cooking, and you don't want to burn the egg mixture or the vegetables. Smoked salmon is salty, so the dish doesn't really need added salt.

INGREDIENTS:

2 TBS butter

½ cup sliced scallions, plus more for garnish

2 cups packed baby kale, chopped
(or grab 2 large fistfuls and skip the measuring)

4 eggs

2 TBS olive oil

4 slices smoked salmon

4 TBS sour cream
or whipped cream cheese

ESSENTIAL TOOLS:

Large skillet

Large spatula

VARIATIONS

Substitute power greens or spinach for kale.

⅓ cup minced red pepper to scallion sauté.

Substitute leftover salmon; flake and evenly distribute.

DIRECTIONS

Heat skillet over high heat for 1 minute. Turn down to medium-high heat, and melt butter. Sauté scallions until slightly aromatic and brightly colored.

Add chopped baby kale and lightly sauté until bright green and reduced to half its original size (don't overcook). Remove scallions and kale from pan and set aside. Wipe out pan to remove the remaining vegetables and any browned butter.

Whisk eggs together until frothy. Distribute olive oil evenly across pan, and heat over medium high for about 90 seconds or until the oil becomes slightly aromatic. Slowly pour in eggs to cover pan completely and evenly. Immediately reduce heat to low and cover.

Once eggs have set up slightly (about 1 minute), lay salmon slices evenly over one half of the egg pancake. Smooth cream cheese or sour cream evenly over salmon. Distribute vegetable mixture over salmon and cream cheese or sour cream.

With a large spatula, lift empty side of egg pancake and fold over filling. Turn heat off and cover. Let steam for about 3 to 5 minutes.

Cut in half and serve immediately, garnished with fresh scallion.

CHEF'S NOTES

The trick here is to make sure the pan isn't too hot for the egg mixture. Make sure you turn to low once you have added the eggs. As the pan cools after removed from heat and the omelet steams to completion, the egg mixture will lift off the pan.

Winter Squash Hasty Pudding

Serves 1

Squash for breakfast is a win-win choice and satisfies most cereal junkies. The fat content of the cream or coconut milk combined with the egg protein and the squash's high fiber content will power you all morning long. Grain-based cereals create an immediate blood sugar spike and then leave you hungry a few hours later. The squash contains almost twice the amount of fiber of oatmeal and no anti-nutrient properties such as phytic acid and goitrogens. It is packed with beneficial anti-inflammatory polysaccharides and has a super-low glycemic load.

Roast a large squash up over the weekend, and have it for breakfast during the work week. Once you get the hang of this, you'll be able to make it in less than five minutes!

Can't eat eggs or don't like them? Leave them out and use nuts instead as protein and more cream to add body.

INGREDIENTS:

¼ cup cream or coconut milk, plus more for serving

1 or 2 eggs

⅛ TSP vanilla

⅛ TSP ground cinnamon

1 TBS butter, plus a pat more for serving

1 cup cooked sugar pumpkin or winter squash meat
(baked butternut the sweetest)

Salt, to taste

DIRECTIONS

In a small pan, whisk together cream or coconut milk, egg(s), vanilla, and cinnamon, mixing thoroughly. Add the butter.

Cook over medium heat, whisking mixture constantly as it heats, for about 1 minute. Don't overheat or egg will curdle, but even if it does, don't worry—it will taste fine regardless.

Add squash meat and salt to taste, and continue cooking for about 2 minutes, until thickened and warmed through.

Serve with additional cream or coconut milk and a pat of butter.

VARIATIONS

Add toasted nuts and/or coconut, dried fruit, and ground nutmeg.

Add ⅛ cup toasted, chopped nuts for protein.

Wild-Caught Fish

Salmon-Cabbage Rolls: Thai Fusion

Serves 6

These salmon-cabbage rolls are the answer to alleviate your egg roll or potsticker cravings! Young and old will gobble them up, and don't forget the dipping sauce for added fun. Common to many ethnic cuisines of Europe and Asia, meat fillings are rolled with cabbage leaves instead of wheat or rice wrappers. Treat yourself to three filling variations: salmon, ground beef, or chicken–the salmon is highlighted, but directions for beef or chicken rolls are included.

Cabbage rolls make a savory on-the-go lunch item that can be eaten cold or hot. For the budget-conscious shopper, this is an instance where you can use cheaper salmon varieties such as coho or keta (aka chum, dog or silverbrite salmon) without sacrificing flavor; however, be careful of bones and pick them out carefully.

Grill or roast two large fillets at once–one to eat immediately for dinner with grilled or steamed vegetables and the other to use for rolls or patties the next day. Somehow, eating leftover grilled salmon just isn't appetizing to most, but repurposed into a patty or a roll? Heck yeah!

VARIATIONS

The process is the same, but substitute 2 lbs uncooked ground beef or ground chicken for the salmon. The cheaper 75 to 85% lean ground beef makes a juicer product. Like with the salmon, pretend you are making a batch of meatballs.

After browning the cabbage rolls, cover and steam with liquid for at least 30 minutes until firm. Since you are starting with raw meat, these need to cook longer than the pre-cooked salmon.

ESSENTIAL TOOLS:

Sauté pan or skillet

Large pot

Small paring knife

Large slotted spoon strainer

Large, deep sauté pan or dutch oven

NOTES:

INGREDIENTS:

Rolls:

5 TBS olive oil, divided

2 lbs salmon fillet(s)

2 TBS toasted sesame oil, divided

1 small red pepper, ¼-inch diced

1 bunch scallions, finely sliced

1 TBS minced fresh ginger *(galangal ginger best)*

1 TBS minced fresh lemongrass

2 extra-large eggs, whisked

2 TBS chopped fresh cilantro

½ TSP dried red pepper, crushed *(optional)*

Salt, to taste

1 large cabbage head

1 cup water or chicken broth

Dipping Sauce:

1 TBS Thai red curry paste *(optional)*

6 TBS gluten-free tamari sauce

¼ cup rice vinegar

2 TSP toasted sesame oil

2 TSP honey or sugar

Pinch of chili flakes

DIRECTIONS

Rolls:

1 *Filling:* Unlike a beef or chicken filling, the salmon is either grilled, pan fried, or oven roasted prior to stuffing cabbage leaves.

To Grill: Coat salmon with olive oil on both sides. Grill 3 minutes each side at 425°F.

To Pan Fry: Cut large whole fillets in half. In a large skillet over medium heat, place salmon skin side up in 2 TBS olive oil and cook for 3 minutes each side. Add more oil if necessary.

To Bake: Preheat oven to 425°F. Rub with olive oil on both sides, place skin side down in casserole dish, and bake for 10 minutes.

Remove fish immediately from heat. Place in dish skin side up, cover and let rest 10 minutes. Peel off skin and remove bones.

Once cool, mash cooked salmon thoroughly using your hands, as this helps locate any undetected escapee bones.

In a clean sauté pan or skillet over medium flame, heat 1 TBS sesame oil. Lightly sauté red pepper, scallions, ginger, and lemongrass until fragrant (about 3 minutes). Don't overcook or burn; at this point you are simply pre-releasing the flavors and mingling them.

Let herb and vegetable mixture cool a bit and combine with mashed salmon, eggs, cilantro, crushed red pepper (if using), and salt to taste.

Mash together all the ingredients with your hands, like you are making meatloaf or meatballs. Refrigerate while you prepare the cabbage leaves.

2 *Cabbage Leaves:* Blanch cabbage leaves to make them pliable for rolling. Remove and discard cabbage core, which extends about 2 inches deep into interior. It will look like a circular cone removed from the bottom. Place cabbage head in boiling water and simmer for 5 minutes; then remove with a large slotted spoon strainer.

Carefully remove leaves one by one with tongs and set aside on paper towel-lined plate to drain. If some leaves still seem too hard, simply return remaining head to boiling water for 1 minute or so.

Once you have all leaves removed from head, remove 2 to 3 inches of hard, triangular portion of rib from base of each cabbage leaf with a small paring knife.

3 *Assembly:* Place ½ to ⅓ cup of filling near base of each leaf where rib was removed. Fold base flaps over each other, put sides in, and roll up toward outer edge until you have a compact package. How full you fill them will determine the thickness; for example, if you would like more of an egg roll end product, go lighter on the filling and roll them longer and thinner.

4 *Cooking:* In a large, deep sauté pan or dutch oven over medium-high heat, heat 1 TBS sesame oil and 2 TBS olive oil. Place the cabbage rolls into the oil seam side down, brown lightly, and then flip and brown until portions of the leaves are golden brown. Flip again with seam side down for the remainder of cook time, adding more oil as necessary. You may also need to make in batches, depending on size of your pan. Once done browning, return rolls to pan. You may layer them if they don't all fit on bottom of the pan.

Pour broth or water into pan (broth lends a superior flavor) to a depth of ¼ inch. Cover and gently bring to a simmer on medium high. Reduce heat to medium low; continue simmering 15 minutes, covered, or until filling is firm to the touch. Check after 10 minutes to make sure there is plenty of liquid and replenish if necessary. When done, liquid will have dissipated, but be careful to not steam dry before cooking process is completed.

Dipping Sauce Directions:

In a small bowl, whisk together Thai red curry paste (if using), tamari sauce, rice vinegar, toasted sesame oil, honey or raw sugar, and chili flakes until well combined. Serve rolls with dipping sauce on the side.

Baked Cod in Sour Cream-Dill Sauce

Serves 4

This recipe creates a gourmet-looking meal that can be ready in no time at all with little effort or expertise required!

Black cod or sablefish is a mild tasting fish that inhabits the deep cold waters of the Pacific and Atlantic Oceans and provides about the same amount of omega-3 fat as salmon. The cod from Alaskan waters is marketed under these names: Alaskan cod, black cod or sablefish, Alaskan rockfish, Gindara (sushi fish) and butterfish. Beware: There are many varieties of fish labeled as cod from warmer fisheries that are not high in omega-3 fats, so I look for wild-caught Alaskan. As of this writing, Seafood Watch has placed Russian- and Japanese-caught cod on their "Avoid" list.

INGREDIENTS:

2 lbs cod fillet

Sauce:

   ¼ cup mayonnaise

   ¼ cup sour cream

   2 TBS minced fresh dill

   2 TSP Dijon mustard

   2 TBS fresh lemon juice

   ½ TSP minced garlic

   Pinch of salt

   2 TBS capers (optional)

   Coarsely ground pepper

ESSENTIAL TOOLS:

Glass or porcelain baking dish

DIRECTIONS

Preheat oven to 350°F.

Pat cod fillet dry with paper towels. Remove any remaining pin bones with large kitchen tweezers or needle-nosed pliers. Locate them by feeling with your fingertips along the fillets centerline. Grasp the bone tip and firmly pull sideways and up towards the head area.

Drizzle with olive oil, rubbing it into both sides of fillet.

Place fish in a glass or porcelain baking dish.

In a bowl, mix sauce ingredients together and spread evenly over fish. Sprinkle with capers (if using) and coarsely ground pepper.

Bake for 30 minutes, or until fish and sauce are obviously heated through.

Serve over wilted or sautéed greens.

CHEF'S NOTES

Salt lightly! The fish has a natural saltiness, and the capers are extremely salty, so use caution when adding salt (if any) to sauce.

VARIATIONS

Works well with any type of white fish, like flounder or sole. Like black cod, look for wild-caught fish obtained along the northwestern waters off Alaska.

Grilled Cod with Meyer Lemon Butter

Serves 4

Simple to prepare yet elegant, this recipe works great for a special dinner occasion or as a quick dinner after work. Sometimes the most economical cut is sold as one large fillet. Buy enough to divide into four 6-inch portions. Look for wild-caught Alaskan codfish, preferably the fatty black cod or sablefish.

Meyer lemons are best, but if not available, substitute ⅓ cup lemon juice with fresh orange juice.

No grill? Directions are provided for oven roasting.

TIP

Use squeezed lemon peel and rind cut into ½-inch slices and run in garbage disposal to freshen.

INGREDIENTS:

Cod Fillets:

    4 (6-inch-long) fillets

    Olive oil, for coating cod

    Salt and pepper

Lemon Butter Sauce:

    6 TBS butter, divided

    2 large garlic cloves, minced

    1 bunch scallions, thinly sliced diagonally *(reserve 2 TBS of green portion as garnish)*

    ⅔ cup fresh lemon juice and zest for garnish

ESSENTIAL TOOLS:

Large shallow baking dish *(if using oven)*

Large skillet for sauce

VARIATIONS

Arrange fish skin side down in a large baking dish lined with parchment paper. Bake oiled and seasoned 1-inch fillets uncovered in a 375°F oven for 20-25 minutes or until the fish is just cooked through (looks opaque in center). Let rest covered 5 minutes before ladling warm sauce over them.

Onion allergies: Instead of scallions and garlic, use a large fennel bulb and greens, diced. Add green portion at end as described for scallions.

Substitute ⅓ cup lemon juice with dry white wine.

DIRECTIONS

Cod Fillets:

Rinse cod fillets and dry completely. Remove any remaining pin bones with large kitchen tweezers or needle-nosed pliers. Locate them by feeling with your fingertips along the fillets centerline. Grasp the bone tip and firmly pull sideways and up towards the head area. Generously coat each fillet with olive oil, and season with salt and pepper.

Heat grill to high until it reaches 450°F.

Grill fish with lid closed for 3 minutes on each side for 1-inch-thick fillets, and for those less than one inch, cook 1 to 2 minutes each side.

Cover and let rest 5 minutes before serving. The resting period seals juices in, and allows the fillets to cook to completion in the thickest part without drying out the thinner sections.

Lemon-Butter Sauce:

In a large skillet over medium-high heat, melt 2 TBS butter. Add garlic and white portions of sliced scallions. Set aside green portions to add later. Sauté until fragrant and becoming tender, about 1 minute.

Add lemon juice, and cook another 2-3 minutes to heat lemon and fuse flavors.

Stir in green portion of scallions, and heat 1 minute more until they turn bright green.

Remove from heat, and add remaining 4 TBS butter, stirring as it melts, so it emulsifies with lemon mixture.

Let cool another 4 minutes, stirring periodically. You will start to see butter thicken sauce as it cools.

To Serve:

Ladle sauce over fish, garnish with lemon zest and reserved scallion greens, and serve immediately.

Grilled Gingered Salmon

Serves 6 to 8

As my daughter once remarked, salmon cooked like this "melts in your mouth like butter." Wild-caught king salmon has the best flesh, and sockeye is the next best choice but won't be as tender. I don't recommend coho or keta salmon for grilling. Directions are also offered for oven roasting. If you haven't yet bought yourself a 9-inch-wide spatula for flipping large cuts of meat, you should consider doing so. It flips fish filets easily without breaking them, and you will wonder how you ever did without it. Fillets thinner than ½ inch thick should not be grilled.

INGREDIENTS:

1 large, full-length salmon fillet, skin on (2 to 3 lbs)

Olive oil

Ginger powder

Garlic powder

2 to 4 TBS gluten-free tamari or coconut aminos sauce

Mango Salsa (pg.240) or Avocado-Lime Salsa (pg.222), for serving

ESSENTIAL TOOLS:

Large glass baking dish

DIRECTIONS

Wash and pat dry the salmon. Let set for 20 minutes. Dry flesh will absorb the oil and seasoning better.

Preheat grill to 425°F (medium-high)—you want it hot to sear in the juices and flavor.

Remove any remaining pin bones with large kitchen tweezers or needle-nosed pliers. Locate them by feeling with your fingertips along the fillets centerline. Grasp the bone tip and firmly pull sideways and up towards the head area.

Coat salmon with olive oil on both sides (about 2 TBS, depending on fillet size). On flesh side, generously sprinkle ginger and garlic powder; rub well into flesh.

On a preheated grill, place salmon, flesh side down and cook for 2 to 3 minutes (generally 3 minutes per side, for a 1-inch-thick fillet at thickest part, maximum 2 minutes for any thinner).

Flip salmon skin side down, and grill for another 2 to 3 minutes, depending on thickness. While salmon is grilling, prepare a large glass baking dish for the salmon by spreading tamari in middle.

Remove fish from grill and place flesh side down in prepared glass dish. Let rest for 3 minutes to soak up the tamari sauce. Peel off skin and flip skin side into tamari. Skin should peel off easily in one piece. Let meat rest covered for an additional 3 minutes before serving.

Hold it—don't throw away the skin! Use skin to make crackles.

Serve with my Mango Salsa or Avocado-Lime Salsa.

VARIATIONS

For Soy or Coconut Allergies: Substitute a balsamic reduction sauce for tamari sauce and rub salmon with dried basil or the powdered ginger.

Oven Roast: Bring fish to room temperature before preparing. Place fish skin side down in shallow pan lined with parchment paper. Season as above, and evenly distribute 3 TBS butter across top or drizzle with a bit of additional olive oil. Roast at 425°F for 10 minutes for a 1-inch-thick, full-length fillet. The general rule for oven roasting is about 5 minutes per ½ inch at the thickest part. Cover and let rest 5 minutes before serving. This will complete the cooking process and seal in meat juices.

Don't have parchment paper? Make sure the skin is well oiled, and place fillet skin side down on a shallow cookie sheet or roasting pan.

Fresh Fish Cakes

Serves: 6 (about 12 patties)

So many of the grain-free or paleo-type fish cake recipes call for the addition of coconut or almond flour. However, like with my beef meatballs, none is needed here. If proper technique is followed, they will not break apart.

This is a versatile recipe where the fish could be swapped out with tuna, cod, or crab. Salmon tends to be the most reasonably priced and readily available. It also has a superior omega-3 fatty acid content. Patties are a great way to entice even the pickiest of eaters into eating fish.

INGREDIENTS:

Salmon:

1 lb sockeye salmon fillet (*see Chef's Notes*)

Olive oil, for coating salmon

½ TSP garlic powder

Coarse ground pepper

Patties:

2 large eggs, beaten

½ TBS dried dill or 1 TBS minced, fresh

1 cup minced scallions (*about 4 large scallions*)

1 cup ¼ inch diced red pepper (*small whole red pepper*)

½ TSP garlic powder

1 TBS Dijon mustard

2 TBS mayonnaise, plus 1 TBS more if needed

1 TBS capers, drained and patted dry (*optional*)

1 TBS fresh lemon juice

½ TBS lemon zest (*optional*)

1 TBS olive oil and 1 TBS butter, plus more as needed in these proportions

For Serving:

Shredded lettuce

Fresh flat-leaf parsley

Remoulade Sauce

_____

ESSENTIAL TOOLS:

Shallow baking or broiler pan (*if oven roasting*)

Large skillet

⅓ or ½ cup measuring cup

DIRECTIONS

Salmon:

Preheat oven or grill to 425F. Pat salmon dry and coat with olive oil on both sides. Rub garlic powder and ground pepper into flesh side until well covered.

To Grill: Grill covered for 3 minutes, flesh side down first, then flip and grill covered another 3 minutes with skin side on grill. Remove from grill, cover with foil, and set aside to cool flesh side down for 15 minutes. Skin should peel off easily in one piece.

To Bake: Coat with olive oil and garlic powder as previously described. Grease a shallow baking or broiler pan and place salmon fillet on top, skin side down.

Bake until just cooked through for about 10 minutes, depending on fillet thickness. Flip to flesh side down, cover and let rest 10 minutes. Peel skin off in one piece while still warm.

Patties:

Flake cooled salmon into a large mixing bowl; carefully remove any bones. Mash with your fingers until flakes are completely broken up. Add eggs, dill, scallions, red pepper, garlic powder, mustard, mayonnaise, capers, lemon juice, and lemon zest (if using) to bowl and mix until thoroughly combined. Mixture should clump together. If mixture seems too dry to form into patties, add 1 TBS additional mayonnaise. Refrigerate for 30 minutes.

In skillet over medium flame, heat the butter and olive oil.

Scoop up meat mixture using an oiled ⅓ or ½ cup measuring cup and lightly pack. This will make a nice patty to drop into the skillet. Slightly press into pan with a spatula. Press too much and they will fall apart when you flip. Patties will spread as they cook. Do not disturb patties while they cook.

Fry until golden and crispy, about 4 to 5 minutes each side. Carefully remove from pan and drain on paper towel-lined plate. They will firm up as they cool a bit. I cook three at a time in my cast iron skillet. Scrape up loose burned bits and discard before adding more oil and the next batch. Keep warm in a 180°F oven until ready to serve.

To Serve:

Place each salmon cake on a bed of shredded lettuce, garnish with parsley, and serve alongside Remoulade Sauce or a fruit salsa. This dish pairs well with a cucumber salad.

CHEF'S NOTES

The best salmon to use for this application is wild-caught Alaskan sockeye, then cojo (not farmed). You can also use wild-caught keta (dog salmon), but be careful of all the fine bones it contains. Save the expensive king salmon to eat whole and grilled.

If you choose to use canned meat, make sure the oil or water is completely drained off the meat and it is completely patted dry with paper towels.

VARIATIONS

Replace red pepper with finely diced celery.

Butter may be substituted with 1 TBS olive oil.

Replace dill with ¼ cup minced fresh parsley or mint.

Replace scallions with ½ cup chives.

Smoked Salmon Roll-Ups

Yield: about 12 rolls

Salmon rolls are so easy, portable, and filling. Use as an appetizer, addition to the lunch box, or as a snack anytime. They are particularly great for road trips. When you consider the price of food bought on the road, a package of smoked salmon used to prepare these isn't all that expensive in comparison.

INGREDIENTS:

8 oz cold smoked Alaskan sockeye salmon, sliced thin *(could also use lox or gravlax)*

Small tub sour cream *(less than ½ cup needed)*

3.5-oz bottle of capers, drained and patted dry *(optional)*

⅛ cup minced chives

Chopped fresh dill, for garnish

Thinly sliced pimiento, for garnish *(optional)*

DIRECTIONS

Carefully separate each slice of salmon. If one breaks in the process, overlay slightly the two pieces or roll as separate pieces.

For each slice of smoked salmon, add ½ TBS sour cream, 6 capers, and a sprinkling of minced chives.

Roll and refrigerate at least 1 hour before serving.

You may wish to slice in half if using as an appetizer, but do this with a sharpened knife after chilling for an extended period.

Garnish with fresh chives, rosemary, or dill. Try crossing two thin slices of pimiento on top.

CHEF'S NOTES

Check the ingredients label before you purchase sour cream. The only ingredient it should contain is organic cultured cream. It should not contain milk or thickeners such as carrageenan. Look for organic brands that contain live and active cultures.

VARIATIONS

Whipped cream cheese substituted for sour cream.

Teriyaki Shrimp

Serves 6

I don't know about you, but if I am eating shrimp, 4 measly ones aren't going to do it. I guarantee you that everyone will want to eat at least 6 to 8 shrimp per serving. My Mango Salsa or the coconut version of Lettuce Jus are excellent choices to serve with the shrimp.

The hardest part about this recipe is shelling and deveining 32 to 40 shrimp; the rest is a snap. I most often would employ my teens for this task, and they were more than happy to oblige, knowing the end result would be incredibly good! Buying yourself a deveiner speeds up the process tremendously.

Teriyaki marinades usually contain vinegar or citrus; however, I have omitted these because acidic liquid starts "cooking" the shrimp. While tamari also tenderizes, it does so less. When using pineapple juice, make sure it is the canned variety so the tenderizing enzyme is deactivated. The shrimp simply doesn't need tenderizing or curing like ceviche. A bit more oil than usual is used to keep them from sticking to the hot grill. This recipe is easily halved.

If possible, mix the marinade up the night before to let the flavors really meld. However, I have made the sauce on the fly only an hour before grilling and the shrimp still tasted great!

INGREDIENTS:

2 lbs jumbo shrimp
(16 to 20 shrimp per lb)

1 cup gluten-free tamari or
coconut aminos

1 cup unsweetened canned
pineapple juice

2 TBS unrefined, unbleached,
whole cane sugar (optional)

2 TBS toasted sesame oil

4 TBS olive oil

2 TBS minced garlic

½ cup minced scallions

2 TBS minced fresh ginger

½ cup minced cilantro, mint,
or flat-leaf parsley, plus 2 TBS
for garnish

Mango Salsa (page 240)

ESSENTIAL TOOLS:

Paring knife or deveiner

Bamboo or metal skewers

Large, shallow baking dishes
or sheets

Broiler pan, if not grilling

DIRECTIONS

Peeling Shrimp:

Start by sliding your thumb under top shell segment by legs, removing shell in a circular fashion around body as you work toward tail; do not remove last shell segment before tail. You will want to leave something substantial to skewer into, plus it adds visual appeal. Legs usually pull off along with shell, and if not, remove any that remain.

Devein by making a shallow slit down middle of back with paring knife; lift vein out with point of knife and discard. Rinse under cold running water. Drain and pat dry.

Teriyaki Sauce:

In a medium bowl, whisk to combine tamari, pineapple juice, optional sugar, sesame oil, and olive oil until sugar is fully dissolved. Add garlic, scallions, ginger, and your choice of cilantro, mint, or flat-leaf parsley to marinade; set aside covered and let flavors meld while you skewer shrimp.

Assembly and Marinating:

Thread shrimp onto skewers, starting at top (head), push through and out other side; catch bottom portion of tail containing shell and push skewer through to opposite side. If you have two-prong skewers, they are easier to use and work best to prevent spinning.

Place skewered shrimp in large, shallow baking dishes or sheets. Spoon teriyaki sauce over prepared shrimp and allow them to marinate for at least 30 minutes covered in refrigerator. Periodically check a few times and remoisten with a spoon or flip kabobs to other side.

Remove shrimp from marinade and place on paper towel-lined plate, being careful not to knock off all herbs and spice; let drain while you prepare grill. Discard marinade.

To Cook:

Grill: Heat grill to 425°F and brush grilling rack with oil to prevent shrimp from sticking. Grill with lid closed for 2 minutes on each side.

Broiler: Preheat broiler to high. Place skewers on a broiler pan brushed with oil; top with any remaining marinade. Position 5 inches from heat and cook for 2 minutes on each side.

Garnish:

Garnish with fresh cilantro, mint, or parsley, minced, while shrimp are still hot.

To Serve:

Mound a ¼- to ½-cup of Mango Salsa in the middle of the plate. Arrange 6 shrimp propped up in a circular starburst design (heads meeting in the middle, tails fanning outward).

Pasture Raised & Grass Fed

Beef Carbonnade

Serves 4

A country Flemish woman moves deftly about her seventeenth-century kitchen with hair tied up in a white woolen cap and blue muslin apron on. Braids of garlic, onions, and herbs hang suspended from the rough-hewn ceiling beams. Rays of late morning sun gently stream through a window and bounce against the white plaster walls, filling her eyes with golden reflections.

Life is good this year. It is winter, but the bountiful summer harvest lines the cellar shelves with ceramic bottles of dark brown ale, sides of smoked pork, and baskets of root vegetables. She creates a stew for the midday meal, and a savory aroma soon wafts throughout the house warming the heart and beckoning one to the table.

Beef, bacon, and beer: Do I have your attention yet? The gourmet name disguises the humble nature of the dish, a sweet-sour beef stew largely comprised of onions. Unlike beef bourguignon made with wine, carbonnade is distinguished by the rich, earthy flavor of dark ale. My interpretation calls for four different members of the allium family, each adding its own individual flavor to the mix, balsamic instead of apple cider vinegar, and LOTS of bacon.

In traditional recipes, root vegetables were boiled and served on the side.

Parslied Vegetables recipe, page 214.

INGREDIENTS:

4 TBS butter, divided

1 lb beef stew meat, cut into 2-inch cubes

6 slices thick bacon, cut into ½-inch pieces

1 large yellow onion, sliced lengthwise

6 large garlic cloves, diced

1 large leek, cut in half, rinsed, and sliced into 1-inch pieces

3 shallots, sliced lengthwise

½ cup water

1 ½ cups dark ale

1 TBS balsamic vinegar

¼ cup chopped, fresh thyme

⅛ cup chopped, fresh tarragon

⅛ cup chopped, fresh flat-leaf parsley, plus more for garnish

Salt and coarse ground pepper, to taste

1 TBS kuzu root starch dissolved in ¼ cup cold water *(optional for gravy)*

For Serving:

Parslied root vegetables, potato dumplings, "frites" *(Belgian french fries)*, or roasted cauliflower

ESSENTIAL TOOLS:

Large skillet

6-qt shallow stock pot or dutch oven

CHEF'S NOTES

While cooking potatoes and carrots directly in the stew is a tempting timesaver, I don't recommend it. The vegetables lose their bright color, become mushy, and render the stew unappetizing in appearance.

While the liquids are thickened during the simmer process, some of you might prefer a thicker-bodied sauce if it seems too soupy, or you may want to skip the reduction process. For a grain-free solution, add thinned kuzu to finished carbonnade and simmer over moderate heat until meat juices are thickened and turned transparent.

The beauty of using kuzu root instead of other thickeners is that it doesn't break down (separate after cooking), has a transparent quality to it akin to cornstarch, and it is a perfect grain- or gluten-free alternative for those using gluten-free beer.

VARIATIONS

Replace leek and shallot with 1 large yellow onion, thinly sliced lengthwise.

Replace ½ cup beer with beef stock if you would like a lighter taste.

DIRECTIONS

In a large skillet over medium-high heat, heat 1 TBS butter.

Add beef and working in small batches, brown each batch for about 8 to 10 minutes. Add 1 TBS more butter for each batch or as needed. The beef needs room to breathe while browning, and if overcrowded, too much liquid will generate and defeat the process. Transfer to pot or dutch oven.

Add bacon to skillet and cook until lightly browned and fat is rendered. Transfer to pot with beef and reserve bacon drippings in skillet.

Add yellow onion to bacon drippings in skillet and sauté over medium heat until translucent and starting to caramelize, about 8 minutes. Add 1 TBS butter if onions start to dry out. Add garlic, leeks, and shallot to onion; continue to sauté for another 8 minutes on medium.

Add the water to onion mixture to deglaze pan, stirring to scrape up browned bits from bottom (about 1 to 2 minutes). Transfer to meat mixture.

Add beer, balsamic vinegar, thyme, tarragon, parsley, and salt and pepper to meat mixture. Stir well and bring to simmer on medium high.

Reduce heat to medium low; gently simmer covered, stirring occasionally, until beef is tender, about 1 ½ to 2 hours. Do not replenish lost moisture unless it seems like it is becoming too thick and will burn. The goal is to thicken the liquid portion by reduction. If the mixture seems too soupy for you once the meat is tender, remove the lid and simmer for an additional 30 minutes or until the juices have thickened to desired consistency.

To Serve:

Garnish each bowl with parsley and serve with root vegetables or other vegetables of your choice. Place the hot meat and onion mixture in the bowl and position a serving of vegetables on top to the side.

NOTES:

Chicken Breast Roulade

Serves 4

This dish is equally at home at a special dinner party or as a part of your weekend meal prep, to give you a stress-free week of lunch or dinner. The beauty of this dish lies in its simplicity. It looks gourmet on the plate, yet is super easy to prepare with no slicing, dicing, or measuring required.

INGREDIENTS:

4 boneless chicken breasts

Garlic powder

Dried thyme leaves (optional)

Salt and coarse ground pepper

4 thin slices prosciutto or other ham

4 thin slices provolone cheese

Large bunch fresh basil

2 cups marinara sauce, warmed

Olive oil for brushing rolls, if grilling

2 TBS butter and 1 TBS olive oil, if oven roasting

ESSENTIAL TOOLS:

Plastic wrap

Meat mallet or rolling pin

14-inch oven-proof skillet (if not grilling)

Butcher's twine

VARIATIONS

Prosciutto is sometimes too costly for the budget to bear. As an alternative, I have used thick-sliced bacon cooked until lightly browned. Do not fry to crispiness; you want it to remain flexible. Cook bacon after you have pounded out chicken, have the cheese and basil prepped, and are ready to roll. Cut each slice in half and arrange side by side lengthwise on chicken breast.

Substitute good melting cheeses such as monterey jack, swiss, or fontina for provolone.

Use roasted red pepper instead of or in addition to cheese.

Cook up my Sautéed Greens recipe; cut in half. Evenly divide among the four breasts, smoothing on top of the prosciutto and cheese.

Substitute 2 cups of my Roasted Red Pepper Coulis or Marinara Sauce recipes, warmed for commercially prepared sauces.

NOTES:

DIRECTIONS

Flatten Breasts:

Remove chicken skin and tenders; pat dry with paper towels. Place 1 breast, smooth side down between 2 sheets of plastic wrap on a cutting board. Using short, even strokes, begin pounding breast starting at center and working your way outward to the edge. Repeat until flattened to ¼ inch thick. A rolling pin, the flat side of a meat mallet, or a rubber mallet from the hardware store will work. Make them thin, because they will become thicker as they cook.

Assembly:

Sprinkle both sides of chicken breasts with garlic powder, dry thyme leaves, salt, and pepper; rub into meat, repeating if necessary to thoroughly cover. Arrange smooth side down on cookie sheet or other work surface.

Lay a slice of prosciutto on breast, follow with cheese, and finally evenly distribute 4 fresh basil leaves.

Carefully roll chicken tightly, tying each with 2 pieces of twine to keep roll together.

Slice remaining basil to use as garnish.

Warm sauce and set aside.

To Cook:

Directions are provided for grilling or oven roasting.

Grill: Preheat grill to 400°F (medium heat). Brush each roll with olive oil. Place rolls on hot grill. Cook with lid down for 15 minutes, rotating every 3 minutes until browned on all sides and cheese has started to melt.

Oven: In a skillet over medium-high heat, melt butter with olive oil; add chicken. Cook 6 to 8 minutes, turning to brown on all sides. Transfer skillet to oven, and bake at 425F for 12 to 15 minutes, just until cheese has started to melt.

Remove breast from heat when done and let rest 3 to 5 minutes, until cool enough to touch.

To Serve:

Remove twine and cut rolls into four equal-sized slices with a sharp knife. Place ¼ cup of warmed sauce on each individual plate and arrange chicken slices on it. Garnish with basil and serve.

Chicken with Leek-Mushroom Sauce

Serves 4

It's the fresh thyme that makes this dish taste so good, so don't cut corners by using dried for the sauce. Boneless chicken breasts are pricey, and while better for presentation purposes, they are not essential. Bone in or bone out, it's all good and cooking directions have been provided for both. The more adventurous may want to learn how to de-bone their own and stretch their food dollars even further by freezing the bones to make broth later. Grilling is my preferred method of cooking the chicken breasts, but directions are also provided for oven roasting or pan frying.

INGREDIENTS:

Chicken Breasts:

  4 chicken breast halves

  Olive oil for coating chicken, plus 2 TBS more if frying

Herb Rub:

  1 TBS dried thyme

  1 TBS dried tarragon

  1 TBS dried rosemary

  1 TSP garlic powder

  Salt and coarse cracked pepper

Leek-Mushroom Sauce:

  4 TBS butter

  16 oz mushrooms, sliced

  Salt and pepper, to taste

  1 large leek, sliced

  2 TBS minced fresh thyme

  1 cup cream

  ½ cup chicken broth

ESSENTIAL TOOLS:

Shallow baking pan (if oven roasting)

Large skillet

CHEF'S NOTES

This dish is great served over a bed of steamed greens or roasted butternut squash puree.

Easy Vegetable Sides: After grilling chicken and removing, grill vegetables like fennel, asparagus, or zucchini brushed with olive oil.

Take to work lunch idea: Chop fresh greens of any type and place on bottom of a glass container; slice chicken and place on top along with sauce. To heat, remove container lid, cover with a paper towel or plate, and microwave about 2 minutes.

VARIATIONS

Add ½ cup white wine to cream. Eliminate water or broth accordingly.

Substitute fresh sage in place of dried rosemary and tarragon.

DIRECTIONS

Prep vegetables for sauce and set aside. You want these ready in advance, so your meat doesn't get cold while you are making the sauce.

Chicken Breast:

Generously coat breasts on both sides with olive oil. In a small bowl, mix together herbs and seasoning, and rub breasts with mixture. Salt and pepper.

Cook times depend on breast thickness and will vary. Chicken is cooked when temperatures reach 160F or juices run clear when pierced with a knife.

To Grill: Preheat outdoor grill to 375°F to 400°F. Place chicken skin side down on grill. Breast without bone cook covered for 12 minutes total, turning once; with bone, 20 to 25 minutes total, turning once.

To Bake: Preheat oven to 375°F. Place chicken in a shallow baking pan and bake for 25 to 30 minutes, skin side up without bone; 30 to 40 minutes with bone in; no turning required.

To Pan Fry: In a large skillet over medium flame, heat 2 TBS olive oil. Place boneless chicken skin side down in skillet and cook 6 to 8 minutes uncovered until nicely browned; then turn chicken, cover, and cook another 6 to 8 minutes. If cooking with bone in, cook 10 minutes each side.

Transfer cooked chicken to a shallow casserole dish, cover, and let rest 5 to 10 minutes before serving.

Leek-Mushroom Sauce:

While chicken is cooking, in a large sauté pan or skillet over medium heat, melt the 2 TBS butter. Sauté mushrooms until golden brown; salt and pepper to taste. Work in batches if needed to avoid overcrowding. Mushrooms need room to breathe, so they shed their moisture and don't become soggy. Remove and set aside. Wipe pan clean before preparing leeks.

In same pan over medium heat, melt remaining 2 TBS butter and sauté leeks until bright green, about 3 to 4 minutes. Add thyme and toss for 1 minute more or until aromatic.

Add cream and stir into leek mixture; adjust seasoning to taste. Simmer until thickened, about 3 to 5 minutes. Add broth, and stir until combined with leeks and cream; simmer two minutes more or until sauce has slightly thickened.

Remove leek-cream mixture from heat, add cooked mushrooms to sauce, and stir in.

Distribute sauce evenly over cooked breasts and serve.

Chicken with Leek-Mushroom Sauce pictured on page 54.

Chicken and Zucchini Sauté

Serves 4

This sauté is an easy and light summer dish to cook when turning on the oven is not an option. If you have not purchased yourself a spiralizer for making vegetable "spaghetti" and other "noodles," treat yourself. They are inexpensive and a fantastic alternative to high-carbohydrate grain pasta.

Not everyone has the luxury of a grill, or maybe you just don't feel like firing it up. Alternative cooking directions are provided for sautéing the chicken.

INGREDIENTS:

Chicken:

2 boneless chicken breasts

Olive oil for coating chicken, plus 1 TBS more if sautéing

1 TBS butter

Vegetables:

2 TBS butter

4 to 6 garlic cloves, sliced

1 dry pint cherry tomatoes *(25 to 30 cherry tomatoes)*

4 medium-to-small zucchinis cut spaghetti style *(with a spiralizer)*

Salt and pepper, to taste

1 cup chopped fresh basil

For Serving:

Fresh ground pepper and parmesan cheese, as garnish

ESSENTIAL TOOLS:

Large skillet or sauté pan

Spiralizer

VARIATIONS

All butter can be replaced with olive oil.

Add sliced Greek olives at end with chicken.

Instead of sautéing tomatoes, skewer and grill after chicken. Grill skewered tomatoes for 1 minute on each side at medium high (400°F); set aside and add to skillet at end with cooked chicken.

NOTES:

DIRECTIONS

Chicken:

To Grill: Pat chicken dry with paper towels, coat generously with olive oil, and grill on medium-high heat (375°F) for 5 minutes on each side. Let rest 5 minutes or until cool enough to touch; slice into ¼-inch-thick pieces.

To Sauté: Slice chicken into ¼-inch-thick slices. In 14-inch skillet over medium-high heat, heat 1 TBS olive oil and 1 TBS butter. Add chicken slices to skillet and leave undisturbed about 3 minutes, or until they have browned on one side, before turning.

Once browned on both sides, remove from pan and set aside to drain on paper towel-lined plate.

Clean skillet before sautéing vegetables.

Vegetables:

In a skillet or sauté pan over medium heat, melt 2 TBS butter. Sauté garlic for 1 minute until fragrant.

Add tomatoes and sauté until they become warm and softened, about 5 minutes. Like the chicken, let them cook undisturbed for a while before turning to other sides.

Melt remaining 2 TBS butter in pan, add zucchini, and sauté about 1 minute, until zucchini becomes bright green.

Add cooked chicken to pan, salt and pepper to taste, and warm until meat is reheated.

Remove from heat and add basil, tossing to blend and wilt.

Enchiladas

Yield: 12 rolls

Once my diet changed to low-carb, I lost one of my favorite dishes—enchiladas. The supposedly "low-carb" tortillas combine wheat with corn and/or use cellulose (wood pulp) to bulk up the fiber to net out a low carb count. Some of the "paleo" tortillas use coconut flour, plantains, flax, almond flour, pumpkin, or cauliflower and eggs. Oh, please; I'll just skip the beans and rice and eat organic, no-GMO, corn tortillas if that is the case. Corn tortillas are paleo, and pre-agricultural corn was hunted and gathered just like the seed and nut alternatives. Like corn, nut and seed alternatives made with egg produce allergenic responses in many people.

There is a gluten-free, non-allergenic, paleo, low-carb alternative to corn or wheat tortillas: cabbage leaves. Cabbage is a ubiquitous vegetable found in the Mexican mercados (markets) and is the perfect stand-in for the tortilla. Don't be daunted by the idea of steaming the cabbage leaves. They are way easier to prepare than pre-frying or dipping tortillas in sauce to soften prior to rolling, and a lot less messy.

Years ago, I never could decide which type of enchiladas to make, they all sounded so good. So I cherry-picked all my favorite ingredients from various recipes and rolled them into one. Except for the chicken and sauce, the balance of the ingredients could be labeled "optional," and this recipe offers a solid foundation from which you can experiment on your own. Almonds and olives are traditional ingredients in Mexican cooking, with their origins rooted in Spanish cuisine. The almonds add an interesting textural contrast against the soft cream cheese and olives.

NOTES:

CHEF'S NOTES

If you like your enchiladas saucy, add one additional cup poured over top for a total of 3 cups used in recipe.

Keep your cream cheese well chilled until ready to cube. I like to throw in the freezer 30 minutes before I'm ready to cut it.

Most of the phytic acid lies in the skin of the almond, so I recommend roasting/toasting before chopping.

VARIATIONS

Some people prefer the green sauce (my fav) over red chili. If you are one of those, this recipe works well using all green or red sauce.

Substitute pork or beef for chicken.

Substitute 2 cups cheddar, queso fresco, or swiss instead of cream cheese.

INGREDIENTS:

Sauce:

1 ½ cups tomatillo sauce or green enchilada sauce

½ cup red enchilada sauce

Chicken:

3 cups cooked chicken, shredded or diced *(meat from 1 whole chicken or 3 or 4 boneless chicken breasts)*

Salt and pepper

½ onion, chopped

2 cloves garlic, minced

Toppings:

1 ½ cups grated cheese

1 cup sour cream

1 to 2 TBS water

Fresh tomato, seeded and diced

Lettuce, shredded

Fresh cilantro, chopped

Filling & Cabbage Leaves

1 large onion, ½ inch diced

1 sweet red pepper, ½ inch diced

2 TBS olive oil

½ cup coarsely chopped raw almonds

1 TBS butter

1 (7-oz) can of Anaheim chili peppers

1 can pitted olives, drained and coarsely chopped

1 cup chopped fresh cilantro

8 oz cream cheese, cut into ¾ inch cubes *(keep chilled until ready to cut)*

1 large green cabbage head

ESSENTIAL TOOLS:

6- to 8-qt stock pot

Large mixing bowl

Large skillet

Extra-large spoon strainer

Small tongs

Paring knife

8 x 12-inch baking dish

DIRECTIONS

1 *Sauce:*

In a bowl, mix together the tomatillo sauce and red enchilada sauce. Set aside.

2 *Chicken:*

There are many ways to prepare the chicken. If using boneless chicken breasts, the easiest way is to poach them.

Place chicken in a large pot in just enough water to cover with salt and pepper, onion, and garlic. Bring to a simmer; do not boil. Turn flame down to medium low and simmer for 10 to 15 minutes. Check one breast to make sure it is cooked through. Drain and cool; keep refrigerated until ready to use.

If cooking whole chicken, simmer as directed for breast. After 30 minutes, remove chicken and cut off breast meat and any other meat falling off bone, return carcass to water, and simmer for another 20 minutes until all meat is falling off the bone. Freeze carcass and water for making broth later.

3 Filling:

Shred or dice chicken into ½ inch cubes and place in a large mixing bowl.

Heat skillet over medium-high heat. Sauté the onion and red pepper (if using) in olive oil. After a few minutes, turn down to medium low and continue to sauté (about 10 to 15 minutes) until translucent and beginning to brown. Transfer to mixing bowl with chicken while preparing the rest of the filling.

Clean and heat skillet to medium, and toast almonds in butter until just browned. Drain on a paper towel-lined plate to cool, coarsely chop, and add to mixing bowl with chicken and onion mixture.

Add Anaheim chili peppers, olives, cilantro, and cream cheese to mixing bowl. Lightly mix together with other filling ingredients, and salt to taste. Refrigerate until ready to roll.

4 Cabbage Leaves:

Blanch cabbage leaves to make them pliable for rolling. Start boiling a large pot of water. Remove cabbage core, which extends about 2 inches deep into the interior. It will look like a circular cone removed from the bottom. Place cored cabbage head in boiling water, and cook for 4 to 5 minutes until softened. Remove with an extra-large slotted spoon strainer. Carefully remove leaves one by one with small tongs, and set aside on paper towel-lined plate to drain. If some leaves still seem too hard, simply return the remaining head to the boiling water for 2 minutes more. The inner core leaves will be too small to use; reserve and set aside for another use.

5 Assembly:

Before you begin rolling, pour ¾ cup sauce down middle of baking dish. Take one leaf and remove about 1 to 2 inches of hard triangular portion of rib from base of cabbage leaf with a paring knife. Place ½ to ⅓ cup filling (depending on size of leaf) near base of leaf where rib was removed. Gently fold base flaps over each other, tuck a bit of the sides in, and roll up toward outer edge.

Preheat oven to 375°F. Once you have all enchiladas in baking dish pour remaining sauce equally over them and bake for 30 minutes uncovered. While enchiladas are baking, prepare toppings.

6 Toppings:

Right out of oven, top with optional shredded cheese and let cool 5 minutes before serving. The cheese will melt as the enchiladas cool, preventing cheese from becoming overcooked.

In a bowl, thin the sour cream with water, whisking to create a creamy, thick sauce. Transfer to a squeeze bottle and drizzle across cooled enchiladas. You can buy these bottles for a buck at the dollar store! Place the tomato and greens in individual serving bowls for people to help themselves, along with the sour cream bottle and maybe some guacamole.

Gourmet Pot Roast

Serves 6 to 8

This recipe cooks up a roast featuring a deep, caramelized color and tantalizing aroma and flavor. Pot roast is a relatively inexpensive but tough cut that needs a long, moist cooking method to tenderize, or in culinary lingo: braise. As a rough guide, figure one hour per pound cook time at the minimum. For example, a 4-lb roast will require about four hours.

Years ago, one could find 5- to 6-lb roasts with no problem, but most are now cut in 3- to 4-lb sizes. If you need a larger roast, buy two, 2- to 3-lb pieces to cook in the same pan. The basic cook time, ingredient list, and measurements stay the same and do not double.

This recipe works well with chuck (the most tender and richest flavor) shoulder, brisket, cross rib, and round cuts. To avoid the dreaded overcooked vegetable syndrome, add them in the last hour of cook time. Even better, amaze and impress your family or friends with vegetables roasted separately and arranged artistically around the roast.

CHEF'S NOTES

Check intermittently to make sure the broth level doesn't dip dramatically.

Water used instead of broth is fine (I do this often), especially if you can't obtain a high-quality organic, additive-free broth. If you have any leftover liquid, freeze it to use with the next roast.

Cover after one hour of browning regardless of roast size. If you don't have a lid for your pan, cover it with an aluminum foil tent. A cover and adequate liquid level is crucial to keeping your roast from drying out.

Olive oil or ghee may replace butter.

If you wish to tie herb sprigs together, make sure it is special butcher string. Non-food-grade string, will add an odd flavor.

Save the trimmed baby onion tops to slice and use in other dishes or salads.

Cross rib roasts, while they slice better, tend to be a bit too lean. Chuck, if available is superior in flavor and moister, containing more gelatinous connective tissue. First-cut brisket tends to be too lean as well, choose a second cut or a whole brisket.

INGREDIENTS:

Meat:

3 to 5 lbs roast meat, removed from refrigerator 1 hour before cooking

4 TBS butter or lard, divided, plus more if needed

2 medium yellow onions, sliced

3 celery stalks, chopped into ½ inch pieces

3 to 5 cups water or beef broth, divided

¼ cup balsamic vinegar or red wine

4 large sprigs fresh thyme

4 springs fresh rosemary *(about 4 inches long)*

4 large sprigs fresh tarragon

6 to 10 whole garlic cloves, peeled

Salt and pepper, to taste

Vegetables:

2 to 3 bunches small carrots, peeled and trimmed

4 to 6 red onions, quartered

2 bunches baby onions, trimmed with 3 to 4 inches of green tops left *(optional)*

1 cauliflower cut in large florets and/or celery root cut into 2-inch chunks *(optional)*

Olive oil, if roasting vegetables

Fresh flat leaf parsley, minced for garnish

Gravy:

Kuzu root or einkorn flour *(optional)*

Salt and pepper, to taste

ESSENTIAL TOOLS:

Large heavy flameproof roasting pan or dutch oven

Large cookie sheet or shallow baking pan *(if roasting vegetables separately)*

Lid or aluminum foil

Butcher string for tying herbs *(optional)*

VARIATIONS

Instead of baby spring onions, add small leeks to the vegetable lineup. Cut in half lengthwise, wash, and trim.

Fennel, quartered and roasted.

Broccoli, cut into large florets and roasted.

Red pepper, deseeded, quartered, and roasted.

Celery, cut into 3-inch lengths, roasted or added to juice.

Large red potatoes quartered, roasted, or added to juice.

Red baby round or fingerling potatoes, roasted or added to juice (1 to 2 lbs).

Cauliflower or broccoli puree/mash served with gravy.

DIRECTIONS

Remove roast from refrigerator 30 minutes before cooking.

Preheat oven to 425°F.

Meat:

Pat meat dry with paper towels. In dutch oven or roasting pan over medium heat, melt 2 TBS butter or lard or a combination of both. Add roast to pan, and brown well on all sides (about 5 minutes a side). Don't hurry the process by turning up the flame; take your time to get a rich caramel color, and don't scorch the butter. Add more butter or lard if the pan starts to become dry. Remove roast from pan and set aside.

Add the remaining 2 TBS butter, onion, and celery to drippings in pan and sauté over medium heat until fragrant and starting to soften, about 5 to 8 minutes. Add ½ cup broth or water to deglaze pan (this means you are dissolving all the brown bits in and stuck to the pan). Add the balsamic vinegar or wine to the onions, and continue to deglaze pan while bringing to a low simmer.

Place roast back in pan with onions and celery. Add enough water or broth to cover roast about a third of the way up. Heat and bring back to simmer. Add herb sprigs (you may wish to tie with string, but not mandatory) and garlic cloves. Place in oven and roast for 30 minutes uncovered.

Turn oven down to 375F, replenish liquid, salt and pepper, and cook covered for another 2 ½ hours for a 3-lb roast. Add 1 hour per pound of roast. Before you pull it out of the oven, check to see if it is done: I check with a fork at the bottom to see if it pulls apart in the middle.

Once roast is done, remove from oven and let rest for 15 minutes before slicing.

Vegetables:

In the last hour of cook time, add your choice of vegetables to juice in pan, cover, and return vegetables and roast to oven.

Alternatively, heat oven to 425°F after roast is done and removed. Cube or cut large vegetables into serving sizes described in ingredient section. Generously coat prepared vegetables in olive oil and spread evenly across a large cookie sheet or shallow baking pan. Lightly salt and pepper, and roast for 30 minutes, turning midway. Arrange around roast, alternating colors to create a pleasing pattern.

Garnish with whole and minced flat leaf parsley.

Gravy:

Remove any vegetables, the garlic cloves, and meat but retain the original sliced onions and celery in liquid–they should be mushy at this point. Discard herb bundles. Moisten meat and vegetables with pan juices. Strain pan juices to remove remaining woody herb stems, and press the original sliced onions and celery through (use a large spoon to do this). Scrape bottom of strainer with spoon to capture puree, and add to strained liquid. Discard remaining pulp left in strainer.

While I prefer the strained juices (or fond) ladled over my meat and vegetables, you may like it thickened to gravy consistency instead. Add 1 TBS kuzu root or 2 TBS flour per cup of strained drippings. Bring to boil, turn down to simmer, and whisk until thick. Salt and pepper to taste.

Italian Meatballs and Marinara Sauce

Serves 6 to 8 (18 to 20 meatballs)

You absolutely do not need to add any coconut flour or grain product such as bread, cracker crumbs, or oatmeal to the meatball recipe. Traditionally, breadcrumbs were added to the mixture to stretch the meat and make for a tender ball. However, when gently simmered in sauce or broth, meatballs are moist and tender without any fillers. I don't recommend browning, baking, or long cook times if you want tender meatballs.

This is where you want to buy the inexpensive ground beef with a larger fat content—the more the better for juicy, tender balls. When crunched for time, buy 2 large jars of your favorite spaghetti sauce and add herbs of your choice, or fix the superior-tasting marinara sauce provided below. Fresh herbs are preferred; dried works, but you sacrifice a little flavor. The secret ingredient? Fresh basil. The flavor is incomparable—don't skimp on this one.

Spaghetti squash makes a great substitute for grain-based pasta, and the flavor blends perfectly with Italian spices.

NOTES:

CHEF'S NOTES

The meatballs and sauce freeze well and will keep up to 7 days in the refrigerator.

The squash gets a bit watery if frozen but will keep up to 5 days refrigerated.

Leftover fresh basil and rosemary freeze well.

VARIATIONS

1 cup grated Parmigiano in meatballs.

Add ½ TSP crushed red pepper in meatballs.

Replace ½ lb ground beef with ground Italian sausage or add 1-inch chunks directly to sauce (my favorite).

Lightly sauté a box of chopped mushrooms and add to sauce.

Onion allergy: Replace onion with sautéed, minced celery in meatballs and dice in sauce.

Finely grated Parmigiano added to meatballs will also boost flavor.

INGREDIENTS:

2 large spaghetti squash

Marinara Sauce:

¼ cup olive oil

1 large yellow onion,
½ inch diced

1 large green pepper,
½ inch diced

4 large garlic cloves, minced

1 can black olives, drained
and coarsely chopped

4 large (28-oz) cans
fire-roasted tomatoes
*(okay to use whole, diced,
or crushed tomatoes)*

½ (6-oz) can tomato paste
(freeze the other portion)

1 TBS minced fresh rosemary
(½ TBS dried and crushed)

1 TBS minced fresh oregano
(½ TBS dried)

1 cup coarsely chopped
fresh basil *(2 TBS dried)*

Salt and pepper, to taste

Water, if necessary

Meatballs:

2 TBS butter

1 large yellow
or white onion, minced

2 celery stalks, minced
(about ½ cup)

1 TSP garlic powder
or 2 large cloves, minced

2 lbs ground beef

2 extra-large eggs, whisked

½ TSP salt

½ TSP black pepper

½ TBS dried basil

½ TBS dried oregano

½ TBS dried rosemary crushed

For Serving:

Fresh basil, thinly sliced

Parmigiano, grated

ESSENTIAL TOOLS:

8-qt saucepan

Large sauté pan or skillet

DIRECTIONS

Spaghetti Squash:

Preheat oven to 375° to 400°F. Cut squash in half and bake before preparing the sauce and meatballs. It needs time to cool a bit. When ready to serve, scoop out of shell and lightly separate meat with a fork. Keep warm until ready to serve, or refrigerate for another time. See "How To" section and recipe, Baked Winter Squash for in depth directions.

Marinara Sauce:

In an 8-quart saucepan over medium flame, heat the olive oil until fragrant. Add the diced onion and diced green pepper, and sauté for 5 minutes.

Add garlic and sauté for another 2 minutes. Personally, I like lots of garlic, so I usually add 6 to 8 cloves, but 4 is a good starting point.

Add black olives.

Add tomatoes and tomato paste to pan. If using whole canned tomatoes, crush before adding to saucepan. Canned or frozen tomatoes vary in their consistency. Usually, the juice from the tomatoes creates a soupiness that needs to be thickened with tomato paste. If it seems too thick, add water to the pot ¼ cup at a time until desired consistency is reached. Alternatively, if too soupy, add more tomato paste. Add the rosemary and oregano. Let the sauce simmer for 30 minutes before adding salt and pepper to taste. Adding salt after the herb flavors have had time to blend into the sauce will reduce the amount of salt need.

Season in steps, tasting throughout cook time and adding more seasoning if required. All herbs have varying degrees of potency according to how they were grown, processed, and most importantly, how old they are.

Simmer sauce covered for 1 hour, stirring and tasting occasionally. The fresh basil will be added in the last 15 minutes of cooking, after you have added the meatballs. If added too early, the flavor is lost. While the sauce is cooking, prepare your meatballs.

Meatballs:

In a sauté pan or skillet over medium-high heat, melt the butter. Add the onions and celery; sauté for about 5 minutes, or until soft and aromatic. Add the garlic and sauté for another 2 minutes. Set aside to cool slightly while you make the meat mixture.

In a large bowl, mix together the meat, eggs, salt, pepper, basil, oregano, rosemary, garlic powder (if using), and the onion/garlic mixture until well combined. I like to toss this mixture with my hands to get it thoroughly blended. Form meat into tightly packed 1 ½- to 2-inch-diameter balls.

Add raw meatballs directly to sauce, and simmer for 20 minutes. After 20 minutes, gently stir to release any meatballs stuck to the bottom. Add fresh basil now, and simmer an additional 10 to 15 minutes. Meatballs should be firm to touch and hold their shape when done.

To Serve:

Ladle sauce and meatballs over squash and garnish with fresh basil and Parmigiano.

Meat Skewers: Chicken, Beef, or Pork

Serves 4

Want healthy but craving fast food? Wow, this recipe is so freaking easy, but cook up lots because they disappear fast! Whip up your own marinade, like my Asian Marinade (page 223) or make it even easier by purchasing your favorite.

INGREDIENTS:

4 boneless chicken breasts or 2 lbs cube steak or flank steak

1 cup your favorite barbecue sauce or marinade

2 TBS vinegar or lemon juice, to thin thick barbecue sauce

ESSENTIAL TOOLS:

Bamboo or metal skewers

Foil-lined broiler pan
(if not grilling)

Tongs for turning skewers

DIRECTIONS

Cutting Meat:

Depending upon selection, cut as directed.

Chicken: Remove any skin and tenders; cut chicken breasts lengthwise into 5/8- to 1/2-inch-thick slices.

Cube or Flank Steak: Cut across grain into 1/4-inch-thick and no larger than 5/8-inch-thick slices. Slice tough beef meat thinner than chicken or pork.

Pork Loin: Cut vertically like chicken into 5/8- to 1/2-inch-thick slices.

Marinate and Assemble:

Place meat in a glass bowl or shallow baking dish. Cover with sauce and marinate in refrigerator for at least 1 hour, preferably 2 hours, and overnight is even better. Stir occasionally to keep moist and distribute evenly.

If using bamboo skewers, place in water and let swell for 30 minutes. This will help to prevent burning while cooking. Thread meat slices onto skewers in accordion fashion. Place on a cookie sheet as you finish each skewer. Brush with additional sauce or marinade before cooking.

Cook:

Directions are provided below for preferred method.

To Grill: Preheat grill to 400°F. Grill with lid closed for 3 to 4 minutes each side, turning once.

To Broil: Preheat broiler to high; line broiler pan with foil; place meat about 5 inches away from flame or elements; cook 3 to 4 minutes each side, turning once.

Meat should be firm when done. Brush lightly with barbecue sauce or olive oil immediately upon removing from grill or broiler and serve.

Sesame-Crusted Chicken Piccata with Lemon-Fennel Sauce

Serves 4

Here is my take on piccata–gluten-free and veggie packed! In this dish, the chicken is typically dredged in flour before tossing into the skillet. I have substituted ground sesame meal and dried minced onion for flour, and I dressed it up with savory fennel in addition to the usual capers. For allium allergies, I have included substitutions and traditional recipes don't include them anyway.

INGREDIENTS:

Chicken:

- 4 boneless, skinless chicken breasts
- ⅔ cup ground sesame seeds
- 1 TBS dried minced onion
- ½ TSP garlic powder
- ¼ TSP salt
- ⅛ TSP pepper
- 2 TBS butter, divided
- Olive oil to brush and 2 TBS more, divided for frying

Fennel Sauce:

- 6 TBS butter, divided
- 1 large fennel bulb, sliced ¼-inch thin and leaves chopped
- ¾ cup fresh lemon juice
- 1 cup chicken broth
- 2 cloves garlic, minced
- 4 TBS capote capers, drained

ESSENTIAL TOOLS:

Plastic wrap

Rolling pin or mallet

Blender or food processor

Large skillet or sauté pan

NOTES:

_____

_____

_____

_____

_____

_____

CHEF'S NOTES

Meyers lemons are best, but if you can't find those, replace ¼ cup lemon juice with ¼ cup fresh orange juice.

Reserve a small portion of un-cut, feathery fennel leaves for garnish.

VARIATIONS

You may omit garlic powder and dried minced onion in rub and substitute 1 TBS additional sesame seed and ½ TSP celery powder. In the sauce, omit garlic cloves.

Capers may be omitted without sacrificing flavor.

DIRECTIONS

Chicken:

Remove chicken skin and tenders; pat dry with paper towels. Place 1 breast, smooth side down between 2 sheets of plastic wrap on a cutting board. Using short, even strokes, begin pounding breast starting at center and working your way outward to the edge. Repeat until flattened to ¼ inch thick. A rolling pin, the flat side of a meat mallet, or a rubber mallet from the hardware store will work. Make them thin, because they become thicker as they cook.

In blender or food processor, grind up sesame seed and dried minced onion to a coarse-looking meal.

In a medium bowl, mix together sesame seed meal, garlic powder, salt, and pepper; transfer to a large plate or pie pan. Brush each breast lightly on both sides with olive oil. Dredge chicken in ground sesame seed mixture and press into meat; gently shake off excess.

In a large skillet or sauté pan over medium heat, melt 1 TBS butter with 1 TBS olive oil. Add 2 chicken breasts and cook for 2 to 3 minutes on each side, until golden brown. Wipe pan clean if necessary to remove burned bits and repeat with last 2 breast. Place on paper towel-lined plate to drain and cover to keep warm.

Fennel Sauce:

Clean pan used for chicken. In pan over medium heat, melt 2 TBS of butter and add sliced fennel bulb; sauté until tender but still firm. Add lemon juice and bring to a simmer. Reduce heat to medium low and simmer until reduced in half, about 2 minutes (do not boil).

Add broth, garlic, and capers; simmer 3-5 minutes more until slightly thick (again, do not boil).

Remove from stove and stir in fennel leaves and remaining 4 TBS of butter. Continue to stir until butter is fully melted and starts to further thicken sauce.

To Serve:

Place one chicken breast on each plate. Spoon sauce over chicken.

Shepherd's Pie

Serves 6 as a full dinner or 8 potluck portions

This shepherd's pie is a fiber-rich, filling dish using inexpensive ground beef but packed with contemporary flavors. Low cost, get-in-my-belly appeal, and portability combine to make this one crowd-pleasing potluck dish. My interpretation uses less meat and potatoes and more carrots and adds greens to bulk up the dish's color, nutrition, and fiber. Choose your favorite combination of leafy greens (e.g., kale, spinach, beet greens, arugula, chard) and add at the end to prevent overcooking.

For nightshade-sensitive people, the sweet potato offers the perfect alternative to the red potato, and white or golden flesh varieties are a better match than the sweeter orange types. Kuzu root is used for thickening in place of flour to keep it gluten free, and unlike other gluten-free thickeners, it will not break.

VARIATIONS

Some varieties of sweet potatoes bake better than they boil or steam. If in doubt, it is easier to bake than spend time peeling, simmering, and draining; however, plan for a longer cook time. Pierce with a fork and cook like a baked Irish potato.

Maybe you don't like greens; how about broccoli chopped into small florets? Not broccoli? Okay, maybe green beans? Steam both for about 3 to 4 minutes until bright green before removing from heat and add in at end, just before removing meat mixture from stove.

Add frozen peas after gravy is thickened.

Substitute tarragon, savory, or marjoram for rosemary.

INGREDIENTS:

Potato Topping:

2 lbs sweet or red potato, peeled and cut into eighths

1 TSP salt, plus more for seasoning

4 TBS butter, melted

1/8 cup whole cream, plus more if needed

4 scallions, thinly sliced

Ground black pepper to taste

Filling:

1 lb ground beef

1 TSP salt, plus more for seasoning

1/2 TSP garlic powder

1 TSP dried thyme

1/2 TSP coarse ground pepper, plus more for seasoning

2 TBS butter, plus 1 TBS more if needed

1 large onion, sliced

4 large garlic cloves, minced

1/3 cup balsamic vinegar

1 cup beef or chicken broth

2 cups 1/2 inch diced carrots

1 TBS minced fresh rosemary or 1/2 TBS dried rosemary, crushed

1 TBS minced fresh thyme

2 TBS minced fresh flat-leaf parsley

1 TBS kuzu root or 2 TBS einkorn flour dissolved in 1/4 cup water

4 cups greens, chopped

ESSENTIAL TOOLS:

4-qt saucepan

Broiler-safe 10-inch skillet; or 10-inch skillet and 10-inch broiler-safe pie dish

Rimmed baking sheet

NOTES:

DIRECTIONS

Potato Topping:

Place potatoes in a 4-qt saucepan, cover with water, and add salt; bring to boil. Reduce heat to medium low and simmer for about 15 minutes, or until soft (a fork penetrates without resistance). Drain in a colander, rinse, and return to saucepan. Heat potatoes on medium low, tossing gently for 1 minute or so until any remaining moisture has evaporated.

Remove pan from heat and mash potatoes. Stir in melted butter; stir in cream starting with 1/8 cup, adding more in tablespoon increments if necessary to achieve a creamy consistency. Stir in scallions; salt and pepper to taste. Set aside uncovered.

Filling:

Drain beef and pat dry; add any drained blood to broth or discard. In a bowl, combine beef, salt, garlic powder, thyme, and pepper, mixing together thoroughly as if making meat loaf. Form into 1-inch balls; set aside.

In a 10-inch skillet over medium heat, melt the butter. Add onion and sauté until slightly charred and beginning to caramelize, about 15 minutes. Add garlic and sauté 1 to 2 minutes more until soft, adding 1 TBS additional butter if the mixture becomes too dry.

Add balsamic vinegar and deglaze skillet, stirring to scrape up any browned bits from bottom to incorporate with onions. Simmer for 1 minute more until onions absorb most of the liquid. Add broth and scrape bottom to dissolve any remaining browned bits. Add carrots, rosemary, thyme, and parsley, salt and pepper to taste, and bring to a simmer.

Drop beef chunks into broth, and bring back to a gentle simmer. Cover and steam for 10 minutes, gently stirring halfway through to release any meat sticking to pan.

To make gravy, push aside meat and vegetables to perimeter of skillet. Broth will run to middle of pan. Slowly drizzle dissolved kuzu root into the broth liquid while whisking with a fork to combine. Bring meat mixture back to middle, and gently fold into liquid with a large spoon. Break in half any pieces of meat which are larger than 1/2-in thick. Simmer for a few minutes, stirring constantly until liquid becomes clear and thickens.

Add chopped greens on top of meat mixture; cover and steam for an additional 2 minutes. Gently fold greens into meat mixture. Greens should be completely wilted but still bright green. Remove from heat and cool 5 minutes uncovered. If using pie dish, transfer from skillet now.

Broil Potato Topping:

Adjust oven rack approximately 5 to 6 inches from broiler element and heat broiler on high (if you have the option). Gently drop mashed potatoes evenly over entire surface of the meat filling. Smooth potatoes with a knife; then use knife to lift up small peaks throughout potato topping (it will sort of look like a meringue). Place skillet or pie dish on rimmed baking sheet and broil until peaks of potatoes are evenly browned and filling is bubbly along edges (10 to 15 minutes).

Let cool five minutes before serving.

Teriyaki Beef Jerky: Oven Dried

It is hard, if not impossible, to find 100% grass-fed organic jerky, and once found, the price is out of reach for most. This is a great winter project to warm up the house, while buzzing about getting other chores done in the meantime. How fast it dries really depends on how thin you slice it.

Shoulder, cross rib, bottom round, or a London broil are easy cuts to slice, so they are the preferred choices in this instance. While the following cuts would also work, I would rather save the flank for stir-fry, the brisket and chuck roasts for the stew pot.

INGREDIENTS:

2 lbs beef

¾ cup soy sauce

¼ cup rice vinegar

⅛ cup unrefined and unbleached whole cane sugar (brown sugar)

1 TBS toasted sesame oil

½ TBS powdered ginger

1 TSP coarse ground pepper

1 TSP powdered smoked paprika

1 TSP garlic powder

1 TSP onion powder

1 TSP red pepper flakes (optional)

ESSENTIAL TOOLS:

Glass bowl or container

2 broiler pans and racks (easy to find at thrift stores)

Aluminum foil

Sharp chef knife

NOTES:

_____

_____

_____

_____

_____

DIRECTIONS

Meat is easier to slice if somewhat semi-frozen. For fresh meat, trim and place in freezer 30 minutes before slicing. Slice meat against grain into ⅛- to ¼-inch strips and place in glass bowl or container. You need glass, so it doesn't react with the vinegar.

In a medium bowl, whisk well to combine soy sauce, rice vinegar, brown sugar, toasted sesame oil, ginger powder, pepper, paprika, garlic powder, onion powder, and red pepper flakes. Pour over meat and let marinate covered for at least an hour and overnight for best flavor. Toss periodically to distribute marinade.

Remove meat from refrigerator 1 hour before roasting. Drain and blot dry.

Line pan with foil and place meat side by side on racks, leaving a small space between strips. Place on broiler pan rack.

Roast at 180°F for about 4 hours, checking and turning every hour.

Crack door open to release moisture if you notice moisture building up inside. Most modern ovens are equipped with moisture venting, though some older ones are inefficient.

It will be done when dark brown and cracking slightly, without breaking, when bent. It will become firmer as it cools, so be careful not to overcook.

Store in air-tight container in refrigerator.

VARIATIONS

Substitute ⅛ cup warmed honey for sugar.

If you would like more of a barbecue flavor: substitute olive oil for sesame oil, substitute apple cider vinegar for rice vinegar, delete ginger, and add 1 TSP smoked paprika, 1 TBS catsup, 1 TSP dry mustard, and 1/8 TSP smoke flavoring (*optional*) to the marinade.

Tex-Mex Fajitas

Serves 6

My first introduction to fajitas was in Texas in the early 80s, and they instantly became one of my favorite dishes. I tend to make this recipe during the summer season when peppers are plentiful, it's too hot for extended kitchen time, and grilling is the perfect answer. You barbecue freaks already know that grilling the meat imparts a smoky flavor that is hard to replicate without it. Whether I choose to grill or not, I still add the liquid mesquite smoke to the chili sauce–it's one of the secret ingredients.

Traditionally, the meat was marinated to soften tough skirt steaks, but who has time or the presence of mind sometimes to plan the night before? I use top sirloin, and it works great without marinating overnight. Chicken is every bit as savory a choice and is often my go-to when budget is a concern.

Cabbage is a ubiquitous vegetable in Mexico, and its blanched leaves seem the perfect choice for wrapping the fajita mixture. Butter or romaine lettuce leaves are also a good choice for wrapping and a far simpler substitute for the high-carbohydrate flour tortillas usually served with them. Cool, crisp lettuce contrasts well against the sizzling vegetables and meat. A large, hot cast iron skillet makes the perfect serving dish. While red and yellow peppers are my favorites, they are definitely not the most economical choice. Choosing to make this dish with all green peppers will not sacrifice flavor or appeal.

NOTES:

ESSENTIAL TOOLS:

Large frying pan (*if not grilling*)

Large cast iron skillet or wok

VARIATIONS

Blanched cabbage leaves for rolling up the fajita mixture.

Substitute tequila for water.

2 lbs skirt steak marinated overnight in the chili sauce (*use a glass container and cover*).

Add chopped cooked bacon.

May use 2 TBS cornstarch or arrowroot to thicken.

INGREDIENTS:

Lettuce:

2 large heads butter or romaine lettuce, for wrapping

Meat:

3 TBS olive oil

2 lbs top sirloin or 4 large chicken breasts

Chile Sauce:

¼ cup fresh lime juice (*lemon works too*)

½ cup organic gluten-free tamari or coconut aminos

¼ cup water

¼ TSP to ½ TSP mesquite flavored liquid smoke (*careful, this stuff goes a long way—try first with the smaller measurement and taste test*)

1 TBS raw cane sugar or honey

½ TBS chili powder

½ TSP garlic powder

6 dashes chipotle or habanero pepper sauce (*optional*)

2 TBS kuzu root starch dissolved in 3 TBS water

Peppers and Onions:

3 TBS olive oil

1 large red, yellow, and green bell pepper, each cut into ¼-inch slices

1 large onion, ¼ inch slices

½ cup chopped fresh cilantro

For Serving:

Pico de Gallo or salsa

Sour cream

Guacamole

Fresh cilantro, chopped

DIRECTIONS

Lettuce:

Remove individual lettuce leaves, wash and pat dry; set aside on a covered plate in the refrigerator.

Meat:

Don't worry if the meat is not entirely cooked through to your taste as the final sauté will do that.

In the Skillet:
Heat a large frying pan to medium-high heat, and add 3 TBS olive oil. Place meat in hot oil and brown. Leave it for about 3 minutes on each side to achieve a blackened effect. Depending on the size of your skillet, you may have to do this in 2 batches. Once browned and slightly blackened, let rest for 10 minutes in a glass dish; then slice chicken into ¼-inch-thick pieces and beef ⅛-inch-thick pieces.

Like to Grill?
Using a gas grill substantially enhances the flavor and makes it easier to obtain the blackened effect. Rub meat with olive oil, and barbecue the chicken for about 6 minutes each side and beef for approximately 5 minutes each side at 425°F. Set aside to cool; then slice chicken into ¼-inch-thick pieces and beef into ⅛-inch-thick pieces.

While the meat cools, prepare the chili sauce.

Chile Sauce:

In a large bowl, whisk together the lime juice, tamari, water, liquid smoke, cane sugar or honey, chili powder, garlic powder, and pepper sauce (if using). Whisk in dissolved cornstarch or kuzu root. Mix into sliced meat.

Peppers and Onions:

Heat a large cast iron skillet or wok to medium-high heat, and add the olive oil. Sauté bell peppers for a few minutes, until they start to char slightly, then add the onion. As you sear vegetables, let them be for about 3 minutes without tossing. The oil should be hot enough to brown and blacken the edges and sides of the peppers and onions, but not so hot as to burn. Don't walk away at this point; the searing process will take about 5 minutes and needs constant attention.

Add meat and chili sauce to bell pepper mixture, and gently stir until sauce coats all and has a translucent quality to it. If sauce coating seems too thick, add a bit of water and stir to thin. You don't want soup or free-flowing sauce but to coat veggies and meat, so add water carefully, one tablespoon at a time, until desired consistency is reached. Remove from heat and stir in the cilantro.

To Serve:

Serve hot from the pan. To eat, generously spread guacamole across lettuce leaves, add the fajita mixture. Garnish with Pico de Gallo or favorite salsa, sour cream, guacamole, and cilantro.

Tri-Tip Roast: Oven-Baked or Grilled

Serves 6 to 8

As with London broil, tri-tip is best-served medium rare to medium, and overcooking will produce a tough, unappetizing meal. Organic 100% grass-fed tri-tip tends to run small, so not to worry if you can't find a 2 lb cut. For a large crowd, buy two. The herb measurements are approximate, as I generously apply them and rub them into the meat without measuring. The best part about cooking this cut of meat is you can do ahead and then incorporate into many recipes. Have it for dinner and then save the rest for cutting up over a lunch salad.

INGREDIENTS:

1 ½ to 2 lbs tri-tip roast

Olive oil

1 TSP coarse ground pepper

1 TSP powdered smoked paprika

1 TSP garlic powder

Salt

2 TBS barbecue sauce

ESSENTIAL TOOLS:

Oven-proof baking dish

Aluminum foil

DIRECTIONS

Pat meat dry with paper towels and place roast in an oven-proof baking dish. Allow to sit 10 minutes to dry.

Generously drizzle with olive oil and rub into meat coating well. Salt lightly. Generously sprinkle with pepper, smoked paprika, and garlic powder, and rub evenly over top of roast. Flip over and repeat on other side. Allow to rest another 15 minutes to bring close to room temperature. Prep your veggies for a side dish while waiting.

To Cook:

Directions are provided for either grilling or oven baking.

Bake: Preheat oven to 425°F. Puncture meat with a fork all over top, and roast for 20 minutes for rare, 30 minutes for medium rare, and 40 minutes for medium (times are approximate, as it all depends on cut of meat, thickness, and how many pounds it weighs). Brush with barbecue sauce if desired.

Grill: Heat grill to 425°F. Cook for 8 minutes for 1 ½ lbs and 10 minutes for 2 lbs on each side. Once removed from oven or grill, brush with barbecue sauce.

Regardless of cook method, cover with foil, and allow to rest 15 minutes before slicing (it will continue to cook as it cools).

To Serve:

The stand time allows juices to settle back into the meat instead of running out when cut. They still will a bit, but not as badly if left to rest before carving.

Thinly carve against grain and spoon juice over cut meat. Pour juices into any sauce you might want to cook, such as a mushroom, a green peppercorn sauce, or caramelized onions.

VARIATIONS

Change up the seasoning with 1 TSP crushed rosemary, 1 TSP dried tarragon, 2 pressed garlic cloves, and eliminate barbecue sauce.

Twice-Cooked Pork

Serves 6

A staple in most Chinese restaurants, this is a Szechuan regional dish using pork that is first cooked and then stir-fried – double cooked!

Looking for something to do with pork belly? Many recipes call for uncured pork belly, which is first simmered with seasonings and then fried. Other authentic versions require "pork hind leg," and again it is first simmered, sliced, and then stir-fried with vegetables. The lack of consensus leads me to the conclusion there are most likely as many versions of twice-cooked pork as there are cuts of pork and cooks. However, recipes are in agreement with three other foundational ingredients comprising the dish, those being garlic sprouts, sweet broad bean paste, and red or green peppers.

In the US grocery world, raw pork belly is a hard commodity to find, let alone pig leg. Garlic sprouts and broad bean paste? Nope; out of luck there too. So, I have adapted the recipe by substituting boneless pork chops, bacon, scallions, and tamari sauce. The bacon, when combined with grilled meat and Asian seasoning, lends a flavor that you will find absolutely addictive.

A word of caution: Go easy on the salt. Plenty is provided from the tamari and optional bacon.

NOTES:

INGREDIENTS:

Sauce:

3 TBS tamari or coconut aminos

½ cup water

1 TBS cane sugar or honey

½ TBS vinegar

⅛ TSP garlic powder

¼ TSP ginger powder

1 TBS kuzu root dissolved in ¼ cup water

½ TBS sesame oil

Meat:

4 boneless fat-on pork chops (about 2 lbs)

Barbecue sauce marinade, for brushing on meat

Powdered smoked paprika, garlic powder, ginger powder, for rubbing into meat

1 TBS butter and 1 TBS olive oil, for frying

4 thick-cut bacon slices cut into 1 ½-inch pieces *(optional)*

Vegetables:

1 TBS toasted sesame oil

1 TBS olive oil

2 red bell peppers, julienned

6 large garlic cloves, peeled and coarsely chopped

2-inch piece ginger root, peeled and minced

12 to 16 scallions, sliced into 1-inch diagonal pieces *(2 bunches)*

½ bunch fresh cilantro, for garnish *(optional)*

ESSENTIAL TOOLS:

Glass dish for marinating meat

Large skillet

Large wok or sauté pan

VARIATIONS

If using pork belly in place of pork chops and bacon:

Simmer 1 ½ to 2 lbs cut into long, 1-inch-thick slices for 30 minutes in salted water with a sliced onion, garlic cloves, a few peppercorns, or any other seasoning like celery, lemongrass, or cilantro. Drain and let cool before browning like the bacon.

4 boneless chicken breasts instead of pork (now it's twice-cooked chicken). Same drill as cooking the pork chops.

Garlic sprouts or 2 large leeks, trimmed and sliced, substituted for scallions.

2 TBS broad bean paste swapped out for 2 TBS tamari sauce.

1 TBS fermented black beans added to sauce in addition to tamari or broad bean paste.

DIRECTIONS

Stir-frying moves at a fast pace and requires attention. Cook time is short and doesn't allow for setup midstream. Organize and prepare sauce, meat, and vegetables in advance of stir-frying and before turning on the wok "mise en place"—a French term meaning "everything in its place."

Sauce:

In a medium bowl, whisk together all sauce ingredients. Set aside.

Meat:

Remove from fridge 30 minutes before cooking and bring to room temperature. Cook times are for chops 1 inch thick or less. Chop vegetables while bringing chops to room temperature.

To Grill: Marinate chops in barbecue sauce overnight or 2 hours before grilling. Heat grill to 375°F (medium) and cook with lid closed for about 5 minutes each side, depending on thickness. Or if you have a meat thermometer, cook until they reach 135°F. As the chops rest, they will reach the recommended 145°F. Really, don't fret about doneness; remember, you will be cooking them again in sauce and bringing to simmer temperature, 212°F. It is better to have them slightly underdone.

To Fry: Generously sprinkle smoked paprika, garlic, and ginger powder over meat and rub in well. In skillet over medium heat, melt 1 TBS butter into 1 TBS olive oil; add chops. Cook about 5 minutes each side until nicely browned. Remove and brush both sides with barbecue sauce.

After removing meat from grill or skillet, let rest for at least 10 minutes before slicing into ¼ inch strips.

Fry bacon pieces (if using) until just browned; remove from heat and drain; set aside.

Vegetables:

In a wok or large sauté pan over medium-high heat, heat sesame oil and olive oil.

Sauté red peppers until they start to brown slightly on edges. As you sear the red peppers, let them be for about 2 to 3 minutes without tossing. The oil should be hot enough to brown and blacken edges and sides of peppers, but not too hot as to burn. Toss again and let sear another 2 minutes without tossing. The searing process will take about 5 or minutes or less and needs constant attention.

Add garlic, ginger, and scallions, and sauté until aromatic.

Add tamari sauce mixture and meat; cook, stirring periodically, until sauce coating becomes clear and thickens.

To Serve:

Eat as is, or ladled over sautéed cabbage, cauliflower rice, or seaweed noodles. Garnish with cilantro, if desired.

Soup Pot

Beef Bone Broth/Stock

I was hesitant to include a beef bone broth recipe in the book, because there are so many recipes floating around on the web and in cookbooks. However, in many, misinformation abounds. Cook times are much too long, vegetables and herbs are added prematurely, and there is no need to spend time skimming "foam" or fat off along the way. It is said the skimming process is necessary to remove odd flavors, but I have not found this to be true. Skimming along with straining is done to achieve clarity, and this can be done at the end. The fat is much easier to remove once it cools and congeals on top.

Why one would want to remove the fat is beyond me, especially when you consider the fat is predominately from the bone marrow itself. The marrow bone you buy is usually from the long bones of the animal (e.g. the femur or round bone and tibia or shank bone), and not from the ends of the long bones, although sometimes these are thrown in an assortment package. Shaft marrow is known as yellow marrow, and it is largely comprised of monounsaturated fat. Yup—why would you go to all the expense of buying marrow bones, simmer them to remove the marrow, and then throw away the most nutritious part you paid good money for?

While there are some excellent organic beef broth products out there, many commercial brands contain a nightmare of ingredients such as hydrolyzed soybean protein, caramel color, yeast extract, safflower oil, and sugar.

Maximum cook time should be about 8 to 9 hours, as long as 10 hours, and never 24 hours. As your broth cools, it is still cooking, so while I may turn it off after 8 hours, it's still cooking for an additional 2 hours or more. Don't worry if you need to run errands in the middle of cooking. Just turn off the stove, keep the lid on, and go.

I do not roast my bones first, because I am striving for optimum nutritional content. Color and a rich flavor can be achieved from deeply browning meat trimmings, stew meat, oxtail, or osso buco and then deglazing the pan. However, if you would like a deeper dark brown color to your broth, I have included directions. Many believe the longer you cook the broth, the better it will be. I have found extended cook times produce a bitter broth, break down the collagen, and subtle flavors are lost. Also, I just can't understand how nutrients could possibly be retained with a 24-hour cook time.

Total Cook Time: 8 to 10 hours

CHEF'S NOTES

Always cook on a low simmer, and *no* boiling; the surface barely bubbles.

Don't use too much water; barely cover bones with water. Using too much water also dilutes the ratio of collagen to water, and your broth won't gel (if you care about that).

Don't worry about exact timing. All my timing is approximate. It will depend on the bones you have and how long it takes to cook the connective tissue off the joint bones and the marrow out of the bone. Start in the morning, and you will be done by early evening.

Invest in a good stock pot. Begin with an 8- to 10-qt size; they are the most versatile. Once you have the cash, invest in a 16-qt size, and you will be able to double this recipe and cook a month's supply.

VARIATIONS

Replace osso buco with 1 lb stew meat deeply browned and have the meat later for a meal.

Neck bones are a great addition.

Save meat trimmings and cooked rib or steak bones in freezer to use in your broths to add flavor and color.

INGREDIENTS:

1 uncut knuckle bone
(for the gelatin)

½ lb oxtail, browned
(optional but advisable)

½ gallon water

4 TBS vinegar

2 TSP salt, divided, plus more as needed

3 to 4 medium-cut marrow bones *(2 to 3 inches long)*

1 osso buco / beef shank
(contains the marrow bone with meat and tendon attached and is sometimes called a soup bone)

2 to 4 TBS butter, divided

10 peppercorns or ½ TSP coarse ground pepper

1 garlic head, trimmed and cut in half through diameter *(or 10 garlic cloves cut in half)*

1 onion, quartered

4 large celery stalks, leaves on, cut into 1-inch pieces

4 large carrots, cut into 1-inch pieces

1 bunch fresh thyme

1 bunch fresh tarragon

1 bunch fresh rosemary

ESSENTIAL TOOLS:

8- to 10-quart stock pan

Large skillet

Tongs

Large fine-mesh strainer

DIRECTIONS

1 Place knuckle bone and browned oxtail (if using) in stock pot and just barely cover with water. Bring to high simmer, and then reduce to low simmer. Add vinegar and 1 TSP salt. Low simmer, covered for 4 hours. I do this first to dissolve the gelatin off the bone without overcooking other ingredients. Pick out any oxtail meat that may have separated from bone and reserve for another time.

2 Roasting Bones (*optional*): Preheat oven to 400F. Brush marrow bones, osso buco, and oxtail with 2 TBS of melted butter or olive oil. Roast bones for 45 minutes to 1 hour. Deglaze bottom of roasting pan with a bit of water, scraping browned bits up from bottom, and add bones and drippings to stock pot.

3 If not using knuckle bones or oxtail, skip first step and add vinegar when adding the osso buco and marrow bones.

4 In a large skillet, melt 1 to 2 TBS butter; brown osso buco. Make sure meat is super dark brown–this is important if you want a light caramel color to your broth. Deglaze pan with a bit of water, and add osso buco and juice to stock pot. (Skip this step if pre-roasting meat and bones).

5 Add marrow bones, and additional water if needed to cover bones completely.

6 Add remaining 1 TSP salt and the pepper. Toss in trimmed and halved garlic bulb (don't worry about peeling).

7 Replace pan lid and bring back to low simmer for another 3 hours.

8 Check marrow bones periodically. Pick up marrow bones with tongs and gently knock remaining marrow into broth. Stir to break up.

9 After 3 hours, remove osso buco, oxtail, and any meat floating around. Strip any remaining meat off bones. The meat should fall off easily and be fork tender. If not, cook 30 minutes longer or until it does. Return bones to pot. Refrigerate or freeze meat to eat another time.

10 Add coarsely chopped vegetables and herbs. Low simmer for another 2 hours. Salt to taste.

11 Remove from heat and let broth cool down to lukewarm. Remove all bones with tongs and discard. Strain remaining vegetables and broth through a large fine-mesh colander placed over a large soup pan or bowl. Using a broad spoon, press through strainer; discard remaining pulp.

Some like to strain through cheesecloth to obtain a clear broth, but I like all the bits of good stuff that make it through a fine mesh colander. I pick out carrots and any meat and save to eat later if they aren't too mushy.

12 Store in glass containers if using within the week, or pour into glass canning jars or plastic containers for freezing.

Canning jars specifically made for freezing hold up well, and I prefer them over plastic. The jars used for spaghetti sauce that look like canning jars are not manufactured for freezing or canning. I don't recommend using them, because you risk a cracked jar. A fill line is usually indicated on the canning jar; if not, I leave a good inch below bottom portion of rim.

13 Let broth cool, and then chill completely in refrigerator overnight. It will slowly gel and fat will congeal at top in a solid mass. If you must remove fat, it is easy to do so now.

14 Don't freeze until you have completed the cool-down period. Let jar freeze solid before you put on lid.

Chicken Broth

Yield: About 6 cups

This is a breeze to make compared to beef broth. Save and freeze all your chicken bones from roasted or grilled chicken meals and throw them in the pot along with the fresh-bought carcass. The previously roasted bones will add savory richness. If your main goal is restoring your broth cache, save the bones from 2 to 3 chickens in the freezer. However, this requires a minimum 16-qt stock pan. The more water you use, the more diluted the flavor and nutritious gelatin become, so use caution when adding more water. Add enough to just keep bones covered.

INGREDIENTS:

1 whole chicken

1 large yellow onion, peeled and quartered

2 carrots, cut into 1-inch pieces

2 celery stalks with leaves, cut into 1-inch pieces

4 to 6 garlic cloves, chopped

1 small bunch fresh thyme

⅓ bunch fresh parsley

4 (4-inch) sprigs fresh rosemary

2 large sage sprigs (optional)

½ TSP salt

1 TSP whole black peppercorns

ESSENTIAL TOOLS:

8- to 10-qt stock pan

Fine mesh strainer or colander

Tongs

DIRECTIONS

Place all ingredients in stock pot. Add enough water to partially cover chicken (about 1 ½ to 2 quarts), and bring to a boil.

Reduce heat and simmer covered for 1 hour.

Remove chicken and let rest until cool enough to handle. Cut under and around to extract each breast in one piece; remove thigh meat that pulls away easily from bone. Set aside or freeze for later use.

Return chicken carcass to pot and continue simmering, covered, for 2 more hours. Stir periodically to break up carcass.

Ladle broth mixture through a fine mesh strainer a cupful at a time, pushing contents through strainer with a broad spoon until all liquid is removed. Discard pulp.

Store in glass containers if using within the week, or pour into glass canning jars or plastic containers for freezing.

Canning jars specifically made for freezing hold up well, and I prefer them over plastic. The jars used for spaghetti sauce that look like canning jars are not manufactured for freezing or canning. I don't recommend using them because you risk a cracked jar. A fill line is usually indicated on the canning jar; if not, I leave a good inch below bottom portion of rim.

Let broth cool and then chill completely in refrigerator overnight. It will slowly gel and fat will congeal at top in a solid mass. If you want to remove fat (I don't), it is easy to do so now. Don't freeze until you have completed the cool-down period.

Let jar freeze solid BEFORE you put on lid.

VARIATIONS

For an Asian twist, try using fresh cilantro, lemongrass, and ginger for the seasoning.

While thyme, sage, and rosemary are common favorites, try using different fresh herb such as tarragon, marjoram, savory, or an herbes de Provence mixture.

VARIATIONS

Sautéed straw mushrooms added at end.

Instead of chicken, use ½ cup frozen cooked baby shrimp, placed in bottom of a serving bowl. Ladle hot soup over them and garnish.

For a creamier texture, dissolve 3 TBS kuzu root starch in water. Add after chicken is cooked, stir until thickened.

ESSENTIAL TOOLS:

5-qt stock pot

Large skillet

Cheesecloth or fine-mesh strainer

Coconut-Lemongrass Soup with Chicken

Serves 4

This dish is also known as tom kha gai. My version uses red sweet pepper instead of the Thai red chili. However, people could always spice up their individual portion with red chili oil served on the side.

INGREDIENTS:

2 TBS olive or coconut oil, divided

1 TBS toasted sesame oil, divided

2 to 4 garlic cloves, minced

8-inch stalk fresh lemongrass, tough outer layers removed, finely sliced

1-inch piece galangal ginger or regular ginger, minced *(about ½ TBS)*

6 scallions, sliced thin, divided into 2 equal portions

6 cups chicken stock

6 to 10 fresh kaffir lime leaves or 1 TBS lime zest

1 can coconut milk *(2 cups)*

¼ cup fresh lime juice *(if not using kaffir lime leaves)*

½ TSP saffron or turmeric

2 chicken breasts, sliced or 2 cups shredded roasted chicken

1 red pepper, sliced ¼ inch thick

1 bunch fresh cilantro, trimmed and chopped, for garnish

DIRECTIONS

Prep all ingredients before you start cooking. Once you start sautéing, you cannot walk away until all is simmering.

In a 5-qt stock pot over medium flame, heat 1 TBS olive or coconut oil and ½ TBS of roasted sesame oil until fragrant.

Add garlic, lemongrass, ginger, and half of scallions and sauté, stirring constantly, until aromatic but not brown, about 3 minutes max. At this point we are coaxing the flavor out but not cooking until done. Everything still looks fresh and bright green.

Add chicken broth and lime leaves or zest, and bring to a slight boil. Reduce heat and simmer for 30 minutes.

Strain broth through a fine-mesh strainer or cheesecloth into a bowl; discard solids. Return broth to pot.

Add coconut milk, lime juice (if using lime zest instead of leaves), saffron or turmeric, and chicken. Bring to a simmer, stirring occasionally, and cook about 10 to 15 minutes, until chicken is done.

While chicken is cooking, in a large skillet over medium-high heat, sauté the remaining 1 TBS olive or coconut oil and ½ TBS toasted sesame oil with the red pepper until soft.

Add remaining scallions to red pepper, and sauté another 2 minutes, until bright green. Add to soup, stir thoroughly, and remove from heat.

Ladle soup into serving bowls, garnish with fresh chopped cilantro, and serve.

Cream of Asparagus Soup

Serves 6

Asparagus is a great spring detoxifier for the body for many reasons. Its sulfurous amino acids bind toxins and transport them out of the body, its antioxidant properties (glutathione) assist with liver and kidney function, and its ample supply of the fat-soluble vitamin K thins the blood. Asparagus is also wonderful for the digestive system, as it is high in fiber and contains a prebiotic known as inulin (soluble fiber) which feeds the beneficial bacteria in our lower gut.

This recipe works great with or without the addition of cream.

INGREDIENTS:

3 TBS butter

2 onions, chopped

1 celery heart, diced

4 cups chicken broth

2 lbs asparagus, cut into 2-inch lengths

Salt and pepper, to taste

½ to 1 cup cream

ESSENTIAL TOOLS:

5-qt pan

Food processor or blender

CHEF'S NOTES

Cream is highly perishable and this soup will last a maximum of 4 days in the fridge.

If you are making in advance or prepping meals for later in the week, wait to add cream until ready to eat.

If reheating by the bowl, stir in about 2 TBS cream to each bowl; add more or less to taste.

DIRECTIONS

In a 5-qt pan over medium heat, melt the butter. Sauté the onion and celery until fragrant. Be careful not to brown the butter and vegetables or they will dull the color of your soup. Add the chicken broth, cover, and bring to a simmer. Continue to simmer for about 5 additional minutes, or until the onion and celery are soft (do this before adding asparagus).

Add the asparagus, cover, and simmer an additional 5 minutes. The asparagus should be bright green and al dente. Remove from heat and uncover. Do not overcook asparagus or it will lose its appealing bright green color. Prepare your food processor or blender, a large bowl, and a spatula while the asparagus is cooking.

This is where you want to move quickly, because your asparagus will continue to cook until you start pureeing it. In batches and with a slotted spoon, place the vegetable mixture in the food processor, puree, and set aside in a separate bowl as completed.

Return puree to broth in pan, salt and pepper to taste, combine thoroughly, and reheat at medium, stirring occasionally. This won't take long, so don't walk away and forget.

If you are dairy intolerant, the recipe ends here. It tastes great without cow's cream, or you may wish to add 1 cup of coconut milk to replace the dairy cream.

Once the mixture starts to reheat, stir in cream. The amount of cream added is really a matter of individual preference: start with ½ cup to see how you like it and keep adding cream to taste (up to 1 cup). Do not boil or the cream will curdle and/or burn to the bottom of the pan.

VARIATIONS

Add 4 raw, sliced chicken breasts to the broth and cook until done before adding the pureed mixture back in.

Toss in pre-cooked chicken or turkey at the end.

Cut bacon into ½-inch pieces, brown, and drain. Add after puree mixture has been remixed with broth.

VARIATIONS

Substitute 1 large white or yellow onion, chopped for scallions and sauté with celery.

¼ TSP fresh ground nutmeg added at end.

1 can (2 cups) coconut milk substituted for milk cream.

Reduce broth by 2 cups.

Cream of Celery Soup

Serves 4 as an entrée or 6 to 8 as a side

Choose the greenest celery you can find. Tip: Using scallions with plenty of green tops instead of white or yellow onion adds an appetizing green color. If not using scallions, add extra carrots and/or parsley to perk up the color. Pictured is a variation of the soup with carrots and nutmeg but no onion. It was cooked for a friend with an onion allergy, and while I love my onions, it tasted fabulous without them.

INGREDIENTS:

6 TBS butter, divided

2 celery heads, chopped

1 cup ⅜ inch diced carrots (optional)

5 to 6 cups chicken broth, divided

½ bunch fresh flat-leaf parsley, chopped

10 scallions, cut into ½ inch slices

Salt and pepper, to taste

4 chicken breasts sliced into strips 2 inches long (optional)

1 cup heavy cream

ESSENTIAL TOOLS:

6- to 8-qt shallow stock pot

Large skillet

Food processor or blender

DIRECTIONS

In stock pot over medium heat, melt 4 TBS butter and sauté chopped celery until slightly fragrant. Be careful not to brown.

Add carrots to celery (if using) and enough chicken broth to barely cover vegetables (about 2 cups). Bring to a boil and immediately reduce to simmer; cover and cook until tender, about 7 minutes.

Add parsley. Remove from heat and let cool 5 minutes uncovered while you sauté scallions. Parsley will cook as the mixture cools.

In a skillet over medium heat, add 2 TBS more butter and the scallions; sauté for a few minutes until bright green, soft, and aromatic. Add to celery mixture and transfer to a large bowl.

In a food processor or blender, puree the vegetable mixture one cup at a time. If it becomes too thick for the blade, add a little broth. Unlike a traditional recipe, no flour is added to thicken. Make sure you don't use too much broth and excessively dilute the creamy texture. Transfer puree to original stock pot in batches as done.

Add remaining broth carefully, stirring in one cup at a time to achieve a consistency you like. Bring soup back to a low simmer. Season with salt and pepper to taste.

If you are adding chicken, now is the time; cook until chicken is done, about another 15 minutes, and keep stirring off and on.

Add cream and stir in until warm and completely blended. Adjust seasoning, remove from heat, and serve.

Cucumber Gazpacho

Serves 4

Stay cool as a cucumber on warm summer days with this easy no-cook soup. Gazpacho is Spanish in origin and served cold. Traditionally, tomatoes are used to create the soup base, but this recipe flips around the ingredients and uses cucumber as the soup's base with tomatoes added as a topping.

INGREDIENTS:

Tomatoes:

1 lb cherry tomatoes, halved or quartered *(depends on size)*

1 garlic clove, minced

¼ cup finely sliced fresh cilantro or dill

Salt and coarse ground pepper, to taste

Cucumbers:

¼ TSP salt

1 lb cucumber, chopped

4 large scallions, chopped

2 TBS fresh lemon or lime juice

¾ cup sour cream or full-fat yogurt

1 cup chicken broth

ESSENTIAL TOOLS:

Food processor or blender

DIRECTIONS

Tomatoes:

Prepare the tomatoes first so they have time to soak up the herb and garlic flavors. Add tomatoes, garlic, and cilantro or dill to a large bowl, and salt and pepper to taste; toss lightly to combine and set aside.

Cucumbers:

In food processor or blender, process salt, cucumber, scallions, lemon or lime juice, and sour cream or yogurt until smooth. Slowly drizzle in chicken broth until well blended. Divide among 4 bowls.

To Serve:

Top with prepared tomato (and optional shrimp), evenly divided among bowls, and serve.

CHEF'S NOTES

Taste your cucumbers to make sure they are sweet and not bitter before preparing soup. While any variety of cucumber works, lemon or English cucumbers are reliably sweet.

Sour cream produces a far richer tasting soup than yoghurt.

VARIATIONS

Add 1 cup precooked baby shrimp to tomato topping.

Don't like the herbs cilantro or dill? Try fresh basil or mint instead. Substitute the juice of one orange for lime or lemon juice. Really good!

For those who cannot tolerate dairy, substitute a cold, gelatin-rich chicken broth for the sour cream (you know, the kind that sets up and shakes). This will help with thickening and provides a filling yet savory experience.

Ground Beef Vegetable Soup

Serves 4

How do you make ground beef more interesting without expending too much energy? With a keep-it-simple soup that cooks in a flash. Use the recipe as is or throw into the sauté whatever other veggies are in the fridge.

Usually a beef soup is made with stew meat or osso buco cooked long and slow to form a savory broth. But more often than not, such a time-consuming method just isn't an option. Sometimes a high-quality beef broth is an elusive commodity, because I forgot to take it out of the freezer, it's not within the budget, or I plain won't buy the usual additive-loaded caramel-colored junk in the grocery store.

In this recipe, a broth is created by replacing the slow-braised meat flavors that usually form its basis with what is called a "fond." Ground meat and vegetables are browned, and then the pan is deglazed to capture the caramelized bits of yum. A tasty meal is ready in no time at all.

INGREDIENTS:

1 lb ground beef

2 TBS butter, divided

1 TSP salt

½ TSP coarse ground pepper

½ TSP garlic powder

1 large onion,
cut into ¼ inch slices

2 large carrots,
sliced thin into rounds

2 pints cherry tomatoes,
cut in half (1 lb)

4 large garlic cloves, diced

3 cups water, divided

1 TSP dried thyme

Salt and coarse ground pepper,
to taste

4 fistfuls baby super greens or
mature, thinly sliced greens
(kale, spinach, beet greens, or
collards)

ESSENTIAL TOOLS:

Large sauté pan or skillet

6-qt stock pot

CHEF'S NOTES

For tender ground beef, use the fattier mix.

Use a large enough skillet; if overcrowded, you will not be able to develop the fond.

DIRECTIONS

Drain beef and pat dry; add any drained blood to stock pot if desired.

In a large sauté pan over medium-high heat, melt 1 TBS butter or oil. Drop 1-inch meat chunks into skillet. Season well with salt, pepper, and garlic powder, and brown for 3 minutes without disturbing. Turn meat, season, and brown for another 3 minutes without disturbing. The goal is to start creating flavor without toughening up the ground beef and reducing it to a crumble. Don't worry if not all meat chunks seem cooked through; they will be later. Transfer browned meat to stock pot.

In same skillet (don't clean) used for meat, over medium heat, melt remaining 1 TBS butter in meat drippings. Add onions and sauté for a few minutes until fragrant; add carrots and sauté until the onions have started to turn a light brown and softened. Keep heat at medium; you don't want to burn, but brown. Bits of caramelized meat and veggie juice will have formed on and glazed over portions of the pan bottom.

Add tomatoes and garlic to skillet; cook until tomatoes start to release juice, about 3 minutes. Add ½ cup water and the thyme, stir to combine, and cover. If using canned tomatoes, add tomatoes with their juice and skip the ½ cup water. Stir periodically to dissolve fond into water. Cook until skillet is fully deglazed, scraping up browned bits from the bottom, and fresh tomatoes are soft or canned are warm; transfer vegetable mixture to meat in pot.

Add remaining 2 ½ cups water to meat and vegetable mixture and gently stir to combine all ingredients. Salt and pepper to taste. Cover and bring to a gentle simmer over medium-high heat.

Add greens to top of meat mixture, reduce flame to medium low and cover. Steam until greens start to wilt, about 2 minutes. Remove from heat and stir greens into soup mixture to complete wilting. Greens should be bright green still. Serve immediately.

VARIATIONS

For tomatoes: use 2 large tomatoes, cut into 1-inch squares; or 1 (14.5-oz) can diced fire-roasted tomatoes.

In onion sauté, replace onion with 1 bell pepper or 2 celery stalks. Instead of greens, add green beans or broccoli at end while bringing to simmer.

Panang

Serves 8

This dish will soon become your all-time favorite. The fragrance arising from the spices, the contrasting colors, and the rich coconut texture on the tongue provide a multisensory experience. Coconut red curry is a great base for any type of meat or fermented soy product you would like to throw in for protein.

CHEF'S NOTES

Try to obtain the galangal ginger for authentic flavor. If all you can find is dried galangal ginger, crush or grind it to a powder or small bits before you put in soup. You can also leave it whole and remove at the end.

Freeze any lemongrass stalks, kaffir and/or basil leaves you don't end up using for next time. The red curry paste and dried galangal ginger can usually be found in the Asian section of your grocery store. I try to buy all herbs fresh, but sometimes it just isn't possible! Whenever I spot kaffir lime leaves, I stock up and freeze them—they last up to a year frozen.

All brands of coconut milk tend to vary in consistency. If your version cooks up too soupy for your taste, try this: After you have added chicken, add 2 TBS kuzu root in a small bowl with water and mix with a fork until a smooth paste forms. Pour into hot Panang and stir until thickened.

It is not a good idea to add greens directly to soup pan, because the greens will eventually turn a grayish looking yuck color. To keep them bright and appetizing, always cook separately and add when serving.

VARIATIONS

Olive oil may be substituted for coconut oil with no off-flavor occurring.

For those that like it hot, add 1 small red jalapeño chili, thinly sliced and chopped at the beginning.

While this recipe cooks the chicken breast directly in the soup base, you can also make the soup base ahead of time and add meat as needed. For example, put ½ cup cooked, frozen baby shrimp in the bottom of a bowl, and then ladle hot Panang on top. The hot soup defrosts the shrimp in a flash. Or try adding previously roasted fish, beef, or chicken; fresh stir-fried chicken or beef; or cubed tofu. This way you can accommodate vegetarians or vegans at the same meal.

Another way to serve is to place a small handful of fresh uncooked greens at bottom of a large soup bowl. Spoon hot soup over and let the soup cook greens. If you would like to microwave the greens first, place a handful of fresh baby kale or super greens in bowl, cover, and microwave for 30 seconds.

NOTES:

_____

_____

_____

_____

_____

_____

_____

_____

_____

_____

_____

_____

INGREDIENTS:

1 (4-oz) bottle Thai red curry paste

8 cups canned unsweetened coconut milk *(equals 4 cans)*

8 fresh or frozen whole kaffir lime leaves *(in a pinch use lime juice)*

1 TBS minced fresh lemongrass

3 TBS minced fresh galangal ginger; or 2 TBS dried, pulverized galangal

1 TBS roasted sesame oil

1 TBS coconut oil

1 large onion, sliced

4 garlic cloves, minced

2 large red bell peppers, julienned into ¼ inch thick strips

4 large skinless, boneless chicken breast halves, cut into ¼ inch-thick slices

1 lb baby kale or other dark greens, chopped

2 large leafy sprigs fresh Thai basil or regular basil, roughly cut *(about 1 cup tightly packed)*

½ cup chopped fresh cilantro *(optional)*

ESSENTIAL TOOLS:

6- to 8-qt stock pot

Large sauté pan or skillet

DIRECTIONS

Prep all ingredients before starting the cooking process.

In stock pot, whisk together ½ of the bottle of red curry paste with coconut milk, and bring to a simmer over medium high heat. Taste, and add rest of bottle if you like it spicier.

Add lime leaves, lemongrass, and ginger to the coconut milk. Bring back to a simmer and reduce heat to medium low. Continue to simmer, stirring often, for about 20 minutes.

While coconut mixture is simmering, in sauté pan or skillet over medium flame, heat the sesame oil and coconut oil. Sauté the onion, garlic, and red bell peppers until slightly caramelized and set aside.

Add chicken to coconut milk mixture, and simmer another 10 minutes.

While chicken is simmering, lightly steam the baby kale or other dark greens and set aside.

Add bell pepper and onion mixture to coconut milk mixture, and simmer until chicken is thoroughly cooked and onion-pepper mixture warmed through, stirring often so it doesn't burn on the bottom (about another 5-10 minutes). Remove from heat and stir in basil and cilantro (if using).

Place a serving of steamed greens in a large soup bowl, ladle Panang mixture over it, and serve.

Winter Borscht

Serves 8

This is a hearty winter borscht served hot, and the bacon lends a wonderful smoky flavor. Traditional borscht usually contains potatoes, but I have substituted celery root and carrots instead. Beets may be cut into ½-inch cubes instead of grated.

INGREDIENTS:

4 medium or 2 large beets
(*2 cups grated*)

3 TBS butter, plus more if needed

2 lbs beef stew meat, cubed

8 cups beef broth or water

6 pieces thick-cut bacon, cut into
1-inch pieces (*about ½ lb*)

4 carrots, cut into 1-inch pieces

4 garlic cloves, minced

1 large onion, sliced

1 celery heart, sliced

1 large leek, cleaned and sliced
(*optional*)

1 large celery root, trimmed,
peeled, and cubed

Salt and pepper, to taste

Sour cream, for garnish

Chives or scallions, finely minced,
for garnish

ESSENTIAL TOOLS:

4-qt saucepan

Grater

Large skillet

8-qt stock pot

DIRECTIONS

Beets cooked first are so much easier to shred, especially if you don't have a food processor. Place trimmed whole beets in saucepan, and add 3 inches of water. Cover and bring to a boil. Reduce heat to medium low and simmer for about 30 minutes, or until a fork easily penetrates the largest ones. Remove from heat and let cool. Coarsely grate beets and set aside.

While beets are cooking, in the bottom of a large skillet, brown beef in 1 TBS butter. You might have to do this in batches, 1 TBS butter for each pound of beef. Transfer to an 8-qt stock pot, cover with the broth or water, and bring to a simmer.

Meanwhile, in a large skillet, lightly brown bacon and add to stew meat. Reserve bacon drippings left in skillet. Don't overbrown, as you want bacon to cook up soft in meat mixture. Let meat mixture simmer for 45 minutes.

Add carrots to meat mixture.

Add garlic, onion, and celery heart to bacon drippings (add 1 TBS butter if needed). Sauté until fragrant. Add to meat mixture and simmer all for another 30 to 45 minutes, or until meat is fork tender.

Sauté optional sliced leek in 1 TBS butter until fragrant, and then add leek, celery root, and beets to soup mixture. Salt and pepper to taste, and simmer for another 30 minutes.

Serve warm, garnished with generous dollops of sour cream, chives or scallions.

CHEF'S NOTES

Unless you make your own broth, it is hard to find a commercially prepared broth made from organic 100% grass-fed meat and bones. Most contain grain products and additives, even the organic brands. Using water is fine and still creates a rich, flavorful soup.

VARIATIONS

Substitute leeks with ½ head shredded cabbage added with cooked grated beets.

Winter Squash Soup

Serves 8

Pumpkins are not gourds but a winter squash. Right around Halloween, I stock up on sugar pumpkins, the ones perfect for making soup and pies. I gradually bake up all of them and freeze for future use over the holidays and throughout the winter. Mashing and freezing them in 2-cup increments offers flexibility to make most pie, pudding, or soup recipes. You may use steamed or canned pumpkin, but it doesn't have anywhere near the flavor of oven-roasted pumpkin.

Butternut squash is available all winter and a great stand-in for pumpkin. It is sweeter, milder tasting, and a better deal for the money than pumpkin, because pound for pound, it has more pulp and less seed cavity. If the squash you are using doesn't seem very sweet, adding apple eliminates the need for refined sugar.

INGREDIENTS:

6 cups cooked winter squash
(5- to 6-lb squash)

8 thick-cut slices bacon,
cut into ¼ inch slices (optional)

2 TBS butter

2 apples, peeled and diced
(optional)

2 cups diced yellow onions

6 cups chicken broth, divided

2 TSP salt

½ TSP fresh ground nutmeg

1 cup heavy cream or
coconut milk

ESSENTIAL TOOLS:

Large sharp knife to cut squash

Shallow baking pan

Large skillet or sauté pan

Food processor, blender,
or food mill

8-qt heavy-bottomed stock pot

DIRECTIONS

Preheat oven to 375°F. Cut squash in half. Place meat side down in a shallow baking pan. Cook until you see juices browning on baking pan, at least 1 hour. Scoop out seeds, before scooping out meat of squash. The seeds can be rinsed, toasted, and used as a garnish–they are fully cooked at this point–or discarded along with skin.

In skillet or sauté pan, fry bacon (if using) until just browned. Remove from pan, drain, and set aside. Reserve bacon grease for apple onion sauté.

In same pan used for bacon, melt butter. Add apples (if using) and onion and sauté over medium heat until soft. Add 1 cup chicken stock and the salt and nutmeg. Cover and simmer over medium-low heat for about 10 minutes.

In a food processor, blender, or food mill, work in batches to process apple-onion mixture with cooked squash meat. Add chicken stock as necessary to keep processor or blender blade moving. Add processed squash mixture to stock pot.

Continue until all squash pulp, apples and onion are pureed.

Add remaining chicken broth and optional cooked bacon to stock pot. Bring to a simmer over medium heat (about 30 minutes), stirring occasionally. Careful; don't let it burn. Add cream and stir for an additional 5 minutes. Remove from heat.

Garnish: With fresh minced scallions, toasted pumpkin seeds, and drizzle rings of thick cream over top.

VARIATIONS

Add 3 TBS maple syrup for additional sweetness.

Substitute cooked and sliced andouille sausage for optional bacon.

Veggies with Pizzazz

Beef-Caper Salad

Serves 4

Prep vinaigrette and vegetable salad ingredients first, so they are ready to go when the meat is. This salad is particularly good when served with hot meat. Exercise caution when salting; the capers add plenty.

If using economical cuts like London broil, skirt, or flank steak, it is recommended you tenderize the meat by marinating the night before. This is especially true for the 100% grass-fed steak. Skirt steak in particular responds well to marinating with its loose grain that readily soaks up the marinade. Poke the meat all over with a fork, so it absorbs better.

Many a time I have skipped the marinade with good results. The secret is to cook the tough cuts no more than medium and use a razor-sharp knife to slice thin. Overcooking the tougher cuts can make for chewy steaks no matter how long you marinate. If you like well-done meat, opt for a more expensive cut like the top sirloin or tenderloin. For cooking your tenderloin roasts, use the Tri-Tip Roast recipe included in this book.

Cook times are approximate and based upon average thicknesses of cuts. Unless you are experienced with feeling the meat for doneness, only a meat thermometer will produce spot-on accurate results. To prevent disappointment, remember the meat will cook further as it rests.

INGREDIENTS:

Salad:

 ½ cup olive oil

 ¼ cup balsamic vinegar

 1 TBS Dijon mustard

 ½ TSP dried whole-leaf tarragon or marjoram

 1 TSP dried whole-leaf thyme

 1 TBS capers

 Salt and pepper, to taste

 1 head butter lettuce

 1 yellow bell pepper, thinly sliced

 1 small red onion, thinly sliced

 1 dry pint cherry tomatoes
 (about 25 to 30)

Meat:

 1 TBS powdered smoked paprika

 1 TSP coarse ground pepper

 ½ TSP salt

 1 TSP garlic powder

 1 lb top sirloin or marinated London broil, skirt, or flank steak

 Olive oil

 3 TBS butter
 (if skillet frying meat)

ESSENTIAL TOOLS:

Large skillet, broiler pan, or grill

Sharp knife

VARIATIONS

4 oz crumbled blue cheese or gorgonzola over top of meat slices.

Apple cider vinegar or fresh lemon juice may be substituted for the balsamic vinegar for a lighter taste.

NOTES:

DIRECTIONS

Salad:

In a medium bowl, combine olive oil, vinegar, Dijon mustard, marjoram or tarragon, thyme, capers, and salt and pepper to taste; set aside to let flavors mingle.

Slice vegetables and add to a large, nonreactive bowl. If cherry tomatoes are larger than ½ inch in diameter, cut in half. Pour vinaigrette over sliced vegetables and toss to mix. Cover and refrigerate for at least an hour, stirring periodically.

Wash lettuce, separate leaves, and pat dry; set aside in refrigerator.

Meat:

Remove from refrigerator 30 minutes before preparing. In a small bowl, mix the smoked paprika, pepper, salt, and garlic powder seasonings. Pat meat dry with paper towels; generously rub both sides of meat with olive oil and then the seasoning mix.

To Pan Fry: Best used with top sirloin steak. In a large skillet over medium-high heat, melt the butter. Add steaks and cook to desired doneness. Cook a half-inch steak about 2 minutes and 1-inch steak 3 minutes per side for medium rare.

To Broil: Best used with London broil, skirt, or flank steak. Position oven rack so the meat sits about 2 to 3 inches away from the flame. Preheat oven on high broil along with the broiler pan inside for about 5 minutes, or until high temperature has been reached. Place meat on broiler pan. Cook 1 to 1 ½-inch thick London broil about 5 to 6 minutes per side for medium rare. The thinner cuts such as skirt or flank broil 2 to 3 minutes per side.

To Grill: Heat grill to medium high (keep between 425° to 450°F). Grill 1-inch thick top sirloin steaks 3 minutes per side for medium rare; 1 to 1 ½-inch London broil 5 to 6 minutes per side for medium rare. Skirt and flank steak, cook 2 minutes per side for medium rare.

Regardless of cooking method, cover and let meat rest at least 10 minutes before slicing.

To Serve:

While meat is resting, divide lettuce leaves among 4 plates and arrange in a circular fashion; using a slotted spoon, divide and place vinaigrette vegetables evenly over greens on plates. Retain remaining vinaigrette to spoon over salad as desired.

Using a sharp knife, thinly slice steaks at an angle and crosswise against grain (about ⅛ inch thick). Divide into 4 portions, arrange slices atop salads, and serve.

Brussels Sprouts and Sausage in Mustard Cream Sauce

Serves 2 as an entrée or 4 as a side

My mother used to cook us macaroni or beans with sliced hot dogs mixed in–sounds gross now. This recipe beats the heck out of that, and all but the pickiest of eaters will like it. If you mess up the measurements, no one will notice. The wine adds a gourmet flavor to the dish, but of course you could always substitute chicken broth for those who don't care for the taste of wine.

INGREDIENTS:

2 TBS butter

1 large shallot, sliced

12 oz andouille beef
or pork sausage, sliced
(about 4 large sausages)

1 lb brussels sprouts,
trimmed and halved

⅛ TSP salt

½ cup chicken broth

½ cup white wine

½ cup cream

1 TBS coarse ground
prepared mustard

1 TBS fresh dill *(optional)*

ESSENTIAL TOOLS:

Large skillet

DIRECTIONS

In a large skillet over medium heat, melt the butter. Sauté shallots for 1 minute, or until fragrant and slightly translucent.

Add sliced sausage and cook another 3 minutes, until lightly browned.

Add brussels sprouts, salt, and broth and cook covered until just tender but still bright green, about 6 minutes. The broth should have been reduced to half its amount, but if necessary, cook uncovered for 1 to 2 minutes until it does so.

Stir in white wine, cream, and mustard, and cook until sauce thickens.

Turn off heat, stir in fresh dill and serve.

VARIATIONS

Andouille tends to be a spicy sausage. You may want to substitute with a milder Thuringer sausage or bratwurst. Or, even use turkey hot dogs, if that is what your kids prefer.

Substitute 1 small sliced onion for shallot.

You may substitute water for broth, but you sacrifice a bit of flavor by doing so.

French Potato Salad with Raspberry Vinaigrette

Serves 10

What would a Fourth of July picnic, or any picnic for that matter, be without potato salad? Even the diehard paleophile must have at least one up their sleeve for the occasional celebration. It's a great make-it-ahead recipe the night before, so you can grab and go. The salad was inspired by Monika Callard, a great Telluride, Colorado, chef who left this earth far too early but whose salad lives on in my memory.

This colorful, light version of potato salad leaves plenty of room for barbecued meat and dessert. Use your favorite bottle of raspberry vinaigrette or make it yourself using my Raspberry Vinaigrette recipes (pages 248-9). While red baby potatoes are preferred, the larger red variety works fine cubed. Many recipes require warm vinaigrette be poured over still-hot potatoes, but here they are chilled prior to cutting and then marinate in the vinaigrette with the rest of the vegetables.

INGREDIENTS:

4 lbs red baby potatoes

½ lb thick-cut bacon, cut into 1-inch pieces

2 red bell peppers, cut into ¼-inch slices

1 large red onion, cut into ¼-inch slices

¼ cup fresh minced dill

Salt and coarse cracked black pepper, to taste

1 cup raspberry vinaigrette

ESSENTIAL TOOLS:

Large stock pot (6- to 8-qt)

Large skillet

DIRECTIONS

In stock pot, place whole potatoes and add enough water to cover by 1 inch. Bring to a boil, reduce heat to medium low, and simmer until just barely fork tender (about 10 to 15 minutes depending on size).

Drain immediately; cool and refrigerate until ready to use. If using large red potatoes, cut into halves, then boil. It is important not to overcook; you are not cooking potatoes for mashing.

In a skillet, sauté bacon until just browned; drain and reserve.

Cut potatoes into halves, quarters, or 1-inch chunks, depending on size; place in a large bowl.

Add bacon, bell pepper, onion, and dill; season with salt and pepper and toss.

Add vinaigrette and toss again until distributed well; cover and refrigerate for 2 hours or overnight prior to serving, tossing periodically to mingle flavors and keep moist.

Prior to serving, add additional vinaigrette if necessary to eliminate dryness; salt and pepper to taste.

Hash-Browned Flying Saucer Squash

Serves 4

You will love these squash, also known as patty pan, with eggs on top or as a side dish with steak. They are a low-carbohydrate alternative for home-style hash brown potatoes.

Their flesh is dense, nutty, and flavorful, and it doesn't mush as quickly as other varieties of summer squash when cooked. Avoid squash that exceed 4 inches in diameter for this recipe because they tend to become mealy, seedy, and less firm. Look for younger ones that are at least 2 inches deep or greater. I have found the yellow, bell-shaped, and variegated green on top and bottom to be the firmest of this variety, but all the patty pans work well.

Pictured on page 67.

INGREDIENTS:

½ cup sliced and cooked bacon or breakfast sausage (*optional*)

5 or 6 squash about 3 inches in diameter

1 TBS olive oil

1 TBS butter

1 cup scallions

Salt and pepper, to taste

ESSENTIAL TOOLS:

Large sauté pan or skillet

DIRECTIONS

Brown and drain bacon or sausage (if using) and set aside.

Cut squash into approximately ¾ inch cubes (do not cut smaller).

Heat skillet to medium high and distribute olive oil and butter evenly. When oil becomes fragrant, add squash.

Spread squash so they have room to breathe and release moisture. Reduce heat to medium and fry uncovered for about 5 minutes without turning.

Add scallions, toss well, and season with salt and pepper.

Cook about another 5 minutes undisturbed, until browned. Remove from flame.

Add browned bacon or sausage (if using) and gently mix in. Serve immediately.

Leek and Orange Salad

Serves 6

Do you ever get super-bored with salads? When going healthy, they seem like the obvious solution, but hey, sometimes they are just so monotonous however you slice them. This salad is the exception. Leeks are the perfect accompaniment to heavy meat dishes, and the organic ones are super affordable. Save the greens and slice them up thin to sauté with other veggies, use for soup and stock, or freeze for later.

To make preparation easier, choose leeks at least 2 inches in diameter; you will need to purchase less and can enjoy the bonus of less greens to deal with later. Look for a nice gradation from green to white in the long bulb portion.

A large, 2-inch-diameter leek serves one, and if using smaller ones, you will need 2 ½ leeks per person. The recipe is broken down into tablespoons to help you scale it down for a serving of four if desired.

CHEF'S NOTES

Oranges and mandarins may be used interchangeably. Purchase about 5 oranges or 7 large mandarins.

Add 2 additional TBS orange juice for a total of 14 TBS (¾ cup) if you would like a little bit sweeter taste without adding refined sugar or honey.

Any unused vinaigrette mixed with herbs is great used over other salads. Will keep up to a week refrigerated.

INGREDIENTS:

1 TBS orange or mandarin zest

Segments of 2 oranges or 3 large mandarins

12 TBS (⅔ cup) fresh orange or mandarin juice

3 TBS rice vinegar

Pinch of salt

9 TBS (½ cup) macadamia oil

6 TBS (⅓ cup) macadamias or walnuts

1 TBS butter

6 leeks *(2-inch diameter)* or 9 *(1-inch diameter)*

Ice water, for blanching

Fresh mint sliced and sprinkled for garnish *(optional)*

ESSENTIAL TOOLS:

Grater or zester

Sharp paring knife

Non-reactive bowl or glass jar

Medium-sized skillet

Large steamer

DIRECTIONS

Zest, Segment, Juice Oranges:

Zest one of the oranges before segmenting and juicing; set aside zest.

You'll need a super-sharp knife for this. Slice off the top and bottom of the orange; cut deep enough so you expose a bit of the fruit.

Stand orange up on a cutting board. Start at top and cut down to peel, following the curve of the fruit. You want to cut deep enough to remove all pith, but shallow enough to avoid cutting away flesh. Be safe rather than sorry while peeling; you can trim up missed portions of pith afterward.

Work over a bowl to capture juice. Cut between the membranes on both sides of segment working toward the orange's center; flatten knife underneath segment toward core to release and lift out. The first one is the hardest; the rest should come out easier. After lifting all segments out, squeeze whole orange and membrane over bowl to capture remaining juice.

Squeeze additional oranges (if needed) to reach the required 2/3 cup juice.

Vinaigrette:

In a nonreactive bowl or glass jar, combine orange juice, vinegar, oil, and a pinch of salt and whisk or shake to mix; set aside.

Toast Nuts:

Roughly cut nuts and reserve a whole one to garnish each serving with. In a skillet over medium heat, melt the butter until it slightly bubbles. Add nuts and toss frequently until lightly browned. Remove from heat and drain on a paper towel-lined plate; set aside.

Leeks:

Wash outside of leeks, remove tough outer layer, and cut off green leafy tops, leaving 4- to 6-inch segments of bulbs. In portioning the segments, you will want to include the color transition from green to white.

Split leek segments lengthwise down to root, but do not remove roots yet; wash out any remaining interior dirt. Cut off root portion at bottom of bulb but retain enough of root base to hold leek together. Slice leek into 2 equal halves.

Place cleaned and halved leek segments lengthwise into a large steamer. Steam 5 minutes for 1-inch diameters and 8 minutes for 2-inch ones. While leeks are cooking, prepare a large bowl of ice water for blanching leeks. Carefully place leeks in ice water to stop cooking process; refrigerate until ready to assemble.

Assembly:

Transfer to a cutting surface and place each leek half flat side down. You may need to remove a top layer of skin to reveal a smooth surface. Slice each leek segment into three equal slices (cut lengthwise), stopping before bottom is reached, without disturbing shape of leek. Using wide, flat portion of knife, lift onto serving plates. Place two to three leek halves on a plate, reversing one leek half against another, so each bulb portion is opposite another bulb portion.

Drizzle 3 to 4 TBS vinaigrette over each leek portion so it soaks into slices cut into leeks and flows around sides.

Arrange 4 orange segments around each plate, sprinkle ½ TSP nuts and a pinch of zest and optional mint over top of leeks, and serve.

CHEF'S NOTES

If applied too early, the lemon zest will discolor the asparagus.

VARIATIONS

½ TSP Dijon mustard and/or ½ TSP dried tarragon added to vinaigrette.

Marinated Asparagus

Serves 10

This crazy-easy make-ahead dish works for a busy work week yet is elegant enough for a party as a side or an appetizer. Once made, it's ready whenever you are and requires no reheating! The optional lemon zest and red pepper flakes provide a nice zing. Large-diameter asparagus makes for less work and is easier for serving.

INGREDIENTS:

Vinaigrette:

½ cup olive oil

¼ cup apple- or raspberry-infused vinegar

½ TSP salt

1 TSP coarse ground pepper

4 garlic cloves, minced finely

Asparagus:

Ice water, for blanching

2 bunches asparagus, trimmed (about 2 pounds)

2 TSP grated lemon zest (optional)

1 TSP red pepper flakes (optional)

ESSENTIAL TOOLS:

Large stock pot (8- to 12-qt)

13-by-9-inch nonreactive dish

DIRECTIONS

Vinaigrette:

In a glass bowl, whisk together the olive oil, vinegar, salt, pepper, and garlic. Set aside.

Asparagus:

Prepare a large bowl of cold ice water and set aside. The addition of more ice cubes may be required.

Fill a large (8- to 12-qt) stock pot halfway with water and bring to a boil. In the alternative, place a stainless steel steamer in the pot, fill with a couple inches of water (or the amount recommended by manufacturer), and bring to a boil.

Add asparagus and blanch until it turns bright green, about 1 minute for thin varieties and 2 minutes for large-diameter ones. It is critical you don't overcook.

Transfer to ice water to stop it cooking. You may need to change water until asparagus is cool to the touch. Drain thoroughly and pat dry. Asparagus should look bright green. Lay asparagus in a 13-by-9-inch non-reactive dish.

Drizzle just enough vinaigrette over asparagus to coat generously, and gently toss. Reserve remaining vinaigrette to recoat asparagus if necessary or to use for another time. Refrigerate for an hour covered, re-tossing periodically to ensure all remains coated.

To Serve:

Serve after an hour or leave overnight. Just before serving, arrange on a platter and sprinkle with lemon zest and red pepper flakes.

Mint-Garlic Roasted Potatoes

Serves 6

The mint adds a burst of flavor to the otherwise ordinary potato, making this the perfect companion to rich main courses. You will want to use a potato that cooks up firm, unlike the varieties you would use to mash. If you haven't already, plant some mint in your yard. It's a hardy herb, foolproof to grow, and thrives in sun or shade. Be careful where you locate mint–it is a vigorous spreader.

INGREDIENTS:

3 lbs sweet potatoes, peeled or red potatoes, unpeeled; each cut into ¾- inch cubes

½ cup fresh mint leaves, chopped

8 to 10 garlic cloves, peeled and diced

¼ cup olive oil

½ TSP salt

Coarse ground pepper, to taste

ESSENTIAL TOOLS:

Shallow baking pan or sheet

DIRECTIONS

Preheat oven to 425°F.

In a large bowl, mix to combine all ingredients. Spread evenly in a shallow baking pan or cookie sheet. Roast for 15 minutes, then turn. Continue cooking for another 15 minutes or until nicely browned. Best served warm.

Orange Roasted Carrots

Serves 4

INGREDIENTS:

1 lb large carrots

1 TSP orange zest

⅓ cup fresh orange juice
(zest orange before squeezing)

1 TBS raw cane sugar or honey

½ TSP salt

4 TBS butter

1 TBS minced fresh flat-leaf
parsley, for garnish

ESSENTIAL TOOLS:

1.5-qt shallow glass baking dish

Grater or zester

Non-reactive bowl or glass jar

Aluminum foil, for baking dish
without a cover

DIRECTIONS

Preheat oven to 425°F.

Peel carrots, cut into 3-inch segments, and cut each segment in half lengthwise. Place in 1.5-qt, shallow glass baking dish.

In a medium bowl, mix orange juice, zest, sugar, and salt together until sugar dissolves; pour over carrots.

Dot with butter; cover with baking dish lid or foil.

Bake for 20 minutes. Remove lid or foil, toss carrots with juice, and bake for another 20 minutes uncovered.

Upon removing from oven, periodically coat carrots with juice glaze in pan for the first 5 minutes as they cool.

Sprinkle with parsley and serve.

Parslied Vegetables

Serves 4

What generally comes to mind is parslied new potatoes, but I find myself adding parsley to carrots, cauliflower, and baby onions to brighten their appearance and flavor. It works best with vegetable colors other than green. Make as a mixture of vegetables or use individually.

INGREDIENTS:

2 lbs prepped vegetables *(cauliflower, baby onions, potatoes, carrots, beets, and other root vegetables like celery root, parsnip, rutabaga, and kohlrabi)*

½ TSP salt, added to water, plus more for seasoning

4 TBS butter

2 to 3 TBS minced fresh flat-leaf parsley

ESSENTIAL TOOLS:

4- to 5-qt saucepan

Colander

DIRECTIONS

Chop, quarter, or leave vegetables whole according to size.

For example, vegetables like carrots, large red potatoes, or sweet potatoes are best peeled, sliced, or cubed into smaller sizes. Fingerling or small red potatoes should be simply scrubbed and boiled whole. Scrub and boil whole small beets by themselves, cool, and then peel—their skins will slide off easily. Divide cauliflower into large florets instead of chopping.

Place prepared vegetables in saucepan. Steam or cover with water and add salt. Bring to a boil, then reduce to simmer.

Cook for 10 to 15 minutes, or until tender. Beets will require more like 20 to 30 minutes, or until a fork pierces easily.

Drain in a colander and return to saucepan. In the case of beets, let cool enough to peel.

Heat on medium-low heat, gently stirring vegetable(s) periodically to remove any remaining moisture for about 30 seconds to 1 minute.

Add butter and parsley, and salt lightly or to taste; gently stir periodically to evenly distribute as butter melts. Keep covered and warm until served.

Sautéed Greens

Serves 4

The sheer deliciousness of the dish pleases the senses, yet its utter simplicity leaves many speculating there must be something more to it than meets the eye. It is remarkable how many people have asked me how to prepare this effortless recipe and quizzically reply, "That's it?"

Use as an all-purpose side, in an omelet, or as a bed base for eggs, fish, or meat, and then drizzle sauce over top. I prefer to use a baby super greens mix (sans lettuce varieties), but you may enjoy using dandelion leaves, spinach, or baby kale—they all work interchangeably.

INGREDIENTS:

4 TBS butter or olive oil

4 to 6 garlic cloves, minced

1 bunch scallions, sliced thin

1 lb baby greens, chopped

Salt and pepper, to taste

ESSENTIAL TOOLS:

Large skillet or sauté pan

VARIATIONS

Substitute 1 TBS roasted sesame oil for 1 TBS butter or olive oil; add dashes of tamari sauce at end for an Asian flavor.

Pictured on page 102.

DIRECTIONS

In a large skillet or sauté pan over medium-high heat, melt butter. Add garlic and scallions, turn down to medium, and sauté for about 60 to 90 seconds, until fragrant and bright green; do not brown onions and butter.

Add greens in portions and sauté until greens have wilted a bit, add more greens, sauté, and repeat until full pound has been added to pan.

Sauté until all greens have been reduced to half their size, about 3 minutes. Salt and pepper to taste, remove from heat, and serve immediately.

CHEF'S NOTES

Toward the end of green season, sometimes I use the large, mature leaves of beet, kale, and chard. For average-size leaves like dino kale, slice them crosswise into ¼- to ⅓-inch ribbons; for the larger varieties, slice them down the middle along their spine first before slicing crosswise into ribbons.

The mature leaves can be used as a pasta substitute and topped with meat, marinara, or red bell pepper sauce. Add a bit of grated pecorino cheese on top and you are good to go.

When using mature greens, add 1 TBS water to skillet after wilting greens and cover. Steam on medium high for about 1 to 2 minutes longer.

Vegetable Puree/Mash

Is it puree or is it a mash? The two terms are used interchangeably as if the same. Puree, known more recently as mash, is an easy way to dress up just about any vegetable or rescue those that have resided in the fridge a bit too long escaping notice. It is a process where food has been finely mashed or strained to achieve a thick, pulp-like consistency.

While I may be accused of splitting hairs, a mash usually retains large, irregular chunks and lacks a smooth texture. To make puree, you need a food processor, blender, or mill. Ricers are handy as well, particularly for potato or beets. For those on a budget, stainless steel food mills and ricers can be purchased for as little as $30 each.

Broccoli puree first crossed my radar in the late seventies and remains my favorite today. There is something about the bright green that says "happy," and it is a good low-carbohydrate choice that pairs so well with any meat dish. Another (but not low-carb) favorite of mine is included here: leek and potato. They are like, well, they just go together like peas and carrots.

While I could devote a whole chapter to puree recipes alone, the following recipes provide a solid template for future forays with other vegetables, such as the ubiquitous cauliflower mash, or for more exotic concoctions, such as spiced butternut squash and apple, carrot and chestnut, beet and apple, or celery root and potato. You are limited only by your imagination.

NOTES:

The keys to perfect puree are:

1 peel, roast, boil, or steam your vegetable/fruit well, so it purees into a dense, smooth pulp;

2 in the case of green veggies, blanch immediately, so the cooking process is stopped and color is not lost;

3 drain well or you end up with soup;

4 add butter and cream or liquid gradually to achieve the desired consistency. You may not need the total amount of melted butter or cream required by the recipe.

Broccoli and Nutmeg Cream Puree

Serves 6

INGREDIENTS:

3- to 4-qts water
(fill pan about ⅔ full)

1 cup cream

4 TBS butter

4 lbs broccoli

Ice water, to blanch

1 TSP grated, fresh nutmeg

Salt and pepper, to taste

ESSENTIAL TOOLS:

Large saucepan or stock pot
(6- to 8-qt)

Small saucepan

Food processor, blender,
or mill

DIRECTIONS

In large saucepan or stock pot, over high flame, begin heating water.

In small saucepan over medium heat, warm cream to lukewarm; add the butter and melt; set aside.

Place colander in sink.

Remove broccoli head from stem and chop into 1-inch florets. Peel stem and cut into ¼ inch slices.

Prepare a large bowl of ice water; set aside.

Drop stems into boiling water, turn down to medium, and simmer 3 minutes. After 3 minutes, drop florets into water with stems and simmer an additional 3 minutes, or until just tender.

Remove from heat, drain, and plunge into cold water to blanch. Repeat if necessary to arrest cooking. Drain thoroughly and place on a clean towel to drain further.

Add to food processor, blender, or mill and puree in batches with cream and butter mixture, adding just enough cream to keep blade moving. Reserve a few small whole florets to use as garnish.

When all is pureed, mix in any remaining cream if necessary to reach a mashed-potato consistency; add the nutmeg, and salt and pepper to taste.

Prep in advance of meal: Place in casserole dish and bake in a preheated 375°F oven for 15 to 20 minutes just prior to serving.

Garnish with reserved small broccoli florets.

Broccoli and Nutmeg Cream Puree pictured on page 217

Leek and Sweet Potato Puree

Serves 6

INGREDIENTS:

Potatoes:

2 lbs large red potatoes or white-fleshed sweet potatoes, peeled, washed, and cut into eighths

1 TSP salt for water

4 TBS butter

½ cup heavy cream *(approx.)*

Salt and pepper, to taste

Leeks:

5 large leeks

4 TBS butter

4 to 6 garlic cloves, chopped

Garnish:

Fresh chives, for garnish *(optional)*

ESSENTIAL TOOLS:

Large saucepan or stock pot *(6- to 8-qt)*

Large skillet

Mixer, mill, or food processor, for potatoes

Food processor or blender, for leeks

VARIATIONS

DIRECTIONS

Potatoes: Place in large saucepan or stock pot, add enough water to cover by 2 inches, add salt, and bring to a boil. Reduce to simmer and cook uncovered until soft (fork easily penetrates), about 20 minutes.

While potatoes are cooking, melt 4 TBS butter; set aside and keep warm. Once potatoes are done, rinse well to remove starch, and drain in colander, return to pot, and heat on medium low until all excess moisture is removed.

Handheld or Stand Mixer: Transfer potatoes to a separate bowl, add butter, and whip. Gradually add cream but only enough to reach a creamy but firm consistency.

Ricer: Rice potatoes into a large bowl; with a whisk, stir in melted butter. Gradually stir in cream to reach a creamy but firm consistency.

Food Processor: Transfer potatoes to a food processor in batches; gradually add melted butter and cream as needed to keep blade moving until a firm yet creamy consistency is reached. Transfer to a large bowl as completed and repeat process until all potatoes are pureed. Salt and pepper to taste; set pureed potatoes aside covered.

Leeks: Trim roots to remove stringy parts. Remove most of tough green leaves, but leave about 1 inch of green above white shaft. Slice lengthwise down to within 1 inch of bulb base; spread layers open and wash out dirt and sand thoroughly. Drain in colander and slice crosswise into ½ inch pieces.

In the large skillet over medium-low heat, melt 4 TBS butter; add leeks and garlic. Cover and cook mixture, stirring occasionally, until soft and tender (about 15 to 20 minutes).

Transfer leek mixture to blender or food processor fitted with a steel blade and purée. Add to potato mixture and combine.

To Serve: Place pureed potatoes and leeks in casserole dish. Reheat in a preheated 375°F oven for about 20 minutes or until steaming just prior to serving. Garnish with fresh chives if desired.

Dairy Allergies: With an appropriate taste match, such as carrot, pumpkin, or sweet potato, thickened coconut milk or cream could be substituted for dairy cream.

It's All About the Sauce

Avocado-Lime Salsa

Serves 4

INGREDIENTS:

2 avocados

4 TBS fresh lime juice

½ red onion, diced

1 garlic clove, minced

¼ cup fresh cilantro, chopped

¼ TSP salt, or to taste

1 small jalapeño, seeded
and minced (optional)

DIRECTIONS

Halve, pit, quarter, and peel avocados.

Cut quartered avocado into cubes.

In a medium bowl, toss avocado cubes with lime juice immediately to prevent browning.

Add remaining ingredients and toss lightly.

Serve immediately.

Asian Marinade for Meat

Yield: About 2 cups

INGREDIENTS:

½ cup gluten-free tamari sauce
or coconut aminos

½ cup water

2 TBS unrefined brown sugar
(optional)

½ cup fresh orange juice

1 TBS rice vinegar

3 TBS olive oil

1 TBS toasted sesame oil

1 TBS minced ginger

3 garlic cloves, minced

½ cup minced scallion

½ cup minced fresh cilantro
(optional)

¼ TSP chili pepper sauce
(optional)

DIRECTIONS

In a large bowl, mix all ingredients together
and use with chicken, beef, or pork.

VARIATIONS

Fresh lemon juice or apple cider vinegar may be substituted
for the milder rice vinegar.

Substitute 1 cup pineapple juice for orange juice and water
to create a teriyaki version.

Add zest of 1 orange.

Lazy Day Version:

Not the gourmet option, but hey, sometimes ya gotta run.
Substitute ½ TSP each of ginger and garlic powder for the
fresh stuff and ½ TBS dried onion for scallions.

Approximate Fresh to Dried Reference:

1 garlic clove = ⅛ TSP powdered

1 TBS fresh ginger = ½ TSP powdered

1 small fresh onion or
1 cup sliced fresh scallions = 1 TBS dried onion

Dried cilantro is just plain nasty, so no conversion is offered.

Balsamic Marinade

Yield: About 1 ½ cups

This marinade is for beef, pork, or poultry—not recommended for seafood. Use a higher quality balsamic vinegar and at the minimum, a product labeled Aceto Balsamico Di Modena, containing no additives, or you will end up with a caustic-tasting result. A sweetener is not optional and necessary to tone down the vinegary taste. Before you purchase, it would be a good idea to read about balsamic vinegar in the Ingredients section.

Save the marinade after use and reduce over medium heat to a thick syrup. Add up to a cup of wine for an even more gourmet flavor before reducing. It is great served as a condiment for drizzling over the cooked meat. Conversions are provided in Variations to change from fresh to dried herbs.

INGREDIENTS:

⅔ cup balsamic vinegar

⅓ cup olive oil

⅛ cup water

1 TBS minced fresh rosemary or tarragon

1 TBS fresh thyme leaves

4 to 5 garlic cloves, minced

¼ cup minced fresh onion

1 TBS Dijon mustard (optional)

3 TBS unrefined brown sugar

½ TSP salt

⅛ TSP ground black pepper

DIRECTIONS

In a nonreactive bowl or container, mix to combine all ingredients.

Keep refrigerated until ready to use.

VARIATIONS

Replace rosemary or tarragon with basil.

Fresh to Dried Reference:

1 garlic clove, minced = ⅛ TSP powdered

¼ cup minced fresh onion or 2 large scallions with green tops, minced = 1 TBS dried minced onion

1 TBS minced fresh herb = 1 TSP whole-leaf dried

Berry Delicious Jam

Yield: 2 ½ to 3 ½ cups

Not just for toast, it is equally at home spooned on top of cheese slices or used as a sauce for fowl and pork dishes. Berry jam is one of the easiest to make–no drudge work required like peeling or de-seeding. While making your own jam may sound challenging, once you learn the ropes, it's a snap. This small batch recipe will be gone in no time, so really, any glass jar you have hanging around will do.

Traditional recipes require LOTS of sugar with fruit to sugar ratios ranging from 5:3 to 1:1. Love jam, but hate the hefty price tag of the sugarless, all-fruit jams? They are not worth the price in most cases. The natural fruit flavor is diluted with grape juice concentrate and many brands contain additives, such as thickeners or artificial sweeteners. Your palate may take a while to acclimate itself to the tarter taste of sugarless jam, but if given the chance, it will. Your tongue eventually learns to appreciate the subtle flavor of the berry instead of being seduced by added sugar.

About choosing berries: The larger varieties of cultivated blueberries and blackberries usually contain more juice and may require a longer cook time to thicken. The acidity, seed, and juice content varies wildly and there is just no telling what you are getting when purchasing them. The store variety raspberry seems to have no juice whatsoever and doesn't work for jam making purposes. Strawberries need to be juicy, ripe, and have a deep red color.

Unless they are marked organic, buying and paying more for "wild" blueberries will not protect you from pesticide residue. The small "wild" blueberries are from the lowbush species and will be sprayed with pesticides in the same manner as their larger highbush cousins. The Consumer Reports' Food Safety and Sustainability Center currently rates non-organic blueberry pesticide residues from Uruguay, Argentina, Canada, Chile, and USA (in that order) in the very low to low categories and are essentially equivalent to organic if properly washed. Cherries from USA and raspberries from USA and Mexico rate low in pesticide residue; strawberries are rated high and should be avoided unless they are organic.

INGREDIENTS:

36 to 48 oz fresh berries

3 to 4 TBS fresh lemon juice

½ TSP lemon zest (optional)

A pinch or up to ⅛ TSP cinnamon

ESSENTIAL TOOLS:

6-qt stainless steel saucepan or stock pot (wide and shallow)

Large stainless steel spoon

1- or ½-pint glass wide mouth canning jars and lids

Canning funnel for filling jars (optional)

NOTES:

CHEF'S NOTES

Cinnamon: careful—too much masks the berry flavor.

Sweetening: Add ⅛ to ¼ cup sugar if you must, but don't cut back on the lemon. The pectin in the lemon will help "set" the juice faster and reduce cooking time.

This recipe accommodates up to 54 oz berries in a wide, shallow 6-qt pan.

If making larger batches, see my instructions in this book's "How to Section" under "Relishes, Sauces, and Jams: Making and Canning."

48 oz of berries will fill two (1-pint) jars.

VARIATIONS

This recipe works with plums, peaches, apricots or cherries.

Try adding a shredded Granny Smith apple to the batch to increase the jelling power and to reduce cook time.

DIRECTIONS

Hand wash and air dry jars and lids you plan to use; set aside.

Wash berries and air dry thoroughly before processing.

Place blueberries in pan with lemon juice. Resist the temptation to add water, because doing so will increase cook time and decrease gelling properties. Err on the side of adding too much lemon juice rather than not enough.

Cover pan, heat on medium high, and don't walk away. Keep covered and gently stir every two minutes until the berries have released their juice and reached simmer point (about 10 minutes). The berry mixture will be soupy and a small bubble or two will break the surface every second or so. Set a timer to remind you to check.

Do not boil–this is critical as you want to keep as many berries whole as possible to prevent seed grittiness.

Once the berries are simmering, you can start to relax. Uncover, turn flame down to medium low, and maintain the simmer. Gently stir from the bottom, taking care not to mash or puncture the berries; repeat every 10 minutes to prevent them from burning on the pan bottom. After 30 to 40 minutes has elapsed, I set the timer every 5 minutes.

The water in the juice will start to evaporate, and together with the natural pectin in the fruit and the lemon, the berry soup will thicken into a jam consistency.

Cook Time:

As mentioned before, it is important to not overcook or the resultant jam becomes gritty from the concentration of all the tiny berry seeds, and the pectin will start to break down. The natural water and pectin content in fruit will vary, so a firm cook time is hard to call. Some batches have taken 30 minutes from simmer time to gel, but I have had others take up to 45 minutes to an hour. You know it is done when it clings to the spoon, and the liquid resembles a thick syrup. Another test is to place a spoonful on a dish and cool five minutes. If the syrup thickens as it cools, you know it is done.

Filling and Sealing:

Ladle hot jam into jars. Cool for one minute until most of the steam is released. Apply lids and cool to room temperature before refrigerating. If using sealing canning jars and lids, the jam will store unopened in the refrigerator up to 6 months and up to a month once opened.

Cranberry Sauce

Yield: about 2 pints

Not just for holidays, cranberries make a great winter sauce for meats and cheeses. Heated and served over warm brie? Oh, yum! When mixed with other fruits, the need for added sugar is reduced by 75%. Fuji, McIntosh, and Gala are the best apples to use, and if you are lucky enough to have access to ripe sweet persimmons, all the better. Apples and persimmons may be used interchangeably, and I also use oranges or mandarins in the recipe to sweeten the sour cranberries.

Make up a batch for the winter holidays and to use throughout winter. If you have a big enough pan, double or triple the recipe and can for gifts. The recipe is easily doubled in a 6-qt pan. In the "How To" section under "Relishes, Sauces, and Jams" you will find canning instructions.

INGREDIENTS:

1 bag fresh cranberries (12 oz)

½ cup fresh mandarin or orange juice

1 TBS coarsely grated mandarin or orange rind

3 apples or persimmons, peeled and cubed

4 mandarins, peeled and chopped (or 2 large oranges)

¼ TSP ground cinnamon

1 TSP grated fresh ginger (optional)

⅛ to ¼ cup sugar or honey, to taste (if needed)

ESSENTIAL TOOLS:

4- to 6-qt stainless steel saucepan (wide and shallow)

DIRECTIONS

Add cranberries and orange juice to pan; bring to simmer on medium high. Do not boil.

Add remaining ingredients except for sugar; reduce heat to medium low. Simmer and stir often to avoid burning on the bottom.

After 10 minutes, sample sauce and add sugar to taste if needed. Simmer until cranberry skins pop and liquid has thickened, about 20 to 30 minutes.

Once liquid has been reduced, you may keep simmering and stirring to achieve a more jam-like texture or remove from heat for a chunkier texture. Liquid in sauce will gel as it cools, and I never worry about gelling with cranberries, because their pectin content is so high.

Cool to room temperature and keep refrigerated or hot-pack into sterilized canning jars for long-term storage.

Guacamole

Serves 4

People often request my recipe, and once shared, they are somewhat dumbfounded with how simple it is. During multiple journeys throughout Mexico, I never experienced added sour cream, mayonnaise, or tomatoes in the guacamole. These embellishments overwhelm and/or obscure the avocado texture and flavor.

Sometimes chili was added but usually chili or the ubiquitous Pico de Gallo was served on the side. The addition of cilantro, tomato and onion mixed directly in with the avocado is more of a New Mexico or Tex-Mex adaptation.

INGREDIENTS:

2 large Hass avocados

2 TBS fresh lemon or lime juice
(about 1 medium lemon)

Salt, to taste

DIRECTIONS

Peel and pit avocados; scoop flesh into a bowl.

Mash avocados coarsely with a fork.

Add lemon juice and blend thoroughly; add salt to taste.

VARIATIONS

Add one small serrano chili, seeded and minced.

NOTES:

Hollandaise

Yield: 1 cup

Unlike traditional hollandaise recipes, this variation uses the whole egg. This sauce pulls together fast and is foolproof—well, unless you burn the butter. After discovering it, I have never understood why one would create hollandaise any other way. It can be made the night before and reheated for later use.

INGREDIENTS:

3 large eggs

¼ cup fresh lemon juice

6 TBS butter or ghee

DIRECTIONS

In a medium bowl, whisk eggs until thoroughly blended.

Add lemon juice to egg, and whisk until blended.

In saucepan or double boiler over medium-low heat, melt the butter while stirring continuously.

Remove pan from heat when butter is 50% melted and continue stirring until it is completely liquid.

Place pan back on medium-low heat.

Slowly drizzle egg mixture into pan, whisking continuously until sauce is just thickened.

Remove from heat immediately and serve.

If sauce becomes too thick, add 1 TBS water and whisk to desired consistency over medium-low heat. Add additional TBS of water if needed, but usually one will do.

NOTES:

Lettuce Jus

Yield: About ¾ cup (will serve 4)

This delicate, elegant sauce is surprisingly rich in flavor without overpowering, and it pairs best with seafood or poultry. Grilled shrimp or salmon, with their orange-pink colors, contrast beautifully with the jus. My Teriyaki Shrimp recipe (page 124) is a terrific choice.

The first time you make the jus, allow yourself some extra time to get the hang of it. After you have made it once, you will be able to throw it together quickly in subsequent attempts. The lettuce jus may be prepared the day before and refrigerated for use the next day.

CHEF'S NOTES

Lettuce jus yield will fluctuate per moisture content of lettuce.

To increase yield, add up to 1 TBS of mildly flavored chicken or vegetable broth after straining.

VARIATIONS

If a thicker sauce is desired, dissolve 1 TSP kuzu root in a ¼ cup of lettuce jus. Combine with the remaining lettuce jus in a saucepan or skillet. Simmer for 1 minute or until thickened and starch taste is gone. If not using jus at once, transfer to a sealed container and refrigerate.

Substitute roasted cashews or macadamias for almond garnish. The nuts provide a contrasting textural element against the jus and delicate meats, but leaving them out is fine too.

If allergic to nuts, try water chestnuts or bacon bits to add texture.

INGREDIENTS:

1 large head romaine lettuce

½ cup cream or coconut milk

½ TBS fresh lemon juice

4 TBS butter or ghee, divided

⅛ TSP salt

1 TSP kuzu root
(optional thickener)

8 almonds per serving
(optional garnish)

Minced fresh cilantro, mint, or
parsley, for garnish

ESSENTIAL TOOLS:

4-qt saucepan or sauté pan

Food processor, blender, or
hand blender

Large fine-mesh strainer

Large skillet

8-qt stock pot

DIRECTIONS

Place 4 plates in the oven warmer.

1 *Lettuce Leaves:*

Separate lettuce leaves, rinse, and drain. Reserve large outer leaves for sauce; refrigerate remaining small inner leaves (about 6 to 8, depending on size) until ready for plating. Slice large outer leaves in half down rib and slice crosswise into 1-inch ribbons.

In saucepan over medium heat, whisk together cream or coconut milk and lemon juice while bringing to gentle simmer; reduce to low and continue to whisk and simmer until slightly thickened for an additional 1 to 2 minutes for cream and an additional 3 to 4 minutes if using coconut milk.

Add 2 TBS butter and the salt; whisk until butter melts.

Add sliced lettuce leaves to cream mixture and stir until they are reduced to half their size. Immediately remove from heat.

In a processor, blender, or in pan with hand blender, puree lettuce and cream mixture.

Transfer the pureed lettuce mixture to strainer and press through until no liquid remains in pulp. Set strained juice aside. Discard pulp.

NOTES:

2 *Nut Garnish:*

In a sauté pan over medium heat, melt remaining 2 TBS butter. Add almonds and reduce heat to medium low; leave without disturbing for 2 minutes or until lightly browned; toss to brown other side. Continue to cook until all sides have browned. The key here is to turn infrequently and keep heat low so nuts have time to brown without burning. Set aside in pan or place in warmer.

3 *Plate and Sauce:*

Divide precooked seafood or chicken into 4 portions; keep warm until ready to plate and sauce. If necessary, reheat lettuce jus and nuts; keep warm, so you can work fast in the plating stage.

Fill 8-qt stock pan halfway with water, and bring to a boil. Place a large colander with a plate under it next to pot of water.

Add reserved lettuce leaves to boiling water. Reduce heat to medium high and simmer until leaves are wilted (3 to 5 minutes). It is critical you cook the lettuce leaves long enough. If prematurely removed, they will turn brown and look unappetizing. I have blanched them as long as 5 minutes without losing color. If in doubt how long to blanch, run a test on one leaf.

Using tongs, remove lettuce leaves one by one by grasping the large bottom portion of rib. Place in colander to drain. When all leaves are removed, transfer to paper towels to drain completely.

Meanwhile, sauce the plates. You will have fun with this! Arrange warm plates on counter. Half fill a tablespoon with jus, and with a horizontal flick of your wrist, splatter one plate. Don't worry about it being messy or splattering the counter or other plates. Take another spoonful of jus and place in an empty space to side of plate. It may run into some of other splatters, and that's okay. Continue saucing the remaining plates.

Arrange wilted lettuce leaves to one side of pooled sauce.

Place warm meat on top. Add a bit more jus to side of lettuce, if you like, but be careful of adding too much and destroying splatter effect. The jus is rich, and a little bit goes a long way.

Finish with almonds dropped here and there. Sprinkle meat lightly with minced cilantro, mint, or parsley.

Mango or Peach Salsa

Serves 4

The mango has always appeared to me as a tropical version of a peach, and I use mangoes and peaches interchangeably. When one is plentiful and sweet, the other is not. This salsa is particularly versatile, and while excellent served with fish, I also like it over a grilled stuffed cheeseburger, served with fowl or pork, or heaped on a slice of cheese. Serve hot or cold, and make a double batch–it freezes up great for later use! This is a perfect accompaniment to my grilled salmon or shrimp recipes.

When choosing mangoes, look for the large variety with red splotches of color. If the mango is not quite soft to the touch, it will have to ripen on the counter before using. To maintain a colorful, fresh appearance, it is important to prep beforehand. Peel and cube the fruit last. This recipe cooks up fast, and you don't want the fruit to brown and the other ingredients to overcook.

Scallion measurements are approximate and not super critical to the success of the recipe. You may leave them out altogether for those with onion allergies.

INGREDIENTS:

2 TBS olive or coconut oil

⅔ cup finely diced red pepper

¼ cup minced white portion of scallions

2 cups peeled and cubed mangoes or peaches

3 TBS fresh Meyer lemon juice
(1 to 2 lemons)

Pinch of salt

½ cup sliced green portion of scallions

½ cup chopped fresh cilantro

ESSENTIAL TOOLS:

Large skillet

Juicer

Fruit and vegetable peeler or sharp paring knife

DIRECTIONS

In skillet over medium-high heat, heat oil until fragrant. Add red pepper and sauté for about 2 minutes.

Add white portion of scallions, and continue to sauté until fragrant, about 1 minute more.

Reduce heat to medium and add fruit; sauté for 2 minutes.

Add lemon juice (or lemon and orange juice if not using Meyer lemons) and simmer for 5 minutes more or until juices are reduced, stirring often.

Once the mixture has thickened, add the sliced scallion tops and stir for a few seconds, until bright green. Remove from heat and stir in the cilantro.

CHEF'S NOTES

The secret here is to use super-ripe fruit. Add 2 TBS sweet fresh orange juice in addition to the 3 TBS lemon juice if the mango fruit is not juicy and sweet.

Don't stress about exact measurements for the juice; a little more or less will not matter. That is the beauty of this recipe: Everyone loves it, and it always ends up a bit different. No reason in this instance to toss the bit of fresh juice left on the bottom of the juicer.

VARIATIONS

Substitute 2 TBS lemon and 1 TBS fresh orange juice for Meyer lemons.

Sauté with ½ jalapeño minced fine with red pepper.

Substitute with ¼ cup minced fresh mint for cilantro.

Add ½ TBS minced fresh ginger to replace scallion whites.

Replace scallion greens with ½ cup finely diced green pepper added with the red pepper.

Substitute green pepper for red pepper.

Mayonnaise: Blender or Food Processor Version

Yield: 1 cup

If you are accustomed to Miracle Whip, or even the organic versions made with soybean, canola, or light olive oil, this mayonnaise might take a little getting used to. Any vacillation in resolve is easily eliminated by reading the labels on grocery store varieties. For a more comprehensive discussion on its history and virtues, please see under "Mayonnaise" in the Ingredients section (page 43).

Homemade mayonnaise is a creamy light yellow, and it bears little resemblance to the familiar grocery store versions manufactured with high-temperature hexane-extracted oil, distilled vinegar, modified food starch, corn syrup, sorbic acid, calcium disodium EDTA, and other additives.

Excepting macadamia oil, cold-pressed extra-virgin olive or avocado oil has the best balance of omega-3 to omega-6 fat ratios out of all the affordable oils. However, quality macadamia and avocado oils are harder to find than olive oil, and particularly at a decent price point.

Like the eighteenth-century recipes, this mayonnaise is chilled ("put to ice") before using. Whether you choose to add a bit of sweetener is totally up to you and will not affect how well it thickens. I include it here, because I feel it tends to cut olive oil's natural acidity.

ESSENTIAL TOOLS:

Blender or small food processor

Glass container or canning jar

VARIATIONS

For a thicker consistency, use 2 egg yolks in place of 1 whole egg. However, now you are confronted with the age-old question of what to do with the leftover egg whites.

For initial forays into the world of gourmet mayonnaise, embellish with fresh herbs like basil, dill, tarragon, or thyme (about 2 TBS) cut and gently folded in after you have made the mayo.

2 to 4 peeled and pressed garlic cloves added to first step for aioli sauce.

INGREDIENTS / DIRECTIONS

Combine in a blender or small food processor:

1 large egg

⅛ **TSP powdered sweet paprika**

½ **TSP dry mustard or 1 TSP wet**

¼ **TSP salt**

1 TBS powdered cane sugar or ½ TBS honey

Blend until thoroughly mixed.

While processor or blender is running (with lid on), slowly drizzle through feeder hole or tube:

½ **cup olive oil** until blended;

3 TBS fresh lemon juice until blended;

½ **cup olive oil more**; continue blending until thickened.

Periodically scrape down ingredients from sides of the container and blend in. With the last ½ cup oil, you will start to see small waves beginning to form. Also, it will start to sound different as it thickens. Magic!

Store refrigerated in a glass container or canning jar. The mayonnaise will become thicker once it cools, and it will last up to 2 weeks.

CHEF'S NOTES

Olive oils vary in how they solidify because of olive variety, age, adulteration with other oils, and processing methods. If you find your mayo consistently lacks body AFTER chilling, add 1/4 cup more oil to egg and spice mixture.

While many recipes will insist the eggs, oil, lemon juice, and bowl must be room temperature, I have never worried about it when using a blender or processor. Machines heat up the ingredients, so I find it better to start cold. Room temperature rule (assuming a 70-degree house) has more to do with whisking it by hand.

The mayonnaise will solidify as it chills, so don't fret if the final product looks a tad thin initially.

If you have a large 10- or 11-cup food processor, you may have emulsification problems unless you are doubling the recipe. This is easily remedied by using a blender or a smaller food processor or by whisking vigorously by hand at the end of the process until the oil is fully incorporated.

Green Peppercorn Sauce

Yield: 1/2 to 3/4 cup

Impress your guests with a chophouse favorite and turn a ho-hum steak into something special. Two versions are offered, with and without cream, and both versions are superb. The depth of flavor will really depend on the quality of your broth. Don't skip the reduction process; it is absolutely essential to concentrate flavor and thicken the sauce.

INGREDIENTS:

2 cups beef broth

2 TBS butter or ghee

⅓ cup minced shallots

3 TBS brandy or wine

2 TBS green peppercorns drained and partially crushed

¼ cup whipping cream
(optional)

DIRECTIONS

Broth Reduction:
This stage you may want to do well in advance of dinner, so the sauce comes together quickly. High simmer broth on medium until reduced in half to 1 cup, about 8 to 10 minutes. A shallow saucepan or skillet works the best and will accelerate the process. If you have purchased broth, you may want to add some fresh or dried herbs such as thyme, rosemary and/or tarragon before reducing to enhance the flavor. Strain herbs out after you have completed the reduction process. You can skip this step if you have 1 cup demi-glace already prepared.

Sauce:
In a skillet, over medium-high heat, melt the butter; add minced shallots and sauté about 2 minutes or until slightly browned.

Add reduced beef stock, brandy, and green peppercorns. Simmer on medium until thickened to the consistency desired (about 6 to 10 minutes); stir periodically. Don't worry if it becomes too thick, merely thin with additional beef stock or water. Add optional whipping cream and bring to simmer, whisking continuously.

Serve warm over meat.

VARIATIONS

Organic shallots are sometimes problematic to find at a reasonable price. In that instance, substitute ⅓ cup minced sweet onion along with 1 large garlic clove, minced.

Tender palates may want to reduce peppercorns by 1 TBS.

Marsala and Cabernet Sauvignon wine are fabulous substitutes for brandy or cognac.

Mexican Red Chili Sauce

Yield: 1 ¾ to 2 cups

Most grocery store varieties contain preservatives, thickeners, and additives. Even the organic ones are guilty of this. Traditional red chili sauce has no tomato added and flour is not needed to thicken. My recipe uses pureed onion to add body and flavor. As the red chili mixture simmers, the sauce thickens as the powder swells and absorbs liquid. If you can find a roasted or smoked chili powder, all the better. Ancho chili is one of the mildest, but mixing in other varieties like habanero or chipotle in addition to ancho chili will certainly spice it up.

INGREDIENTS:

4 TBS olive oil, divided

2 large garlic cloves, minced

1 medium onion, chopped

½ cup red ancho chili powder
(*dried ripe poblano*)

2 cups water, divided
(*plus more if necessary*)

1 TBS lime juice

1 TSP salt

ESSENTIAL TOOLS:

Large skillet

Blender or food processor

Glass jar

DIRECTIONS

In skillet, over medium flame, heat 2 TBS olive oil. Sauté garlic and onion until soft and translucent. Combine with ¼ cup water and puree in a blender or food processor until smooth; set aside.

In same skillet over medium heat, heat 2 TBS olive oil. Once the oil is fragrant add chili powder, whisking in a bit at a time to form a thick paste.

Whisk in onion and garlic mixture; add remaining water, lime juice, and salt; continue to whisk until smooth. Bring to a simmer while whisking; simmer up to 30 minutes, stirring occasionally, until thickened to a medium consistency. Patience: the chili sauce will become bitter if cooked at too high a temperature.

Remove from heat, cool, store in a lidded, glass jar, and refrigerate. Freeze if not using within a week.

VARIATIONS

If you would like a more "Americanized" taste, add ½ cup tomato sauce and ¼ to ½ TSP cumin to the mix.

For richer flavor, substitute warm chicken broth for water.

Toast 12 whole dried ancho chilies lightly in a comal or skillet over medium-high heat until aromatic. Cool, then remove stems and seeds. Toasting is the secret step to increase flavor. Place in about 2 cups boiled water (enough to cover) and soak 1 hour. Add chili and about 1/8 cup soaking water to a blender and puree. Add to skillet and stir to blend with onion-garlic mixture. If necessary, thin with remaining soaking water.

Pico de Gallo (Salsa Fresca)

Yield: 2 cups

A colorful, fresh salsa is an indispensable element when cooking Mexican dishes. It's good spooned over fajitas and enlivens your everyday meals, especially breakfast!

Make it as hot as you like with the addition of jalapeño. Adding between ½ to 1 fresh jalapeño, or the little bit hotter serrano, finely seeded and minced to every cup salsa will dramatically add fire. A true Pico de Gallo is not cooked. Meaty plum tomatoes work best and keep it from becoming too soupy.

INGREDIENTS

1 cup Roma (plum) tomatoes, seeded and diced (about 4 to 5)

½ cup diced white onion

½ cup seeded and diced green bell pepper

1 garlic clove, minced

½ cup finely chopped fresh cilantro

1 to 2 TBS fresh lime or lemon juice

1 small, finely minced jalapeño or serrano chili (optional)

Salt, to taste

DIRECTIONS

In a non-reactive bowl (glass preferred), mix together all ingredients.

Chill at least 1 hour prior to serving. Store refrigerated in lidded glass containers.

NOTES:

Raspberry Vinaigrette: Two Versions

Each recipe yields about 1 cup

Fresh Raspberry Vinaigrette 1:

Uses fresh raspberry; won't keep long and should be used within a few days of making.

INGREDIENTS:

6 oz fresh raspberries

2 TBS fresh lemon juice

2 TBS apple cider vinegar

½ TSP sugar (optional)

½ TSP prepared mustard

¼ TSP salt

⅛ TSP pepper

½ cup olive oil

ESSENTIAL TOOLS:

Blender or food processor

Glass or non-reactive bowl

Small mesh sieve

Glass container with lid

DIRECTIONS

In a blender or food processor, puree raspberries; strain through a small mesh sieve, pushing through with a spoon to remove seeds.

In a glass bowl, whisk together strained raspberry puree, lemon juice, vinegar, sugar, mustard, salt, and pepper.

Whisk in olive oil in a slow, steady stream until emulsified.

Store refrigerated in a lidded glass container until used.

NOTES:

Raspberry Vinaigrette 2:

Has a fainter raspberry taste and uses raspberry vinegar instead of fresh berries.

INGREDIENTS:

⅓ cup raspberry vinegar

½ TSP sugar *(optional)*

½ TSP prepared mustard

¼ TSP salt

⅛ TSP pepper

⅔ cup olive oil

DIRECTIONS

In a glass bowl, whisk together raspberry vinegar, sugar, mustard, salt, and pepper.

Whisk in olive oil in a slow, steady stream until emulsified; store in a glass container with lid in the refrigerator until used.

Remoulade Sauce - Creole Style

Yield: about 1 ½ cups

Such a versatile sauce! Served cold, it pairs well with any variety of fish and it's fantastic with hamburgers.

INGREDIENTS:

2 large scallions, chopped

2 TSP minced or pressed garlic or ½ TSP garlic powder

1 TBS capote capers

1 cup mayonnaise

1 TBS Dijon mustard

½ TBS powdered sweet paprika

2 TBS catsup

1 TBS fresh lemon juice

½ TBS prepared horseradish *(optional spicy ingredient)*

1 to 2 TSP pepper sauce *(optional)*

ESSENTIAL TOOLS:

Food processor or blender

DIRECTIONS

In a food processor or blender, pulse scallions, garlic, and capers to convert into a fine mince.

Add remaining ingredients and mix until smooth.

CHEF'S NOTES

The remoulade is better if made a few hours ahead so the flavors meld. Keep refrigerated in a glass container.

NOTES:

Roasted Red Pepper Coulis

Yield: 1 ¾ to 2 cups

Coulis is the French term for a pureed vegetable or fruit sauce. They offer a refreshing change from the usual tomato-based sauces, pair well with spiralized vegetables like zucchini, and are perfect as a bed for or drizzled over chicken, pork, and fish. Two variations are offered here: a nondairy and a dairy. The nondairy version freezes well.

INGREDIENTS:

2 large, fresh red bell peppers, roasted; or 1 cup canned, roasted red peppers, chopped

1 cup chicken broth or ½ cup (*if using cream*)

2 TBS butter or olive oil

2 TBS minced garlic or 3 TBS minced shallots

½ cup fresh basil leaves

Salt and coarse ground pepper, to taste

ADDITIONAL INGREDIENTS FOR DAIRY VERSION:

½ cup heavy cream

1 TSP fresh lemon juice

¼ cup grated Romano or parmesan cheese (*optional*)

ESSENTIAL TOOLS:

12-inch skillet or sauté pan

Blender or food processor

DIRECTIONS

Roast red peppers, and then seed and stem; coarsely chop. (*see "How To" section, "Roast and Peel Peppers"*) If using canned peppers, drain and pat dry with paper towels before chopping.

In 12-inch skillet or sauté pan, high simmer stock until reduced in half, about 4 to 7 minutes; set aside to cool.

In skillet over medium heat, warm the butter or olive oil. Sauté garlic or shallots until fragrant, about 1 minute. Add roasted red peppers, and simmer an additional 5 minutes.

Nondairy Version:

In a blender or food processor, combine garlic and pepper mixture with basil until thoroughly blended. Drizzle reduced broth in slowly until you reach desired consistency; puree until smooth.

Return puree to skillet and reheat to a low simmer; salt and pepper to taste. Serve warm.

Dairy Version:

In a blender or food processor, combine garlic and pepper mixture with reduced broth, basil, and lemon juice; puree until thoroughly blended. Drizzle cream in slowly until you reach desired consistency; puree until smooth.

Return pureed mixture to skillet and reheat to a low simmer. Add optional cheese, and heat until melted. Thin with additional broth if necessary. Salt and pepper to taste. Immediately remove from heat and serve warm.

Almost Healthy

Desserts and Sweets

It was with great hesitation that I included a dessert section, but ignoring it seemed akin to repressing an emotion that later manifests as severe dysfunction. Are you really never going to have a birthday cake again because you are on a new diet? Then I remembered this cookbook is not about beating yourself up over occasional indulgences.

While for the most part I have eliminated grains and nuts out of my diet on a daily–or even a weekly basis–realistically, everyone has a basic human need to partake in celebrations and holidays or special events. If you are aware of the quality and source of the ingredients used and limit the frequency of splurges, the long-term detriment to your body can be mitigated or avoided altogether. Also, as you practice healthier choices by limiting the toxins ingested, you become more sensitized to their negative effects. The ill feeling you experience after a splurge becomes a self-regulating motivator for not going off the deep end continually.

Using organically grown einkorn wheat, nut, or coconut flour, minimally processed sugars, and fruit in moderation brings your treat back into alignment with unadulterated ingredients available at the turn of the century in 1900. But even so, sweets in those days were reserved for holidays and special occasions, not for daily consumption. Don't delude yourself by replacing desserts with a "cleaner" or "paleo" version. Cooking fruit-sweetened coconut or nut flour confections is not Paleolithic eating–there are no "paleo diet" desserts. When you consume sweeteners and/or grains, you are eating something our bodies were never meant to eat on a regular basis. There is no fundamental difference between how your body processes the various sugars, starchy tubers, and grains (whole grain, gluten free or not), whether they are from bananas, honey, cane, agave, or coconut, nut, rice, sweet potato, or quinoa flours.

Any type of high-carbohydrate food (this includes sweet potatoes and fruit), causes a huge spike in your blood sugar levels. Rising blood sugar levels induces an insulin response, which in turn, causes your bones, muscles, and connective tissue to shed stored magnesium and calcium. To add insult to injury, phytates in seeds, nuts, and grains bind with the magnesium and calcium contained within them and renders those substances largely unavailable. Eating these foods in any form day in and out eventually wears out the endocrine glands, creates deficiencies, and springboards us into all sorts of diseases; not just diabetes.

Cooking with honey and other alternative sweeteners is not new stuff. Back in 1978, William Dufty's book *The Sugar Blues* (Dufty 1976) inspired my switch from cane sugar to baking with alternative sweeteners like honey, bananas, and maple sugar. While he was right on a number of issues, he was grossly inaccurate on many. His gig of recreating desserts using natural substitutes like honey and whole grains sent me down a glycemic rabbit hole. The logic of "hey, this cookie must be good for me, it's made with whole grain oats, bananas, nuts, and honey" was a total disaster. The 30 years of taste deprivation were not ultimately any healthier and totally ruined the sublime dessert experience.

Included here are recipes chosen with discrimination. The recipes range from ones naturally gluten free to those using nut and non-hybrid grain flours. Sugar contents are lowered but are still in keeping with conventionally made desserts. There are so many killer dessert cookbooks out there, and I am not here to compete with them but to share with you how to have your cake and eat it–and still have it taste good too.

Orange Nut Cake

Serves 8 to 12

This dessert is a perfect union of nuts and a refreshing citrus flavor that always enlivens any occasion, summer or winter. It is completely grain and dairy free, and eggs are used in place of flour to create a moist yet light crumb. Don't let the egg whites and springform pan intimidate you, it is a failproof recipe and you can't go wrong.

Blanched almonds are recommended to eliminate the bitterness from their peel and reduce the phytic acid content. While the recipe uses almonds, macadamias are a fantastic alternative, although more expensive. Macadamia offers a wonderful buttery flavor that almonds just can't imitate. Walnuts may also be used, but they lend a more rustic look and bitter flavor. Nut oils are volatile, and I recommend using freshly ground nuts over the packaged almond meal.

INGREDIENTS:

2 large oranges
(should equal 2 cups puree)

2 ¼ cups blanched, ground almonds

½ TSP salt

1 TSP non-aluminum baking powder

6 large eggs, separated

1 cup cane sugar, divided

½ TSP almond extract

⅓ cup blanched sliced almonds,
toasted, for topping *(optional)*

Powdered sugar, for topping
(optional)

ESSENTIAL TOOLS:

9-inch round springform baking pan

Parchment paper, cut to fit inside pan bottom

Food processor or blender

2 large mixing bowls

Mixer

VARIATIONS

Topping: In a small bowl, use a fork to combine 1 TBS sugar and 1 TSP lemon zest; set aside. Before placing cake in oven, sprinkle top evenly with ⅓ cup sliced almonds followed by zest mixture.

Serve with whipped cream and fresh berries.

DIRECTIONS

Line 10-inch round springform pan with parchment paper. Adjust oven rack to middle position and pre-heat to 350°F.

1 *Cook Oranges:*

Oranges will be soft and squishy to touch when done.

To Simmer: Place washed, whole oranges (peel included) in a 4-qt pan; cover with water and bring to simmer; cook covered for 1 ½ hours or until soft (periodically check water level); or

To Microwave: Place oranges in water, cover, and microwave on high for 15 minutes; or

To Pressure Cook: Place steaming rack in pan with enough water to fill to bottom of rack, but not covering rack; place oranges on rack and cook for 15 minutes.

2 *Almond Meal:*

While oranges are cooking, prepare almond meal. If using whole almonds, coarsely chop before placing in processor. In a food processor or blender, pulse until almonds are ground into a meal, about 20 or more pulses. Add salt and baking powder and pulse to blend. Transfer almond mixture to a large mixing bowl and set aside.

3 Eggs:

Separate and set aside in advance of preparing batter, so they have time to reach room temperature.

4 Puree Oranges:

Cool oranges and cut tops and bottoms off; slice into quarters, and be sure to remove the seeds. In a food processor or blender, puree oranges, including peels; if using a blender, puree one orange at a time. Mixture will not puree to a fine texture; it will be a bit lumpy looking like a mash and as if the peel was zested. Measure out 2 cups' worth and use no more, but a bit less is fine.

5 Batter:

With a mixer, beat egg yolks with ½ cup sugar until pale yellow; add almond extract; slowly add orange mash and mix until volume has doubled. Gently fold egg yolk mixture into almond mixture in the separate bowl until just blended.

Whip egg whites until they start to increase in volume and become foamy. Gradually sprinkle remaining ½ cup sugar in, a bit at a time, so it slowly dissolves into egg white before you add more; whip until stiff but not dry. Peaks should fold over a bit as you remove the beater blade and not be standing straight up.

Fold ⅓ of egg white mixture into almond mixture to lighten. Transfer remaining egg whites to top of lightened almond mixture. Using a rubber spatula or a large spoon, gently fold starting from center working straight down, out, and up against side of bowl, and fold back to center. Fold until just blended.

Transfer batter to prepared pan.

6 Bake:

Bake until center of cake is set, bounces back slightly when gently pressed, and toothpick inserted in center comes out clean, 50 to 65 minutes. Center of cake may collapse a bit, but that's okay. Place on a wire rack and cool 15 minutes. Run a knife around the edge then release outer rim.

To Serve:

When cake has cooled completely, dust with powdered sugar (made with tapioca instead of corn starch for corn allergies) and toasted almond slices.

Berry Cobbler

Serves 6

Hot out of the oven cobbler will be a favorite with your bunch and watch it disappear fast! This recipe works best with 32 oz (2 lbs) of ripe, sweet berries but can be made with as little as 24 oz in a deep 9-inch glass pie dish.

INGREDIENTS:

Filling:

 32 oz blackberries or blueberries

 3 TBS fresh lemon juice

 ¼ TSP ground cinnamon

Dough Topping:

 1 ½ cups einkorn wheat flour

 1 TBS cane sugar

 ¼ TSP salt

 1 TBS baking powder

 5 TBS softened butter

 ½ TBS lemon zest

 ¼ cup cream

 3 TBS water

 1 egg

 1 to 2 TBS coarse cane sugar

 1 cup heavy cream,
 for topping (optional)

 Fresh-grated nutmeg,
 for topping (optional)

DIRECTIONS

Preheat oven to 400°F.

Filling:

Wash berries and dry thoroughly. Spread berries evenly throughout a glass, non-greased baking dish. Sprinkle with the lemon juice and cinnamon. Toss lightly, evenly coating berries. Bake for 25 to 30 minutes while you make dough topping. Berries should release their juice and bubble before adding topping.

Dough Topping:

In a large bowl, combine the flour, sugar, salt, and baking powder. Cut in softened butter until it resembles coarse sand. Sprinkle with lemon zest and toss lightly. In a separate bowl, combine the cream, water, and egg and whisk until thoroughly blended. Drizzle into dry ingredients, lightly mixing with a fork until just combined.

Remove berries from oven. With a small spoon, quickly drop dough, distributing evenly over the berries. You will have gaps between the drops, but don't worry—they will spread. Sprinkle dough with coarse cane sugar.

Pop back into oven and cook an additional 20 minutes, or until top is golden.

To Serve:

Cool for 10 minutes, and serve warm. For extra deliciousness, whip 1 cup heavy cream to soft peaks. Place a dollop of cream on each serving with a pinch of fresh-grated nutmeg.

ESSENTIAL TOOLS:

7-by-11-inch glass baking dish *(2-qt)*

Zester

VARIATIONS

Substituting 5 to 6 cups of cherries or peaches for berries are fantastic seasonal alternatives. When using peaches, substitute fresh ground nutmeg for cinnamon and add ½ TSP almond extract to peaches.

Sometimes I use a mixture of about 2 heaping TBS sour cream mixed with enough water to equal ¼ cup to replace cream in batter. Consistency should mimic heavy cream. Works great and saves a trip to the grocery.

Blueberry or Pomegranate Chocolate Drops

Serves 8

Do you love chocolate and berries? Get ready for a juicy explosion of deliciousness when you bite into one of these. Hard to eat just one of these once you get going! The fun is in the making, and you will become mesmerized playing with little glistening pomegranate rubies.

Don't like the seeds in pomegranates? Neither do I, but I hardly notice them when eating these. Choose ripe ones and use immediately, before the pomegranate starts to dry out.

Still don't think you would like pomegranate seeds in and amongst your chocolate? Make them with blueberries, still an awesome, juicy chocolate experience. Plus, blueberries don't come with the added deseeding hassle.

If you use the 85% cacao chips or bars, all the better to reduce the sugar content when indulging. This recipe allows for wide variations in the amount of chocolate used. I try to use as little chocolate as possible, just enough to coat the berries or pomegranate seeds and still have them stick together.

INGREDIENTS:

2 **pomegranates** (*2 cups seeds*) or **18 oz blueberries**

6 oz chocolate chips or bars

ESSENTIAL TOOLS:

Colander

Cupcake pans lined with paper baking cups or cookie sheet lined with wax or parchment paper

DIRECTIONS

Wash blueberries or deseed pomegranates.

Reserve ¼ to ½ cup to place on top of chocolate drops.

Place berries or seeds on paper towels and blot gently with more paper towels. Periodically rotate them and blot them again. Let them air dry for up to an hour. Seeds or berries must be completely dry before you coat them or they will fall apart.

Keep at room temperature if using immediately. Berries or seeds must be room temperature when mixing with chocolate.

Line cupcake pans with paper baking cups. Use the minis when using pomegranate and step up to the next larger size with blueberries. Don't have cupcake pans? Place the paper baking cups on a cookie sheet or simply line a cookie sheet with wax paper or parchment.

See directions for melting chocolate in the "How To" section (page 80).

Pour liquid chocolate slowly into room-temperature fruit, gently tossing to coat. Drop by spoonfuls into muffin liners or onto lined cookie sheet. Don't worry if this gets messy; you will be able to clean up the presentation later. Keep working so it doesn't set up before you are done dividing up the batch.

Scatter reserved berries or seeds on top to brighten and enhance eye appeal. Lightly press into mounds.

Allow to harden and cool on the counter. Store in refrigerator for up to a week—if they last that long.

Once hardened, you can transfer to clean baking cups / liners to spruce up presentation.

Prior to serving, allow to soften at room temperature.

Flourless Chocolate Torte

Serves 8 to 12

Decadence at its finest—chocolate freaks, this is for you! An over-the-top cake that is gluten and nut free using only ¾ cup added sugar and no leavening. Shop around for premium chocolate that isn't loaded with sugar at the expense of chocolate and is made with chocolate liquor (contains equal amounts of chocolate solids and cocoa butter).

INGREDIENTS:

6 large eggs

9 oz dark bittersweet chocolate
(72 to 88% cocoa content)

8 TBS butter

¾ cup cane sugar

¼ TSP salt

1 TSP vanilla

For Serving:

Whip cream

Fresh berries

½ cup homemade fruit jam

1 TBS fresh orange juice

ESSENTIAL TOOLS:

8-inch round springform baking pan

Parchment paper, cut round to fit inside pan bottom

Mixer

CHEF'S NOTES

88% cacao chocolate, packaged in 3.2-oz bars, was used to create recipe. The total amount of chocolate used was rounded to 9 oz, as an additional .6 oz seemed inconsequential to worry about.

If using 72% cacao chocolate, you may want to reduce sugar to ½ cup. If sugar is the first ingredient on the chocolate label, you definitely will want to reduce sugar to ½ cup.

A conventional gas oven was used to develop recipe. Adjust convection ovens by reducing the temperature and cook time. I recommend you check your stove's owner guide for guidance. It is better to undercook this cake rather than cook too long.

Uneaten portions may be kept unrefrigerated up to 3 days (if they make it that long). Refrigeration tends to dry out the cake and create a dense texture.

DIRECTIONS

1 Preheat oven to 350°F. Line springform baking pan with parchment paper; set aside.

2 Separate egg whites from yolks; set both aside. Separate before starting recipe, so they have time to reach room temperature.

3 Cut chocolate and butter into tablespoon-size pieces.

4 Melt Chocolate: In a double boiler, melt butter and ¼ cup sugar; add chocolate and stir periodically until chocolate is almost melted. Turn off heat and stir to melt final lumps. You may also melt chocolate mixture in a bowl set over simmering water to simulate a double boiler. Bowl should not sit in water and water should not be boiling under chocolate but simmering. The trick here is to gently heat chocolate so it doesn't seize up and become thick. The mixture should fall off a spoon in a liquid stream that is thin and smooth.

Or microwave butter and chocolate mixture in a glass bowl in 30-second increments, stirring after each time, until chocolate has just started to melt. Remove from microwave. Stir until chocolate and butter are completely melted into a thin, smooth consistency; continue in 10-second increments if necessary. I don't recommend this method unless you are experienced melting chocolate in a microwave.

5 While chocolate and butter are melting in the double boiler, in a large mixing bowl, whisk yolks until frothy. Whisk in salt and vanilla.

6 Here is where it gets a bit delicate. Chocolate must be cooled down before adding egg yolks. Chocolate should still be warm but hotter than room temperature so it stays in a thin consistency. Cooling chocolate should only take about 2 minutes, stirring periodically. Slowly drizzle ⅓ of chocolate into egg yolks while gently stirring ("tempering"

egg yolks). Add remaining chocolate mixture to yolks; mix to incorporate thoroughly. Set aside while you prepare whites.

7 Add egg whites to mixer and whip until they start to become foamy. Gradually add remaining ½ cup sugar, a bit at a time, so it slowly dissolves into egg whites but doesn't deflate them; whip until almost stiff but not dry. Whites should be foamy, increased in volume, and just beginning to form peaks.

8 Fold ⅓ of egg white mixture into chocolate to lighten. Transfer remaining egg whites to top of lightened chocolate mixture. Using a rubber spatula, gently fold into chocolate, starting from center, working straight down, out, and up against side of bowl, and fold back to center. Fold until just blended. Do not over-fold, and a few streaks are okay.

9 Transfer batter to prepared pan; smooth and equally distribute with a spatula. Cook times are approximate: Bake 30 to 35 minutes. When done, cake center will have risen. Crumbs of cake will still cling to a toothpick and look like it is not quite done yet, but it will not be liquid. Do not overbake; cake will continue to cook as it cools. Center will fall slightly when cooling, but that's okay.

Place on a wire rack and let cake cool 10 minutes. Run a knife around edge and then release outer rim. Cool an additional 30 minutes before slicing. Best served same day.

10 Serve with fresh berries and whip cream or with ½ cup homemade fruit jam thinned with about 1 TBS orange juice to form a sauce.

Chocolate-Dipped Strawberries

Yield: 1 lb (12 to 20 chocolate covered strawberries, depending on size)

Tried and failed before? There couldn't be an easier dessert recipe to make, but there are secrets you must know. Does your chocolate seem too thick for dipping or your berries look like unattractive lumps? The answer to success lies in the strawberry and chocolate preparation. In this recipe, I reveal the secrets, so you can make rockstar chocolate-covered berries.

INGREDIENTS:

1-pt basket (*1 pound*) fresh large strawberries

12 oz dark chocolate chips or chocolate bars, chopped

ESSENTIAL TOOLS:

Baking sheet

Wax or parchment paper

Microwave-proof glass bowl or stove-top double boiler, for melting chocolate

Small deep glass bowl, for dipping

VARIATIONS

Melt 3 oz of white chocolate while chocolate strawberries are drying on counter (do this before refrigerating).

Dip a small spoon into melted white chocolate, let excess drip back into bowl, and drizzle across each strawberry.

DIRECTIONS

Wash strawberries under cold water, drain, and spread out on a towel covered with paper towels. Pat moisture away with additional paper towels. Air dry and rotate occasionally until each strawberry is completely dry, about 30 minutes. As they are drying, gently coax the leaves up and away from strawberries.

Line a baking sheet with wax paper or parchment paper; set aside. Berries must be room temperature before dipping. See directions for melting chocolate in the "How To" section.

Choose a deep glass bowl with a bottom smaller than the top and just big enough to contain the total chocolate amount needed. The point here is make dipping easy by concentrating the chocolate in a deep, small area rather than having it spread out over a shallow wide bowl. If using a double-boiler for melting, you may want to have a small bowl ready to transfer chocolate to for dipping.

Grasp strawberry by top leaves and gently pull leaves back and away from berry until all leaves are nestled in your fingers; lower bottom tip into chocolate, rotating strawberry as needed to completely coat. Lift strawberry straight up and let excess chocolate drizzle back into bowl. If the chocolate starts to set up before you are done dipping, place glass bowl in microwave and heat in 15 second increments until thin again.

Transfer dipped strawberry to lined baking sheet; do not disturb once you have placed strawberry down. Repeat dipping process until all remaining strawberries are coated. Let strawberries rest until chocolate coating is set. I like to refrigerate to speed the hardening process, and it is perfectly fine to do so. However, make sure you bring them to room temperature before serving (about 30 minutes).

If not eaten within the day, cover when completely cooled and refrigerate. They will keep up to a week.

Meyer Lemon Curd

Yield: 2 ½ cups

Lemon curd is the perfect accompaniment to any sort of berries or as a layer in a cream pie. Meyer lemons are preferred to reduce the amount of cane sweetener needed, but the recipe works fine with the tarter varieties. To mimic Meyer lemon, substitute ⅓ cup fresh orange juice for ⅓ cup of the lemon juice.

This version is a tad tarter than traditional versions. Add a minimum ½ cup (up to ⅔ cup sugar if not using Meyer lemon) for you who like it sweet.

INGREDIENTS:

¼ lb butter (1 stick), cut into ½ inch chunks

3 to 4 large Meyer lemons

¼ cup sugar if using Meyer lemons and ½ cup if not

4 large eggs

⅛ TSP salt
(if using unsalted butter)

Fresh berries, for garnish
(optional)

Whipped cream, for garnish
(optional)

ESSENTIAL TOOLS:

Paring knife or large fruit-vegetable peeler

Food processor or blender

3-qt saucepan

Lidded glass container

DIRECTIONS

Remove butter from refrigerator to soften while you prepare lemons.

Peel 3 lemons, removing the white, bitter pith.

Place peel in a food processor or blender. Add sugar and pulse until peel and sugar resemble coarse sand.

Juice the peeled lemons until a total of ⅔ cups fresh juice is obtained.

Whisk eggs together in saucepan. Add lemon-sugar mixture, lemon juice, and salt (if using unsalted butter) to eggs and whisk until thoroughly combined.

Add butter.

Warm over high heat, stirring with a whisk. Once butter melts, reduce heat to medium. It is important that you don't burn the bottom; keep stirring and don't stop.

Continue to simmer over medium heat. After about 5 minutes, curd will thicken, hold whisk marks, and begin to periodically bubble; this indicates it is done.

Patience is a virtue in this instance. Too high a heat for too long will curdle the egg and the lemon will separate from the mixture. Once thickened, remove from heat and transfer to a glass container or canning jar. Cool uncovered at room temperature and then refrigerate covered.

To serve, place a large dollop of lemon curd onto a small plate and generously top with fresh berries. Especially yummy topped off with a small dollop of whipped cream.

Shortbread Cookies

Yield: 24 cookies

Great for dipping in chocolate anytime and these cookies are also perfect for decorating over the holidays. Important: Butter should still have a chill to it when creaming. It should not be softened to a temperature warmer than 60°F. Einkorn wheat has less gluten proteins than hybrid varieties. When combined with the recipe's high butter content, the dough is almost impossible to roll out and cut if the butter is too warm. Use too little butter and the final cookie is too tough.

INGREDIENTS:

½ lb butter, semi-softened

½ cup cane sugar

½ TSP pure vanilla extract

2 large eggs

3 cups einkorn flour, plus more for dusting

1 TBS coarse cane sugar, for topping (optional)

9 oz dark chocolate - 75 to 88% cocoa content, for dipping (optional)

ESSENTIAL TOOLS:

Mixer

Baking sheet

Wax or parchment paper

Airtight container

DIRECTIONS

Preheat oven to 400°F.

Cream slightly softened butter with a mixer until smooth, creamy, and lighter in color.

Mix the butter and sugar until well combined.

Add vanilla and eggs, and blend until fluffy.

Add einkorn flour to butter-sugar mixture, and mix on medium-low speed until all is well blended and forms a dough.

Shape into a flat round and place on a flour dusted surface. Roll out dough to form a long oblong ⅜-inch thick. Cut with 2½-inch-diameter cookie cutter. Gather unused portions. Form into another flat round, roll, cut, and repeat until all dough is used. Place cookies on an ungreased baking sheet.

If you are not planning on dipping in chocolate, sprinkle cookies with coarse sugar before baking.

Bake for 13 to 15 minutes. Some edges will brown, but not all. Remove from oven and cool to room temperature.

While cookies are cooling, prepare a baking sheet lined with wax or parchment paper.

See directions for melting chocolate in "How To" section (page 80). Dip each cookie in chocolate, coating half of its exterior. Place on prepared cookie sheet to harden.

Refrigerate in an airtight container between wax paper layers.

References

Alaska Department of Environmental Conservation (DEC). Press Release: "No Fukushima-Related Radiation Detected in Alaska Seafood." January 9, 2017.

American Society for Clinical Nutrition (ASCN). "Supplementation with flaxseed alters estrogen metabolism in postmenopausal women to a greater extent than does supplementation with an equal amount of soy." *Am J Clin Nutr.* vol. 79 no. 2 318-325. February 2004

Andrews, James. "Formaldehyde Detected in Supermarket Fish Imported from Asia." *Food Safety News.* September 11, 2013.

Atkins, Robert C., M.D. *New Diet Revolution.* New York: Avon Books, an imprint of HarperCollins Publishers. 1992, 1999, 2002.

Bolton, Jason; Bushway, Alfred; Crowe, Kristi; El-Begearmi, Mahmoud. Bulletin #4336: "Best Ways to Wash Fruits and Vegetables." University of Maine and the U.S. Department of Agriculture. 2004, 2011, 2013.

Canola Council of Canada. "Canola: The Myths Debunked." Website article: www.canolacouncil.org/oil-and-meal/canola-oil/canola-the-myths-debunked/#Lubricants. 2016.

Centers for Disease Control and Prevention (CDC), Department of Health and Human Services. Report: "Antibiotic Resistant Threats in the United States." 2013.

Chassaing, Benoit; Koren, Omry; Goodrich, Julia K.; Poole, Angela C.; Srinivasan, Shanthi; Ley, Ruth E.; Gewirtz, Andrew T. "Dietary Emulsifiers Impact the Mouse Gut Microbiota Promoting Colitis and Metabolic Syndrome." *Nature.* 519, 92–96. 2015.

Connecticut Agricultural Experiment Station, Department of Analytical Chemistry (CAES) Summary Report: "Removal of Trace Pesticide Residues from Produce." 2000.

Consumers Union (CU). Letter re Comments of Consumers Union to the Food and Drug Administration on Use of the Term "Natural" in the Labeling of Human Food Products. Docket No. FDA-2014-N-1207. May 10, 2016.

Cordain, Loren, Ph.D. *The Paleo Diet.* Hoboken, New Jersey: John Wiley & Sons, Inc. 2002, 2011.

Cornucopia Institute. Report: "Carrageenan: How a 'Natural' Food Additive Is Making Us Sick." March 2013.

Cornucopia Institute. Report: "Carrageenan: New Studies Reinforce Link to Inflammation, Cancer and Diabetes." April 2016.

Davis, William, MD. *Wheat Belly.* New York: Rodale Inc. 2011.

Dean, Carolyn, MD, ND. *The Magnesium Miracle.* New York: Ballantine Books, an imprint of Random House, a division of Random House LLC, a Penguin Random House Company. 2014.

de Vrese, Michael MD, et al. "Probiotics: Compensation for Lactase Insufficiency." *American Journal of Clinical Nutrition.* February 2001

Dufty, William. *The Sugar Blues.* New York, NY: Chilton Book Company and Warner Books, Inc., 1975, 1976, 1993.

Fallon, Sally and Enig, Mary G., PhD. "Why Butter is Better." Weston A. Price Foundation. http://www.westonaprice.org/know-your-fats/why-butter-is-better/. January 1, 2000.

Food and Drug Administration (FDA). "Use of the Term 'Natural' in the Labeling of Human Food Products; Request for Information and Comments." *Federal Register.* Vol. 80, No. 218. Docket No. FDA-2014-N-1207. 21 CFR Part 101. FR Document No. 2015-28779. Thursday, November 12, 2015.

Gedgaudas, Nora, T., CNS, CNT. *Primal Body Primal Mind.* Rochester, Vermont: Healing Arts Press. 2009, 2011.

GRAS Notification. Primex Shrimp-Derived Chitosan Resubmission 000170.000132. Section IV, pg. 28. May 31, 2005.

GRAS Sec. 184.1555 Rapeseed oil. 21CFR184.1555(c)(1). TITLE 21--Food and Drugs Chapter I--Food and Drug Administration Department of Health and Human Services Subchapter B--Food for Human Consumption (Continued) Part 184--Direct Food Substances Affirmed as Generally Recognized as Safe Subpart B--Listing of Specific Substances Affirmed as GRAS.

Grocery Manufacturers Association (GMA) Letter re Use of the Term "Natural" in the Labeling of Human Food Products: Request for Information and Comments; Docket No. FDA-2014-N-1207. May 10, 2016.

Kucinich, Dennis, former U.S. House of Representatives, Ohio's 10th district. "Genetically Engineered Food Right to Know Act." Originally introduced in House, 1999 and reintroduced in House, 2003, 2011, 2013, 2015.

Lukasik J, Bradley ML, Scott TM, Dea M, Koo A, Hsu WY, Bartz JA, Farrah SR. "Reduction of poliovirus 1, bacteriophages, Salmonella montevideo, and Escherichia coli O157:H7 on strawberries by physical and disinfectant washes." *Journal of Food Protection*. 2003.

Masterjohn, Christopher. "On the Trail of the Elusive X-Factor: A Sixty-Two-Year-Old Mystery Finally Solved." *Wise Traditions in Food, Farming and the Healing Arts*. Washington, DC: Weston A. Price Foundation. 2007.

Masterjohn, Christopher. "Fatty Acid Analysis of Grass-fed and Grain-fed Beef Tallow" *Wise Traditions in Food, Farming and the Healing Arts*. Washington, DC: Weston A. Price Foundation. 2013.

McAfee, Mark, Chairman of the Board Raw Milk Institute. Position Statement to American Academy of Pediatrics dated December 20, 2013. "Not All Raw Milk is Produced Equally." *Weston Price Foundation Action Alert*. December 22, 2013.

National Honey Board (NHB). "Definition of Honey and Honey Products" Fact Sheet. June 15, 1996; Updated September 27, 2003.

National Pesticide Information Center. "Methyl Bromide" General Fact Sheet. 2000.

Oceana. Warner K Ph.D., Timme W, Lowell B, Hirshfield M, Ph.D. "Oceana Study Reveals Seafood Fraud Nationwide" www.oceana.org/fraudnationwide. February 2013.

Pizzuti D, Buda A, D'Odorico A, D'Incà R, Chiarelli S, Curioni A, and Martines D. Lack of intestinal mucosal toxicity of Triticum monococcum in celiac disease patients. Scandinavian Journal of Gastroenterology Vol. 41 , Iss. 11, 2006.

Rombauer, Irma S., and Becker, Marion Rombauer. *Joy of Cooking.* New York: Bobbs-Merrill Company, Inc. 1975.

Schmemann, Alexander. *For the Life of the World; Sacraments and Orthodoxy.* New York: St. Vladimir's Seminary Press. 1973.

Seaman, Andrew M. "Celiac Diagnoses Rose During 2000s, Study Finds" New York: Reuters Health. March 29, 2013.

Tobacman JK. "Review of harmful gastrointestinal Effects of Carrageenan in Animal Experiments." *Environmental Health Perspectives*.109(10):983-994. 2001

Vogelsang, GB, M.D. Integrative Medicine & Digestive Center, News and Events. The Johns Hopkins University, The Johns Hopkins Hospital, and Johns Hopkins Health System.

World Wildlife Fund (WWF). Which Everyday Products Contain Palm Oil? http://www.worldwildlife.org/pages/which-everyday-products-contain-palm-oil. 2017.

Acknowledgments and Gratitude

The creation of this book has been overwhelming at times, yet I feel like I have been preparing for it all my life. I owe a great debt to all who made me think–yeah, this is really possible.

I am grateful for and constantly inspired by renegade health-minded individuals and companies who courageously step outside of the box to inform and bring new ideas to the collective consciousness. Risking censure and profit, they stimulate change for the betterment of our planet.

THANK YOU

Thank you for your interest in my book and to show my appreciation, I would like to give you the: *New Era Healthy Eating Resource Guide.*

In it, I share my go to websites, books, and product suppliers to propel you along in building a healthier you and planet.

Please visit www.NewEraHealthyEating.com and download your **FREE** copy.

I WOULD ESPECIALLY LIKE TO ACKNOWLEDGE AND THANK:

MY FATHER AND MOTHER, who have always been there for me. Mom was the first person to encourage me to write this book, and from whom, I acquired my invaluable and acute olfactory ability. I inherited my artistic skills from my dad, and he always provided ample food for the family table with untiring devotion.

MY GRANDMOTHER, who introduced me to *Prevention* magazine in 1964 and prepared amazing down home comfort food all from scratch.

GRACE ENGBRING, who always brings out the best in me and makes me laugh. Without her pep talks and support, this book would have never happened.

KEN MCKENNA, who gave me one of my first cookbooks, *the Joy of Cooking*. He loved everything I cooked, including my disasters (he actually thought they were good). What more encouragement could a budding cook desire?

CHRIS NISHI, a creative chef and friend, who died far too early. He provided invaluable culinary inspiration and direction.

ALL MY FAMILY AND FRIENDS too numerous to mention, who encouraged and stood by me in the good times and the bad.

ALL MY SOCIAL MEDIA AND BLOG FOLLOWERS, who constantly validate my efforts. You are awesome.

A COLLECTIVE CADRE OF BOOK PUBLISHING AND IT PROFESSIONALS who assisted with the technical side and oftentimes shared information without compensation. A special shout-out to Christopher Pradzinski of Print Pros, the production artist wizard with the patience of a saint.

LASTLY AND MOST IMPORTANTLY, TO MY CHILDREN, who represent my greatest achieve-ments. My desire to keep them healthy as well as of all their millennial generation provided the main motivation for writing this book.

About the Author

Jacqueline on left

Cooking has been a lifelong pursuit. I remember watching Julia Child as a kid when her shows were still in black and white. My first cooking experiences were inspired by my mother's *Betty Crocker's Cookbook* (kind of embarrassing to admit) and later the *Joy of Cooking*, cookbook bibles for the average American at the time. Eventually, I spread my wings and discovered other cookbooks rich in gourmet opportunities as I explored the world of culinary arts. A mother of two, socially responsible foodie, cookaholic, writer, health nut, born-again carnivore, and outdoor junkie—that's me. When I am not in my kitchen cooking, photographing, researching, or writing, I am in the mountains skiing, fly-fishing, or hiking.

While always passionate about healthy food and its production and preparation, I wandered in a dietary wilderness without a compass. I have watched fads come and go, and feel betrayed by past nutritional guidelines and gurus. Their collective recipes and philosophies, however well-meaning, fostered beliefs and eating habits that paved the road to health crises not only for me, but worldwide. These epidemics include mood and anxiety disorders, cancer, diabetes, gut, endocrine, joint, and heart disease so rampant in modern affluent societies, but virtually unknown in 1900.

Like a crash test dummy, I ricocheted through multiple persuasions as each new authority announced their definitive answer to healthy eating and its curative powers. Wide-eyed, I earnestly listened as our Girl Scout leader championed the government's nutrition propaganda epitomized by the "The Basic Four" guide. During the 1970s, I suffered through Adelle Davis' heavy cheese, grain, and legume recipes, and god-awful nut loaves laden with savorless wheat germ. I became a devotee of a vegetarian macrobiotic meat- and dairy-free ideology (extremely similar to veganism), but soon grew weary of dishes such as tofu "scrambled eggs" and "quiches," adzuki bean seaweed stews, and mock mashed potatoes concocted from millet. Ultimately bailing, I escaped into the greener pastures of nouveau vegetarianism. But this didn't last long either. By the mid-1980s, I drifted out of macrobiotics and vegetarianism, and added small quantities of fish and meat. Low-fat became my mantra by the mid-1990s, and I became obsessed with lean meat and protein powder fruit smoothies. I continued baking "nutritious" desserts (totally delusional) and cooking with soy products well into 2008.

High-carbohydrate grain- and legume-based diets dominated my eating habits for most of my adult life. I took B-vitamin and calcium-magnesium supplements daily to make up for nutrients in the meat and dairy I wasn't eating. I thought I was eating healthy and by most standards, I was. Although I began experiencing endocrine dysfunction in my late 20's, particularly noticeable in my thyroid and ovaries (holding a pregnancy was problematic)—I never correlated this to the way I was eating.

Slender well into my early 50s, and even though I looked good on the outside, I couldn't maintain health as I aged. Gone was my energy and my muscles became weaker, despite regular exercise and weightlifting. Inflammation developed in my joints, and I could not enjoy high-performance sports without developing injuries. As I ate less and steadily gained weight–I thought I must be eating too much meat and not getting enough fiber. Animal protein became yet again almost absent from my diet, while I upped my consumption of fresh fruit, smoothies, grains, and legumes.

Teetering on the brink of a health disaster, I stumbled upon the Dr. Atkins' New Diet Revolution, then segued into the Paleo Diet™. Atkins opened my mind to an alternative way of thinking and provided a natural progression into paleo. These diets introduced me to the concept that excess carbohydrate consumption drives fat storage and disease. My favorite recipes were soon adapted to help me achieve long-term faithfulness to a low-carbohydrate diet, without sacrificing taste and the pleasure of eating.

Once on a low-carbohydrate diet, weight and inflammation melted away and cravings disappeared. The noon-time crash was gone, and I could go many hours without eating. By eliminating grains and legumes, adding small amounts of animal protein daily, upping my vegetable consumption, and limiting my fruits to those low on the glycemic index, my restoration to health was miraculous–or so it seemed. After three years of eating low-carb, there was still a puzzle piece missing. Faithfulness to a low-carb diet is a great detox and I had lost 20 pounds and kept it off. However, I still wasn't sleeping well, experienced anxiety, and hadn't recovered my endurance and muscle tone. Something was still wrong.

Eventually it hit me. Toxins, toxins and yet more toxins were the culprits, they were messing with my hormones. Unbelievably, the doctors weren't the ones to figure this out. The great purge then commenced. I cleaned up my water, food, and vitamin sources, and threw out everything in the cupboard containing any ingredient unrecognizable as real food. Every amalgam filling in my teeth was removed. I got rid of gardening pesticides, cleaning and personal care products; this included everything from herbicides for weeds, anti-bacterial soap, fluoride toothpaste, to acetaminophen and ibuprofen. Finally, there was improvement. It wasn't gluten, meat, fat, dairy, or even sugar that was making me feel off–it was the poisons hiding in every crevice of my environment!

Spending time with my children, yoga, and meditation are important components of my life, as are my ski lines at Squaw Valley, California. Sighting animals in the wild elicits spontaneous exclamations of wonderment and scares the heck out of anyone standing near me. I find bliss rowing down a river and casting dry-flies to disinterested trout. Nights out are rare but it gives me an excuse to dress up in my Cowboy boots and Southwest jewelry. I would much rather cook amazing food for an intimate home gathering and find it fun creating new recipes to share, especially if it involves a food processor. For some reason, I have a strange preoccupation with food processors–I have three and love using them.

My health at 63 is better than it was at 55 and progressively getting better every day, as I work out a lifetime of stored toxins. Hopefully, the tide was stemmed and years of excessive grain and legume consumption combined with noxious substances haven't done permanent damage. Will I live well into my 90s like my great- and great-great-grandparents? Only time will tell, but in the meantime, I am taking the advice of another nonagenarian, Julia Child, to "...enjoy food and have fun. It is one of the simplest and nicest pleasures in life."

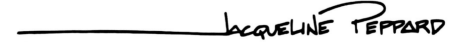

Index

*Please note: page numbers in bold indicate photographs.

Recipe Index

*Please note: page numbers in bold indicate photographs.

Made in the USA
San Bernardino, CA
23 September 2018